A Guide to

RURAL
BUSINESS

WITHDRAWN

A Guide to

RURAL
BUSINESS

OPPORTUNITIES & IDEAS FOR
DEVELOPING YOUR COUNTRY ENTERPRISE

EDITED BY
JONATHAN REUVID

PUBLISHED IN ASSOCIATION WITH

CLA Country Land &
Business Association
RURAL ECONOMY IS OUR BUSINESS

KOGAN
PAGE

Publisher's note

Every possible effort has been made to ensure that the information contained in this book is accurate at the time of going to press, and the publishers and authors cannot accept responsibility for any errors or omissions, however caused. No responsibility for loss or damage occasioned to any person acting, or refraining from action, as a result of the material in this publication can be accepted by the editor, the publisher or any of the authors.

First published in Great Britain 2003 by Kogan Page Limited

Kogan Page Ltd
120 Pentonville Road
London N1 9JN
www.kogan-page.co.uk

British Library Cataloguing-in-Publication Data

A CIP record for this book is available from the British Library.

ISBN 0 7494 4077 5

Typeset by Saxon Graphics Ltd, Derby
Printed and bound in Great Britain by Clays Ltd, St Ives plc

Contents

Contents

Foreword

The well-being of rural England is important to everyone – to the 12 million people who live there and, nationally, as the home to a highly-valued asset and powerful economic force. Recent estimates suggest and that over 5 million people work in rural locations, with 36 per cent of businesses generating some 30 per cent of national GDP. Where rural economic activity is well integrated into urban and regional economies, rural areas often thrive and even out-perform that of their region as a whole.

However, the countryside has undergone rapid change since World War Two. That change has produced many benefits, but rural economic challenges remain. Often these are in areas that are less integrated into wider regional and national economies or rely heavily on troubled business sectors. We need to support communities and businesses where they need help as the continuing process of change impacts on them. And we need to develop capacity in rural areas. Our challenging Public Service Agreements cover a range of key issues for rural areas. In particular we aim to reduce the gap in productivity between the least well performing quartile of rural areas and the English median by 2006, and to improve the accessibility of services for rural people.

This includes improved services for rural communities. One main reason for the decline in service provision in market towns and villages is that each service provider – especially in the public sector – has considered separately whether local outlets are financially viable. The police station, the council office, the library and the pub might have closed, one after the other, when they could have shared a building and support services and remained viable. Some interesting work has already been done under the Vital Villages scheme to pilot increased use of multi-service outlets in villages and in market towns, for example, at Waters Upton in Shropshire. We are now looking, with other Departments, at how we can encourage wider adoption of this approach, including shared premises, shared staff and innovative changes.

Rural areas offer distinctive business opportunities – for example, horse enterprises can harness the special qualities of the countryside to meet growing demands for sport, recreation, tourism and leisure, often in combination with other rural businesses. And raising the skills base of rural businesses is vital. That is why DEFRA has a Learning, Skills and Knowledge Programme. I hope this publication will help us to achieve easier access and better support for business.

The key to all this is co-operation. The Government's key objective is sustainable development, which means a better quality of life for everyone, now and for generations to come. That can only be achieved if we work at it together.

Alun Michael
Minister of State
Rural Affairs and Urban Quality of Life

Foreword

Even 30 years ago the term rural business was synonymous with agriculture. Government policy towards the countryside was then delivered primarily through the medium of agricultural policy. Accelerating change since has greatly increased the importance of diversified rural businesses in relation to traditional primary production. By 2002 only 3.8 per cent of jobs in rural England were in agriculture and fishing.

The structure of business in rural areas has come to mirror that of urban ones in most respects, but indelible differences remain arising from the effects of remoteness. The delivery of every form of utility and service is made more difficult by added distance. Facilities such as 3-phase electricity or mains water, which are taken for granted in towns, can be expensive or impossible to access. Of all the difficulties for business in rural areas the most significant currently is the absence of Broadband access, indeed in many areas the lack of any prospect of getting it.

Despite these natural drawbacks, businesses are increasingly tempted to relocate to the countryside; the benefits of living and working in a peaceful, attractive environment are clearly felt to outweigh the problems, and the overall picture of the rural economy is a positive one. Rural areas consistently generate more business start-ups and better business growth than do towns, and unemployment rates are significantly lower.

This book sets out to clarify the matters that distinguish business in the countryside. The CLA welcomes its publication. It will act as a help and encouragement to entrepreneurs, current and prospective, in the countryside.

Sir Edward Greenwell
President, CLA

Introduction

Living and working in the countryside becomes ever more challenging with the passage of time. Today, with the evolution of 21st century communications and an overloaded transport infrastructure, 'living in the country' has taken on a variety of new meanings.

At one end of the spectrum, the readily accessible rural retreat for city dwellers craving idyllic sylvan weekends has become increasingly unattainable, with the escalation in residential property prices placing second homes out of reach to all but the few. The alternative of living throughout the week in a deeply rural area and working in cities has become steadily more unattractive, with expensive, unreliable public transport and congested roads making the daily commute a misery. Thanks to ICT, relief for many has arrived in the new opportunities to work remotely from the organisation at home for most of the week. Twenty years ago, when PCs were in their childhood and written communication was paper-based, at best by fax, working from home was widely regarded as a euphemism for 'out of work'. Today, hundreds of thousands of professional and creative people and office workers, in employment or self-employed and connected electronically by e-mail, the telephone and the Internet, are able to live and work in the countryside either from home or in rural offices in local towns or villages, often in converted agricultural buildings. The evolution of the rural office worker proceeds apace.

At the other end of the scale, the farming community has suffered economically from a series of setbacks; many farms are no longer profitable and traditional rural occupations are under threat. Survival for some and, for others the maintenance of a livelihood in farming, depends on the redevelopment of redundant farm buildings to release capital or generate much needed income. Alternatively, diversification into non-farming business offers opportunities to develop completely new income streams. The evolution of the rural entrepreneur is a parallel phenomenon to that of the rural office worker.

In the last few years additional economic pressures have arisen which impact on people living in the country, particularly the middle-aged and elderly, whose financial security has been damaged by the crisis in pension and endowment assurance funding brought about by collapsing equity values and imprudent fund management. For many, their only significant wealth lies in the value of the land and buildings where they reside. For this embattled community of country dwellers who had looked forward to a modestly comfortable retirement, their dilemma is similar to that of the farmers. In order to continue living where they are, they need to extract value from under-utilised or developable buildings or to supplement their incomes by setting up in business.

A Guide to Rural Business is intended, therefore, for three categories of reader:

☐ those living in the country already who want to capitalise on the value of their assets, either by developing land and buildings or engaging in a business;
☐ farmers and smallholders who need to diversify;
☐ those moving to the countryside who want to explore opportunities and ideas for developing a country enterprise.

The book is a collaboration between the Country Land and Business Association (CLA), the foremost organisation caring for the countryside and providing advice and guidance to rural communities in England and Wales and to Government, and Kogan Page, the leading independent UK publisher of business books for privately owned businesses and the self-employed.

The book is arranged in four sections. Part One focuses on the development of land and rural buildings, with chapters written by CLA resident experts in planning, the management of compulsory purchase orders, tenancy law and taxation. In Part Two the content is expanded to the range of key issues which are most pertinent to the general operation of country businesses. Topics include business tenancies and regulations, the issue of self-employment versus incorporation, business taxation, audit and accountancy and employment law. Legal liability, litigation and insurance are also covered and there are overviews of alternative marketing and business promotion techniques, and the use of ICT and broadband in rural business. Again, the more technical chapters have been written by CLA resident experts and associates.

Part Three is devoted to the subject of financial management and funding, including approaches to the buying and selling of businesses and, for the pessimists or those facing problems, the management and mitigation of insolvency. Finally, in Part Four we have assembled a collection of country business case histories highlighting the recent achievements of seven countryside dwellers in a variety of business activities.

The credentials of all authors are set out in the Contributors' Notes section at the beginning of the book and my sincere thanks are due to each of them individually for their informative contributions into which they have successfully condensed a vast amount of knowledge. Hopefully, *A Guide to Rural Business* will provide useful preliminary guidance to those embarking on rural enterprises or facing specific problems in the development of their land and buildings or the start-up of country businesses. However, the technical topics cannot be mastered in a single book of this length and readers are referred to the recommended texts listed at chapter ends and in Appendix I, many written by the expert professionals who have authored this publication.

We are indebted to Alun Michael, Rural Affairs Minister, and to Sir Edward Greenwell, President of the CLA, for their Forewords. Finally, I must add my personal thanks to Geoff Litchfield and his colleagues in the management of the CLA who have supported the development of this book with enthusiasm since its conception.

Jonathan Reuvid
Wroxton, Oxfordshire, May 2003

List of Contributors

Brian Castle is Senior Taxation Adviser at the Country Land and Business Association (CLA). He is a former Inspector of Taxes and has advised landowners and rural businesses for over 15 years on all aspects of taxation. He writes articles and lectures regularly on demystifying the complications of capital gains tax and inheritance tax. He is also a local councillor with a London Borough and is a spokesman on planning and regulatory matters.

Philip Coysh is National Business Manager of Farming & Agricultural Finance Ltd. (FAF), part of NatWest and the CLA's recommended lenders for agricultural and rural mortgages. A banker by training, he has specialised in agricultural and rural finance for almost 20 years.

Jeffrey Hansen was a Legal Adviser at the CLA until June 2003. As a member of the CLA legal team, he specialised in all aspects of liability and litigation under contract law and tort. He has returned to private practice with Landons in Essex.

Oliver Harwood is Head of Rural Economy at the CLA, leading a team of economists, planners and surveyors in delivering advice to Government and some 45,000 members and 130,000 rural businesses in England and Wales. Oliver graduated in Land Economy from the University of Cambridge in 1982, trained as a surveyor and has since been involved in the delivery of a wide variety of land management and professional advice in firms in Devon and East Anglia and, for the last six years, with the CLA, where he leads on compulsory purchase and valuation issues.

Matthew Howard is a Licensed Insolvency Practitioner with Norfolk chartered accountancy firm Larking Gowen. Based in Norwich, he is head of the business recovery department, which specialises in all aspects of personal and corporate insolvency work. Matt joined the firm in 1966, having graduated from the University of East Anglia with a degree in Accountancy.

Sean Johnson is the Senior IT Analyst for the CLA; he specialises in local and wide area networking using Microsoft BackOffice and Cisco technologies. He has worked in IT for 15 years and is actively involved in lobbying for greater broadband access in rural areas. He is currently advising Government departments on the methods and benefits of achieving further rollout of Broadband to isolated areas.

Dr Karen Jones is Chief Legal Adviser at the CLA, leading a team of lawyers who give specialist advice to some 45,000 members and to Government. She qualified at the Chancery Bar and has worked for the CLA since 1997, advising and lecturing on legal issues, such as occupiers' liability, which affect land-based businesses.

Mark Jones is Senior Associate at Cunnane Town Planning. He is a Chartered Town Planner and a member of the Royal Town Planning Institute. Until May 2003 he was employed at the CLA as its Senior Planning Adviser and worked previously, in similar roles, with the National Farmers Union (NFU) and as a Local Planning Officer. He has served as a member of various Government planning steering groups.

Roderick Millar is an experienced writer on business practice and development. He is well placed to advise on small business issues and has run his own London-based company for the past five years. He is the editor of several Kogan Page titles and co-author of *Start Up and Run Your Own Business.*

Jonathan Reuvid has edited and written a series of books on international business, and on business development for SMEs and the self-employed for Kogan Page. A graduate in PPE at Oxford University, he worked first as an economist for the French national oil company (Total) and, subsequently, as an investment banker, a financial and marketing consultant and the European director of operations for a US multinational before embarking on a second career in business publishing.

Stuart Rootham is the Commercial Director of R K Harrison Brokers Ltd, one of the UK's leading independent insurance broking groups with extensive experience of insurance for farms, estates and rural communities. This expertise led to the creation of an exclusive partnership with the CLA, resulting in the formation of CLA Insurance Services in November 2002. The new service offers a full range of insurance products for the CLA's 45,000 members with exclusive products and special member discounts.

Helen Shipsey is Senior Legal Adviser, employed by the CLA since 1997, and currently advises on agricultural tenancies, residential landlord and tenant law, employment law and game laws. Previously, she practised at the Common Law Bar in Chambers in London.

Duncan Sigournay is Senior Legal Adviser at the CLA. He qualified as a solicitor in 1996 having graduated from Keele University with a joint honours degree in Law and Economics. Prior to joining the CLA, Duncan worked in private practice in Warwickshire for a large provincial practice. He specialises in all aspects of commercial property and, particularly, agricultural property law.

John Skinner is a partner at Whitley Stimpson, an independent firm of business advisers and chartered accountants in Banbury, where he has worked since 1989 after graduating from university. Working in this medium-sized practice environment has provided him with a broad range of experience in auditing, tax and business management. The Whitley Stimpson practice has been in existence for over 70 years and is also a member of Moores Rowland International, a global association of 170 accountancy firms. Its diversified client base stretches from the rural economy of North Oxfordshire to Scotland and into the West Country.

James Stephenson is joint senior partner of Stephenson & Son, York, established in 1871, with an earlier record of an ancestor's valuation activities going back to the post-1645 Civil War period. The Stephenson Group now run two livestock markets, a professional rural practice and a Yorkshire network of 10 agency offices. The 19th century business was founded by Jacob Stephenson, working first through Tadcaster market and then on to York. Under Reg Stephenson, father of the present senior partners Nigel and James, the firm's professional rural activities were expanded into Estate Agency. Edward Stephenson, the sixth generation of the family, is now a partner.

Charles Trotman is the Rural Economics Adviser to the CLA. His work focuses on all aspects of the rural economy, in particular ICT policy, rural tourism and competition in the market place. Previously, he worked for the National Farmers Union and in Brussels as a political consultant for over five years.

Part One:

The Development of Land and Rural Buildings

1.1 Local authority plans, planning applications and appeals

Mark Jones, formerly Senior Planning Adviser, CLA

INTRODUCTION

Whether you are considering setting up a new rural business or expanding an existing one it is likely that your proposal will bring you into contact with the planning system. The main principle of the planning system is to regulate the use of land in the public interest. The broad aim is to ensure that the right development takes place in the right location. The main responsibility for day-to-day planning issues and implementing planning regulations involving individual development lies with the local planning authority, both for policy creation and development control.

LEGISLATION

The main piece of legislation controlling planning is currently the Town and Country Planning Act 1990. There are separate provisions relating to listed buildings contained within the Planning (Listed Buildings and Conservation Areas) Act 1990. Following on from these Acts there are a number of different regulations covering all aspects of the planning system.

At the time of writing, a fundamental review of the planning system is taking place. The Planning and Compulsory Purchase Bill is progressing through Parliament. Its proposals, if implemented, will bring a number of changes to the system, particularly, but not exclusively, in relation to development plans.

NATIONAL PLANNING POLICY

Government planning policy is contained in Planning Policy Guidance Notes (PPGs), circulars and ministerial statements. Supporting these policies there are often government Good Practice Guides.

General planning policy guidance for the countryside is contained within Planning Policy Guidance Note 7 – The Countryside – Environmental Quality and Economic and Social Development (PPG7). There are other planning policy guidance notes that may be relevant to diversification ventures, in particular:

☐ PPG13 – Transport;
☐ PPG11 – Regional Planning;
☐ PPG15 – Planning and the Historic Environment;
☐ PPG17 – Sport and Recreation;
☐ PPG 21 – Tourism;
☐ PPG22 – Renewable Energy;
☐ PPG24 – Planning and Noise.

Many of these guidance notes can now be viewed and downloaded from the government website: www.planning.gov.uk/ppg/index.htm.

Whilst policy guidance notes provide general guidance as to planning policy, local planning documents provide more detailed guidance.

REGIONAL PLANNING GUIDANCE

Regional Planning Guidance sets out the broad regional strategy; it sets a framework for the preparation of development plans. Regional Planning Guidance generally covers a period of 15 to 20 years. It will consider the broad provision distribution of employment uses and also the broad objectives for the rural economy.

LOCAL AUTHORITY PLANS

Section 54A of the 1990 Town and Country Planning Act places a presumption in favour of development that is in accordance with the development plan. The development plan at present constitutes the County Structure Plan, the Local Plan and, if the local authority is a unitary authority, the Unitary Development Plan.

Structure Plans

These are prepared by the County Council and cover the key strategic policies and frameworks for a particular county, taking into account national and regional policies. They do not provide specific policies but will set the broad framework; subsequent Local Plan policies need to be in accordance with the Structure Plan. This plan will probably contain a section on the economy of an area, including any strategic rural economic issues.

Local Plans

The Local Plan sets out specific policies and land use allocations for a particular area. The policies in a Local Plan are likely to be the key consideration when determining a planning application for a specific development. There will be detailed policies on re-use of rural buildings, highway issues and environmental constraints.

Unitary Development Plans

As the name suggests, Unitary Development Plans (UDPs) are prepared by unitary authorities. They are made up of two parts: Part I is the strategic framework and Part II has specific policies similar to a Local Plan.

It should be noted that the importance of these documents cannot be overstated and it is vital to involve yourself in the process if you wish to secure positive policies and allocations. Each plan has a specific timetable and process with opportunities to make representations and/or be heard at any public examination or inquiry. Further details can be obtained in the former Department for Environment, Transport and Regions publications: *Structure Plans – A Guide to Procedures*, DETR (1999) and *Local Plans and Unitary Development Plans – A Guide to Procedures*, DETR (1999).

Supplementary planning guidance

In addition to the statutory plans, many local authorities produce plans that supplement the development plan policies. These may be prepared on specific issues in a particular area. It is possible that such guidance could be prepared on rural economic development. This guidance will be taken into account when considering an application, although it does not carry the same weight as a development plan policy.

PLANNING APPLICATIONS

Making a planning application

Before a planning application can be processed, all the necessary documents must be completed in full and the appropriate fee paid to the local planning authority.

The necessary documents are:

☐ four copies of the completed application form (all signed and dated);
☐ a copy of the appropriate certificate relating to land ownership and any notice required;
☐ four copies of the relevant plans;
☐ the relevant application fee.

The application forms are straightforward and ask a number of questions relating to applicant, site, development and type of application.

Types of planning application

Outline planning application

This type of application deals with the principle of development. Matters such as siting, design, external appearance, landscaping and means of access can be reserved for subsequent approval. Outline applications cannot be used for change-of-use applications. This type of application may be appropriate where there is doubt about the likely success of the applications since it avoids the expense of drawings, etc. However, another fee will be required when submitting the subsequent details for approval. The local planning authority is entitled to request further details if it is considered necessary.

Full application

This type of application deals with all matters of the application at the same time. Therefore, full drawings etc are required.

Reserved matters application

Once outline permission has been granted, a subsequent approval of details/reserved matters will be required. This is usually submitted within two years but the exact date will be stated on the outline consent. A fee will be payable per application of reserved matters.

Determining planning applications

Once the local planning authority receives an application it will be checked. If the documentation is correct, it will be entered on the planning register. An acknowledgement will be sent out to you.

A planning officer will be allocated to deal with the application. Consultations will be sent out, allowing comments to be made within a certain time period, for example 14 or 28 days. A number of these consultees will be statutory; the Government lists certain bodies who must be consulted on certain developments before a decision is made. In addition, the local authority can also consult any other person/body it considers necessary. Neighbours or adjoining landowners must be consulted either by letter or by posting a site notice. Some applications, usually major developments, are advertised in a local newspaper.

The Planning Officer will make a site visit to consider the application and, once they have obtained all the necessary information, will prepare a report and a recommendation, which will be presented to the Planning Committee. It is the Planning Committee that makes the decision. In some cases, the Planning Officer may have delegated powers to deal with an application, ie it will not need to go to Committee. These powers are normally used on straightforward applications.

There is a statutory period of eight weeks in which a planning authority should determine an application. If no decision is made in this period you could appeal to the Secretary of State on the grounds of non-determination. However, planning appeals can be a lengthy process and you will probably obtain a quicker decision by agreeing with the local planning authority to extend the determination period. You should always check the progress of the application with the local planning authority before making such a decision.

Planning appeals

Should planning permission be refused or be approved subject to planning conditions, there is a right of appeal to the Secretary of State within six months of the local planning authority decision. Appeals are carried out by the Planning Inspectorate. There is no fee for making a planning appeal, but professional costs may be incurred in preparing a case.

There are three types of appeal:

☐ Written representations: this process is an exchange of written statements between the parties. The Inspector will make a site visit and, based on this and the statements, will make his decision.

☐ A hearing: again there is an exchange of statements between the parties. However, in this type of appeal both parties can present their case verbally. The hearing takes the form of a discussion, with the Inspector acting as Chairman. Again a site visit will take place before the Inspector makes a decision.

☐ An inquiry: this is a quasi-judicial procedure with the Inspector sitting as 'Judge'. All parties present their case, which is subject to cross-examination and may be represented legally. Again written statements will have been exchanged and proof of evidence submitted in advance. A site visit will take place before a decision is reached.

Before deciding upon an appeal on the appropriate procedure it is important to consider whether any way can be found to overcome the objection and to ask what the main issues are. Further advice can be found in DETR Circular.

LISTED BUILDINGS

An additional factor that needs to be considered when using buildings to operate a rural business is whether the building is listed. These are buildings that are considered to be of special architectural or historic interest. These buildings fall into three categories: Grade I, II* or II. You can check whether your property is listed by viewing the Statutory Lists. These should be available at your local planning authority offices.

The implications of a property being listed can be significant. Firstly, any alterations or works that affect the building will require

Listed Building Consent (LBC). This is a separate procedure to obtaining planning consent. Furthermore, alterations or changes will need to take account of the various historic elements. Therefore, there are likely to be stricter controls of alterations/additions and materials used to ensure the quality of the building is retained. Many modern building materials such as UPVC windows, for example, will be unacceptable.

It is an offence of strict liability (ie it is no defence that the defendant was unaware that the building was listed) to carry out works for the demolition of a listed building, or which alter or extend it in such a way as to affect its character as a building of special architectural or historic interest, or to fail to comply with the conditions of a listed building consent. The maximum fine for such an offence is £20,000.

Full guidance on these issues is given in Planning Policy Guidance Note 15 – Planning and the Historic Environment.

Listed Building Consent

Applications for Listed Building Consent must be made to the local planning authority on a form obtainable from them and accompanied by sufficient particulars and drawings so that the impact of the works on the building can be assessed. It is not, therefore, possible to make an outline application. Conditions may be applied to LBC in the same way as for a normal planning consent. Appeals may be made against a refusal to grant LBC, or against any conditions imposed, by application to the Secretary of State within six months.

Note that such an appeal provides one of the few opportunities to appeal against the listing itself – one of the grounds of appeal may be that the building is not of special architectural or historic interest and should therefore be removed from the listing. The Secretary of State is empowered to remove the building from the list, if he thinks fit.

ALTERNATIVE USES FOR LAND AND BUILDINGS

The conversion of rural buildings to alternative uses offers the opportunity to make use of buildings that are no longer required for agriculture in order to provide an alternative income. Any proposal for conversion should follow the general principles applicable to all diversification projects, particularly in relation to business planning, choice of alternative enterprise, demand, accessibility etc. However, a key matter in pursuing such a proposal will be how it is considered by the planning system.

PPG7 offers guidance that is generally supportive of employment-generating uses in rural areas. It states (para. 3.8):

'The range of industries that can be successfully accommodated in rural areas is expanding. Many commercial and light manufacturing activities can be carried on in rural areas without causing unacceptable disturbance... there are benefits to the local economy and employment. These firms also help to bring new life and activity to rural communities and so are generally welcomed and quickly assimilated.'

PPG 7 supports the conversion of rural buildings to business use. It states: 'the reuse and adaptation of existing rural buildings has an important role in meeting the needs of rural areas for commercial and industrial development, as well as tourism, sport and recreation'. However, it cautions that: 'local planning authorities... should avoid major developments in locations not well served by public transport or otherwise readily accessible... to a local residential workforce'.

Nonetheless, all proposals will be judged against criteria that allow the local planning authority to balance the many competing objectives of countryside policy.

Within PPG7 there is a requirement that 'the countryside should be safeguarded for its own sake'. It therefore states that: 'the guiding principle in the countryside is that development should both benefit economic activity and maintain or enhance the environment'.

Proposals that can take account of these considerations are likely to be significantly better received than those that do not.

Planning Policy Guidance Note 13 – Transport also offers advice as to transport planning and the need to link to the rest of the development system. Within some rural areas, it has, however, been interpreted as a disincentive to rural development. The guidance states that:

'In order to reduce the need for long-distance out-commuting to jobs in urban areas, it is important to promote adequate employment opportunities in rural areas. Diversification of agricultural businesses is increasingly likely to lead to proposals for conversion or re-use of existing farm buildings for other business purposes, possibly in remote locations. PPG7 indicates that for development related to agriculture and for farm diversification, appropriate new buildings may also be acceptable. In plan policies and development control decisions, local authorities should encourage farm diversification proposals particularly, but not exclusively, where this enables access by public transport, walking and cycling. They should be realistic about the availability, or likely availability, of alternatives to access by car. Similarly, they should not reject proposals where small-scale business development or its expansion would give rise to only modest additional daily vehicle movements, in comparison to other uses that are permitted on the site, and the impact on minor roads would not be significant.'

Whilst it is clearly appropriate to place employment uses where there is a variety of means of transport, it does not need to be exclusively so. The guidance also suggests that the need for alternative means of transport is greater the larger the employment development.

Note that the building does not have to be redundant. However, proposals for the conversion of a new building are likely to come under greater scrutiny than those for traditional buildings, particularly where they have been erected under agricultural permitted development rights.

The primary consideration for planning purposes should be whether the nature and extent of the proposed new use is acceptable in planning terms. In this respect all proposals should satisfy the following basic criteria:

☐ The building should be permanent and substantially constructed.
☐ The conversion should not lead to business activity being dispersed to such an extent that it has a detrimental effect on the activity of towns and villages.
☐ The building's 'form, bulk and general design' is in keeping with its surroundings.
☐ Any planning concerns (eg on environmental or traffic grounds) can be overcome by imposing reasonable conditions.
☐ If the building is in open countryside, then it should be capable of conversion without the need for major or complete reconstruction.

In addition, proposals will clearly be more acceptable if they respect local building styles and materials, and for listed buildings, or buildings in sensitive areas, use of such design and materials may be a necessary precursor to obtaining permission.

PERMITTED DEVELOPMENT

Another possibility for using agricultural land and buildings for business use is to explore possible permitted developments for temporary uses, ie those that do not require consent. The Town and Country Planning (General Permitted Development) Order 1995 specifies various classes of development that may be undertaken without seeking permission from the local planning authority. However, these provisions for permitted development may be restricted by any previous grant of planning permission on the property, or by the making of an 'article 4' direction by either the local planning authority or the Secretary of State. It is advisable to check with the local planning authority as to whether any such provision is in force.

Although the General Permitted Development Order has 33 parts, the one that may be particularly relevant for diversification purposes is Part 4 'Temporary Buildings and Uses'. This part permits: a) temporary buildings and structures which are needed in connection with works being carried out on the land and which will be removed as soon as those works are complete; and b) the use of land for up to 28 days a year for any purpose except the holding of a market and motor car or motorcycle racing (including trials of speed and practising for these activities), which are restricted to 14 days a year.

There are a number of uses that are *not* permitted as a temporary use. These are where:

☐ the land involved is a building, or within the curtilage of a building;
☐ the use of the land is for a caravan site;
☐ the land is within an SSSI and the use is for a market, motor car or motorcycle racing (including trials of speed and practising for these activities), clay pigeon shooting, or any war game;
☐ the use is for the display of an advertisement.

It is important to note the difference between a temporary use and a permanent one. The way in which the land is used is likely to be a relevant consideration. The case of *Ramsay v Secretary of State for the Environment and Suffolk District Council* (1997) JPL B123 gives a useful illustration of the point. In this case it was held that the use of land for vehicular sports and leisure activities for not more than 28 days per year was a permanent, *intermittent* use of the land and not a temporary use, which would have been permitted. The reason was that the vehicle tracks, tyres, fences and markers remained on the land for the rest of the year and were not removed, as would have been expected with a temporary use.

CHECKLIST FOR ACTION

It is important to check the following:

☐ Is the building listed? If so Listed Building Consent will be necessary.

☐ Do local policies restrict certain types of uses in rural areas? (Storage and distribution uses are often restricted.)

☐ Note that different planning policies will apply for conversion to differing uses, whether holiday or business.

☐ If the building is within a designated area (eg a conservation area or Area of Outstanding Natural Beauty 'AONB') then planning regulations are likely to be more stringent. Check also whether permitted development rights have been withdrawn. Contact with the local planning authority at this stage may avoid the need for a retrospective application for work done without planning consent.

☐ Is the building affected by any restrictive covenants? These are particularly likely to apply where a group of buildings has been split and sold off separately. These may restrict potential uses of the building.

☐ Try to arrange a pre-application meeting with the Planning Officer to discuss your proposal. This can identify issues early on and make the application process smoother.

Members of the CLA have access to a wide range of Guidance Notes, downloadable free from the members' area of the CLA website, covering planning matters, including:

☐ Diversificaton: Government planning advice GN04/02
☐ Development control and agriculture GN18/02
☐ The lifting of agricultural ties GN19/02
☐ Certificates of Lawful Use or Development (CLEUD) GN23/02
☐ Conversion of farm buildings to business use GN24/02
☐ Reuse of farm buildings GN29/02

1.2 The compulsory acquisition framework and practical advice

Oliver Harwood, Head of Rural Economy and Chief Surveyor, CLA

INTRODUCTION

Rural businesses face compulsory powers of acquisition in a number of frameworks. Acquirers may be seeking land for road or rail improvements, for planning purposes, or for new public buildings. In some cases the powers are used to address unneighbourly activity. In many cases the use of compulsory powers for construction affects business profits, for example through road closures or works on adjacent land. Less frequently, a rural business may find that part or all of its premises are required for an acquirer's scheme.

Parliament is currently considering a significant change in the planning framework, and a modest reform of Compulsory Purchase powers and compensation in the Planning and Compensation Bill (2003).

New roads continue to be planned and built and rural businesses will remain affected by such proposals where they arise. Equally, rail and canal projects will threaten disruption and severance to business interests, while at the same time perhaps offering opportunities for diversification. Whilst many statutory undertakers in the utilities sector have compulsory rights both to acquire rights in land and freeholds, there is not space to address this here. This chapter covers the major issues for rural businesses and suggests a number of approaches designed to enable them to protect their interests. It is not a substitute for professional advice.

Background

Some elements of the statutory framework are common to acquisitions under each of the alternatives, including the planning system, the environmental impact assessment regime and the compensation code. However, the procedures and requirements of the enabling Acts and secondary legislation differ in detail.

New legislation

Some changes to planning procedures will come about when the Planning and Compensation Act Bill (currently in Parliament) is passed into law. This process will take some time and existing plans will continue to have validity until replaced by the proposed new system. Eventually, Structure and Local Plans will be replaced by Regional Strategic Frameworks and Local Development Frameworks.

At the same time, the Planning and Compensation Bill will increase compensation for Compulsory Purchase when enacted, by introduction of a 'Loss Payment' amounting to a 10 per cent addition to existing compensation payable for land taken, damage and other losses.

Government policy

Government policy is outlined by a number of methods including:

- [ ] White Papers (on subjects such as transport and housing);
- [ ] ministerial statements;
- [ ] Planning Policy Guidance Notes and Statements;
- [ ] circulars;
- [ ] advice publications.

It is important to be aware of any new policies: for example, the Government has recently reviewed much of the guidance it gives to acquirers and claimants. There is a new Compulsory Purchase Manual designed for acquirers' use (costing £250), and new policy guidance to acquirers. If you are a member, your CLA Regional Director may well have the latest information, or alternatively CLA staff at Belgrave Square will be willing to help.

Advice and help available from the statutory authority

The Government (the Office of the Deputy Prime Minister 'ODPM') has published a number of pamphlets to help owners and occupiers of property affected by transport proposals, and others involving Compulsory Purchase. These are:

Booklet 1 – *Compulsory Purchase Procedure*
This deals with the process by which acquiring authorities decide that specified land is needed in the public interest and how they obtain the powers to purchase it compulsorily.

Booklet 2 – *Compensation to Business Owners and Occupiers*
This sets out the compensation available to business owners once a Compulsory Purchase Order (CPO) comes into force.

Booklet 3 – *Compensation to Agricultural Owners and Occupiers*
This sets out the compensation available to agricultural owners once a CPO comes into force.

Booklet 4 – *Compensation to Residential Owners and Occupiers*
This sets out the compensation available to residential owners once CPO comes into force.

Booklet 5 – *Mitigation Works*
This describes the physical help available to reduce the impact of nuisances (such as noise) caused by public works.

Who needs which booklet?

Everyone whose property is affected by a CPO should receive Booklet 1 and either Booklet 2, 3 or 4 as appropriate. If only part of their property is being taken, or they will be close to a scheme of public development, but none of their land is being taken, they should have Booklet 5 as well.

ODPM guidance requires acquirers to send these out at an early stage, but those likely to be affected should ensure they obtain a copy.

THE IMPACT OF THE PROPOSED COMPULSORY ACQUISITION

The impact on the property

There is a need to establish whether the whole or any part of the property is likely to (or will be) acquired for the scheme. Where no land is to be taken, any impact will still need to be addressed. The main factors to be considered are:

- ☐ land taken;
- ☐ physical damage;
- ☐ vibration;
- ☐ noise;
- ☐ air quality/pollution;
- ☐ access to the property;
- ☐ severance (if part of the property is to be taken);
- ☐ services to the property;
- ☐ visual impact;
- ☐ historic and cultural interests.

The impact on existing and future business enterprises

A detailed assessment will need to be made by considering whether it is possible to continue with or carry out the existing and/or proposed business enterprise(s). Professional advice will be needed to assess the position.

Assess the opportunities, if any, which the scheme opens up for development

Transport schemes may open up opportunities for development, for example:

- ☐ petrol filling stations/roadside development;
- ☐ housing;
- ☐ industrial and commercial development;
- ☐ facilities linked to rail transport interchanges or new stations;
- ☐ marinas or facilities linked to canal development;
- ☐ any opportunities for borrow pits or spoil deposition arising from the works.

There is a need to determine whether to object to the scheme, or to put forward an alternative or seek a re-alignment of the route in order to accommodate any such development opportunities. The CLA recommends that professional advice is obtained where such opportunities may be identified as a possibility.

Assess whether or not the property is so seriously affected by the scheme that the statutory blight provisions apply

Land is 'blighted' when its market value is reduced because it will be affected by or required for proposals for development for public purposes under CPO. Some properties will become unsaleable. Procedures have therefore been devised whereby an owner can serve a notice on the authority, known as a 'blight notice'. It operates as a form of reverse compulsory purchase. The owner can require the authority to purchase the property at a market price unaffected by the proposals. The procedures are described in more detail in CLA advisory handbooks.

Assess the basis upon which any compensation would be payable

The Land Compensation Code provides for those who are affected by a CPO proposal. The Code is principally contained in the Land Compensation Acts of 1961 and 1973, the Compulsory Purchase Act 1965 and the Planning and Compensation Act 1991, The Proposed Planning and Compulsory Purchase Act 2003, and case law.

The provisions of the Code are complex and it is essential to obtain professional advice from a suitably experienced chartered surveyor. Whilst the reasonable professional fees incurred in preparing and negotiating a claim for compensation will normally be paid by the acquirer, it does not assume liability for fees incurred until after the CPO is confirmed and entry is taken, or alternatively after notice to treat is served or a general vesting declaration is made and entry is taken. The basis of compensation payments is set out in the section 'Compensation' below.

It is important to know whether the scheme will take the whole or any part of your property, or whether no land is to be taken, as the provisions for compensation differ markedly between these two scenarios.

The government pamphlets on land compensation, described above, are not intended to be a complete guide to the law and have no legal force, but they do provide very helpful information on compensation and procedures.

The Royal Institution of Chartered Surveyors offers a free CPO helpline for those affected by Compulsory Purchase. Owners and occupiers are entitled to up to 30 minutes free advice from a local qualified chartered surveyor, whom the RICS state will be skilled in Compulsory Purchase and compensation. *The number to ring is 020 7222 7000, extension 589.*

DRAWING UP AN ACTION PLAN

Having gathered the necessary background information and established the impact of the scheme on the property and/or business the next step is to draw up an action plan.

It is necessary to decide whether or not to object to the scheme and/or, if applicable, to seek to take advantage of the blight provisions and/or to seek an alternative route or design that removes or minimises the threat to the property. You should also consider whether or not to seek accommodation works, including environmental protection work such as bunding (building up earth banks to protect against noise and other factors) or off-site planting that will involve a greater land take.

An objection can be put forward on the basis that there is no need for the scheme and/or any detail relating to it. In looking at the detail then, consideration has to be given as to whether an alternative route or a re-alignment of the proposed route is practical or can minimise any impact on the property.

Any argument on the need for the scheme must be confined to the specific proposal rather than the general policies of Government, such as Highways Agency or local authority policies. Promoters are not expected to defend their general policies relating to forecast and design but will be expected to justify their application to the case in point.

The main line of objection is therefore to try and bring out local factors which make the proposal adopted inappropriate when judged against specific issues. Professional advice is essential for guidance on the details, including the effect on the environment, traffic appraisals and forecasting, and cost benefit analysis.

Environmental and amenity grounds, including the impact on open countryside and effects on any habitats, are often important to making a sound objection.

Checklist for use when drawing up an action plan

You will need to consider:

☐ The procedures to be adopted by the acquirer (in order to identify every opportunity for objecting and making representations).

☐ An overall assessment of the impact of the scheme on adjoining owners/occupiers of property which may be affected by it.

☐ The overall impact of any alternative route or re-alignment of the proposed route put forward by you or by adjoining owners/occupiers.

☐ Any proposals for development in an approved or draft development plan or which may form the basis of any planning applications and/or approvals.

☐ Whether joint action to maximise opposition to the scheme is appropriate. The formation of an action group, or alternatively a group of professional advisers (who may be acting for more than one affected landowner), to discuss matters of mutual concern can be of advantage during all stages up to and including the public inquiry and also during the construction stage.

☐ The basis of any objection or representations at the public inquiry you may wish to make in order to support any such objection or negotiation.

☐ The need for professional advice (if it has not already been sought).

THE ACQUISITION OF LAND FOR A SCHEME

Land required for a scheme can be acquired by the promoting authority either by agreement or by Compulsory Purchase. In addition, the acquiring Authority can be required to purchase the land under the blight provisions. It is usual for Compulsory Purchase procedures to be run alongside planning procedures. Where feasible, ODPM will seek to run the planning inquiry and CPO inquiry simultaneously, so that a single inspector will hear both planning and CPO objections and make a single combined report to the Minister.

Acquisition by a local authority

The following are the steps involved in a typical local authority (LA) scheme:

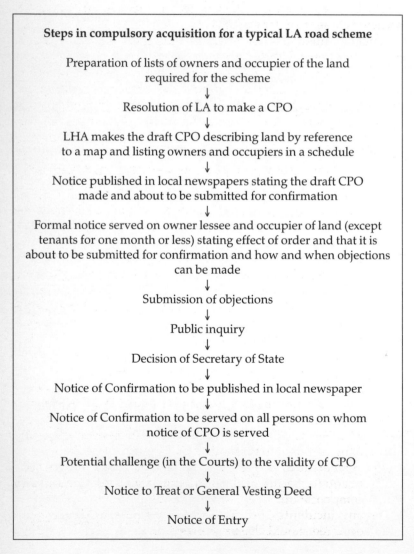

Steps in compulsory acquisition for a typical LA road scheme

Preparation of lists of owners and occupier of the land required for the scheme
↓
Resolution of LA to make a CPO
↓
LHA makes the draft CPO describing land by reference to a map and listing owners and occupiers in a schedule
↓
Notice published in local newspapers stating the draft CPO made and about to be submitted for confirmation
↓
Formal notice served on owner lessee and occupier of land (except tenants for one month or less) stating effect of order and that it is about to be submitted for confirmation and how and when objections can be made
↓
Submission of objections
↓
Public inquiry
↓
Decision of Secretary of State
↓
Notice of Confirmation to be published in local newspaper
↓
Notice of Confirmation to be served on all persons on whom notice of CPO is served
↓
Potential challenge (in the Courts) to the validity of CPO
↓
Notice to Treat or General Vesting Deed
↓
Notice of Entry

THE RIGHT TO ENTER LAND FOR A SCHEME

Entry to land may be required in the pre-construction phase, for surveys of all kinds, and will be required to build the scheme.

Pre-construction entry

Normally, the acquiring authority requires the permission of the owner/occupier to enter private land.

Where permission is not forthcoming, various Acts of Parliament provide for entry without the consent of the owner. For example, Section 189 of the Highways Act 1980 enables a person authorised in writing by the Highway Authority to enter any land for the purpose of surveying it. There is no appeal against a right of entry. If the owner objects, the Highway Authority need only give seven days notice of intended entry in order to be able to demand admission as of right under Section 290(3).

Notwithstanding any compulsory powers of entry, it is advisable to consider the following in connection with pre-construction entry:

☐ To ask for the request to be made in writing, setting out the reasons for entry, the work involved and the time to complete the works and reinstate.

☐ To agree in writing the terms and conditions upon which entry is to be given before permitting entry. The written agreement ideally should include:
  – a written schedule of condition of the property (dated photographs are desirable);
  – a payment for the right to enter;
  – an agreement to pay for any damage to property;
  – if appropriate, measures to protect the enterprise;
  – a copy of the report (where the entry is for the purposes of collecting information) to be made available to the owner or occupier free of charge;
  – an indemnity against all costs, claims, damages ensuing out of the entry on to the land;
  – agreement to pay the fees for a professional surveyor to negotiate terms and conditions and settle claims and compensation.
  – any incidents and occasions when loss or damage has occurred should also be recorded.

☐ Compensation for losses occasioned by early entry is payable under Statute. If the land or any chattels on it are damaged, the owner or occupier can recover compensation in respect of the damage. In addition, if a person is disturbed in his enjoyment of his land or chattels, he can make a claim for the disturbance.

Entry for construction

Entry for construction is preceded by two separate notices, which must be served on the owner and occupier. These are the Notice to Treat (alternatively in some cases the notice of intention to make a General Vesting Declaration), and the Notice of Entry.

It is advisable to seek a pre-start meeting with the acquirer and the project manager for the scheme. A formal record will need to be made (and if possible agreed with the acquirer) of the state of the property before entry. It will be necessary to discuss certain practical matters with the Highway Authority, for example fencing-off temporary access roads, provision of gates and other temporary accommodation works, but it should be remembered that the acquiring authority is responsible for the road scheme and for compensation to owners for injurious affection and disturbance arising from it.

Contractors' work sites

In some cases contractors may wish to make arrangements for occupation by them of land outside the road scheme for some purpose such as parking vehicles or storing apparatus. These arrangements should be looked at very carefully and professional advice sought before concluding any agreement. They should be the subject of a separate written agreement between the contractor and the owner or occupier: the acquiring authority will not be a party to them. Such written agreements should contain adequate protection for the landowner as to payment and indemnities for damage or loss. It should be noted that receipts gained from the letting or sale of such sites may be offset against the compensation payable, and care is needed to ensure the net benefits can be maximised.

BLIGHT

Claimants should be clear that the legislation has a very different definition of blight from the way the word is commonly used in practice. Blight which confers a legal duty on the acquirer to do something about it is called 'statutory blight', in order to distinguish it from general blight. General blight may be observed in an area affected by any major building or infrastructure project, whether or not the property affected is subject to compulsory acquisition. Statutory blight is limited to only those cases where the property is to be taken in its entirety by compulsory acquisition for the purposes of the scheme, or is so badly affected by the scheme that it is unsaleable on the open market. Blight procedures enable a qualifying owner to serve a notice on the acquirer, known as a 'blight notice'. It operates as a form of reverse Compulsory Purchase: the qualifying owner can require the acquirer to purchase the property at a market price which ignores the effects of its proposals. Where an owner does not qualify under the statutory blight regime, he may be able to persuade the acquirer to use its powers of discretionary purchase, but these powers are again subject to limitations.

DISCRETIONARY PURCHASE PROCEDURES

There will be occasions when an owner cannot legally qualify for the protection of the blight provisions, but is still suffering hardship. A property can easily be blighted during the period between the announcement of the preferred route. In these circumstances, Government has introduced a power for acquirers to consider making discretionary purchases in cases of proven hardship.

COMPENSATION

The principles of compensation

Space does not permit a discussion of the details of the 'compensation code'. The code is an amalgam, comprising statute law laid down in the Land Compensation Acts 1961 and 1973, the Planning and Compensation Act 1991 and the Compulsory Purchase Act 1965, together with other legislation and substantial amounts of case law.

The basic principle of compensation is that the acquirer is required to put a claimant into the same position that he was in before the acquisition, but ignoring the fact that the owner had no choice but to sell part or all of the property. This principle is described as 'equivalence'. The owner is assumed to be a willing seller of the land that is taken.

Accordingly, when the land is valued, no account is taken of the particular benefit that the land has for the scheme, and its market value is assessed on the basis of what any other purchaser would pay in the market. In addition, an owner is entitled to 'injurious affection' (literally the injury done to his adjacent property interests), being the loss in value of his adjoining property arising from the purchase, and 'disturbance' (the added costs arising from the purchase, including professional fees and the like).

The acquirer is entitled to offset benefits that flow to the claimant as a result of the scheme. For example, if the scheme brings direct benefit (for example, by opening up land for development) the increase in value of the retained land can be offset against the claim for injurious affection. This is a specialised and contentious area of the compensation code.

The question of compensation has been separated, in consideration of the principle, from the question of whether or not the scheme should be approved. Compulsory Purchase law enables the acquirer to take possession of the land without reference to the eventual price that may be agreed (or imposed) for the loss suffered by the claimant. The compensation code works separately. The claimant is required to set out his claim in response to the Notice to Treat (referred to above). The acquirer is required to pay 90 per cent of its own estimate of the compensation due if claimed by the claimant (and subject to the claimant giving three months' notice and sufficient detail to enable the acquirer to calculate the amount) on taking entry to the land.

In many cases, particularly in the rural sector where the acquisition rarely extends to the whole of the property owned by the claimant, it will be difficult to assess accurately the amount of compensation due until the works are at least started, if not complete. Nonetheless, the acquisition, if approved by the Secretary of State, can go ahead, leaving the question of compensation (in default of agreement) to be decided by the specialist valuation court known as the Lands Tribunal. This is a specialist area, and a separate CLA advisory handbook on the Lands Tribunal is available.

Accommodation works

The acquirer is able (but not required) to ameliorate the effect of its scheme on the claimant by including the provision of accommodation works in its proposals. Such works range from the small and obvious, such as the provision of alternative new means of access where the original access is cut off, through to large-scale works such as the provision of overpass bridges or access tunnels.

It is necessary to negotiate all such matters with the acquiring authority in the first instance to try and have them incorporated in the scheme. If the scheme design does not include accommodation works, they will be dealt with within the compensation code provisions. This means that the acquirer may still be willing to provide them in order to reduce the amount it would have to pay by way of compensation, but negotiations are handed over to the valuer acting for the acquiring authority for compensation to be assessed.

Compensation where no land is taken

Where a business owner does not lose land but is affected by the opening of a new public works, he may be entitled to compensation under Part 1 of the Land Compensation Act 1973. This permits a claim to be made where the property is affected by the physical impact of the works and its use. Claims must be made within a 12-month period beginning one year after the new scheme is opened; which allows the normal pattern of usage to become established.

Later claims are not allowed. If, for example, a road becomes much busier because it acts as a feeder into a motorway junction, no claim can be made unless the road was part of the improvement scheme and physical works were undertaken to it. Compensation for a Part 1 claim is assessed on a 'before and after' basis.

References

A Campaigner's Guide to Compulsory Purchase, CLA Advisory Handbook, CLA 11 (1997)

The Lands Tribunal: resolving disputes on statutory compensation, CLA Advisory Handbook, CLA 24 (2001)

New Transport Schemes, a new CLA Advisory Handbook, (available from summer 2003)

1.3 Tenancy law and the management of agricultural tenancies

Duncan Sigournay, Senior Legal Adviser, CLA

INTRODUCTION

Agricultural land within England and Wales is occupied in a number of different ways. These range from owner-occupation through to different types of letting arrangements such as farm business tenancies (governed by the Agricultural Tenancies Act 1995) or protected tenancies (under the Agricultural Holdings Act 1986), as well as share farming and other contractual arrangements. Indeed, many farmers occupy land under a combination of these arrangements.

Given the current state of the rural economy, and in particular the agricultural sector, both owner-occupiers and tenants alike are increasingly looking towards non-agricultural activities to generate much needed income. That is not to say that diversification will be the solution for everyone but it is certainly an avenue worth considering.

In this chapter diversification in the context of let agricultural land will be considered – from both the landlord's and the tenant's perspective. Accordingly, the following issues will be addressed:

☐ Agricultural tenancies – an overview
☐ Agricultural holdings under the Agricultural Holdings Act 1986:
  – Characteristics
  – Security of tenure
  – Notice to Quit of whole
  – Notice to Quit of part
  – Compensation
  – Diversification by tenant under the 1986 Act

- ☐ Farm business tenancy under the Agricultural Tenancies Act 1995:
  - Characteristics
  - Termination
  - Break clauses
  - Compensation
  - Diversification by tenant under the 1995 Act
- ☐ Possible reforms

AGRICULTURAL TENANCIES – AN OVERVIEW

By virtue of the Agricultural Tenancies Act 1995 agricultural tenancies can now effectively be divided into two separate legislative camps: those granted on or after 1 September 1995, which will typically be farm business tenancies – save in a number of limited circumstances – and those agreements preceding that date, which will be governed by the Agricultural Holdings Act 1986.

Since the two governing statutes are quite distinct and adopt a totally different approach to the letting of land, it is imperative that the parties are aware of the status of their agreement. The differences impact greatly upon landlords and tenants wishing to diversify away from traditional agricultural activities. Accordingly, if in any doubt, professional advice should be sought.

AGRICULTURAL HOLDINGS ACT 1986

The 1986 Act effectively provides security of tenure for the tenant as well as imposing certain conditions on the parties, in particular, in relation to compensation. Furthermore, agricultural tenancies entered into prior to 12 July 1984 will typically benefit from succession rights – that is not automatic succession for close members of the tenant's family but merely enabling such members to apply for succession with all the incumbent qualifying criteria.

As such, although new 1986 Act tenancies cannot be created, the succession provisions will ensure that such tenancies endure for some time to come.

What is an agricultural holding?

Essentially an agricultural holding is a letting of agricultural land that is used for a trade or business. However, that is not to say that the land must be used exclusively for agriculture – the main criterion is that the actual use of the land at its commencement and subsequently is predominantly agricultural.

As will be seen later, with farm business tenancies there is scope within agricultural holdings to diversify into non-agricultural commercial activities without the tenancy necessarily losing the protection afforded by the 1986 Act.

Diversification by landlord – security of tenure under the 1986 Act

The security of tenure provisions within the 1986 Act effectively treats most agricultural holdings as yearly tenancies. Furthermore it imposes restrictions on the operation of notices to quit. As such it can often be quite difficult for landlords to regain possession in order to pursue their own diversification objectives.

So what can be done by the landlord when a development potential arises (eg. a change in the local plan, etc)? In the absence of a negotiated surrender by the tenant, the landlord will be faced with having to serve a Notice to Quit on the tenant based upon one of the statutory grounds.

Incontestable notices to quit

The 1986 Act prescribes a number of circumstances in which a valid Notice to Quit of the whole of the holding can be served on the tenant without the tenant having a right to serve a counter notice. Indeed, the only action available to the tenant in such circumstances is to challenge whether the ground stated in the Notice to Quit in fact exists. The statutory grounds for incontestable notices comprise:

- ☐ Case A – retirement from smallholding where suitable alternative accommodation is available;
- ☐ Case B – the land is required for a non-agricultural use for which planning permission has been obtained;
- ☐ Case C – a Notice to Quit is served within six months of a certificate of bad husbandry having been granted by the Agricultural Land Tribunal;
- ☐ Case D – non-compliance with either a notice to pay rent or notice to remedy;
- ☐ Case E – the landlord has been materially prejudiced by a breach of the tenant not capable of being remedied;

☐ Case F – insolvency of the tenant;
☐ Case G – death of the tenant – though such a notice does not prevent a close relative applying for succession where qualifying criteria and procedural steps have been fulfilled;
☐ Case H – Minister's amalgamation scheme.

In practice, the statutory ground most likely to be used by the landlord in order to gain possession in pursuit of developing the land will be Case B since it is particularly concerned with non-agricultural activities. However, in certain circumstances other statutory grounds may also be appropriate.

Case B Notice to Quit

Landlords must be aware that the planning permission must be obtained prior to the service of the Notice to Quit. Furthermore the Notice to Quit must relate to the whole of the holding and not just part of it unless the landlord can show that he has the ability to serve a Notice to Quit of part.

Notice to Quit – length

On the basis that the landlord has a planning permission for non-agricultural use, what is the timescale involved? In essence, the Notice to Quit would terminate the tenancy 12 months from the end of the current year of the tenancy. However, there are exceptions to this general rule. Consequently, timing can be crucial with a landlord possibly having to wait a further year for possession if the notice is not served before the end of the tenancy anniversary. The matter is further complicated by the fact that many agricultural tenancies are oral in nature and therefore there may be some confusion as to the actual anniversary date.

Notice to Quit of part

If the holding is large and the permission only relates to part of it then there are three circumstances in which a Notice to Quit of part can be valid:

☐ Where there is an express provision within the agreement. Importantly, such a provision will not be implied into a tenancy agreement.
☐ Section 31 of the 1986 Act sets out certain statutory exceptions allowing notices to quit of part. This section contains a collection

of socially desirable objects for which the landlord should be entitled to resume possession of part only of the holding (eg erection of cottages or other houses for farm labourers, provision of allotments, adjusting boundaries between agricultural units).

☐ Where there has been a severance of the landlord's reversion, ie the freehold owner of the land sells off a part of the freehold to another legal entity. There still exists only one tenancy, although in practice the tenant would be paying two landlords apportioned rent.

Enlargement of notice

One point that must be borne in mind is where Notice to Quit of part is served arising out of either a severed reversion or under section 31 of the 1986 Act, the tenant would be entitled to enlarge the notice to cover the whole of the holding, not just that part of the holding mentioned in the Notice to Quit. That may or may not be desirable to the landlord.

On the basis that such a Notice to Quit was valid the tenant would have very little recourse but to submit a claim for compensation. Although not applicable to all scenarios, compensation can be based upon disturbance, improvements, tenant right matters and other miscellaneous issues.

In October 1999 a joint Guidance note was issued by the Country Land & Business Association, Tenant Farmers' Association and the National Farmers' Union in relation to compensation and Case B notices to quit. This is available from the respective organisations.

Disturbance compensation formula

In the event of a successful Case B Notice to Quit the disturbance compensation formula would be one year's rent, and possibly up to two years' rent if additional loss can be proved, and in some circumstances a further four years' rent on top of the one or two may also be allowed.

Diversification by tenant under the 1986 Act

As highlighted earlier, provided the character of the holding remains 'predominantly' agricultural the tenancy will continue to fall under the provisions of the 1986 Act notwithstanding that non-agricultural activities take place on the land.

Many landlords have granted consent to tenants with 1986 Act tenancies to undertake limited diversification activities, such as bed and breakfast in the farmhouse, or a camping site on the farm.

Even though the 1986 Act provides a suitable framework in which modest diversification proposals can be incorporated, tenants must be aware of any 'user covenants' which are commonly applied within their tenancy agreements which restrict the use of the land to a particular purpose (eg agriculture, dairy farming, etc). Such covenants will be binding on the parties and, therefore, in such circumstances the tenant will need to seek his landlord's consent to the diversification proposal.

Although tenants may be reluctant to approach landlords for such consent they should not assume that consent will not be forthcoming. Indeed, in a survey commissioned by the CLA and undertaken by the National Farm Research Unit in 2002 it was found that some 82 per cent of landlords questioned provided positive indications of the availability of consent to tenants wishing to diversify.

Generally landlords want their tenants to be successful; success brings the incentive that the landlord may also benefit from enhanced rent and the knowledge that his tenant's business is more viable. The fact that many owner-occupiers have also benefited from diversification projects often makes them more predisposed to consider such approaches from their tenants.

At the time of writing there is no mechanism in place to force the landlord to either grant consent or for any conditions attached to consent to be adjudicated upon. However, it is essential that tenants present to a landlord a well thought out, structured and costed proposal – such an approach is much more likely to win approval than one which is not so well prepared.

The landlord may welcome the proposals; alternatively he may have legitimate concerns about it – in which case some conditions may be attached to the landlord's consent. Alternatively, the landlord may consider that the proposal is not suitable or even that such a project, if implemented, should not remain under the provisions of the 1986 Act. The landlord may be able to argue legitimately that the matter would be better suited to a surrender of the particular building/land with an immediate grant of a business tenancy to the tenant under the provisions of the Landlord and Tenant Act 1954.

AGRICULTURAL TENANCIES ACT 1995

The essence of the Agricultural Tenancies Act 1995 is freedom of contract and in only limited areas – fixtures, compensation, rent and certain elements of dispute resolution – is compliance with statute mandatory. There are other areas in which the Act provides a fallback should the parties not make other arrangements but, generally speaking, there is far greater scope for the imagination than was the case under the Agricultural Holdings Act 1986.

Tenancies under the 1995 Act do not carry security of tenure, other than for the term contained within the tenancy agreement, nor do they grant succession rights to agricultural tenants.

One of the main aims of the Act was to encourage landowners to let land where previously they were inhibited from doing so by the strictures of the former regime. This has broadly been achieved, and owners are increasingly adopting the 1995 Act.

Although farm business tenancies can be created orally, the lack of statutory default provisions makes such an approach hazardous and it is certainly not recommended.

What is a farm business tenancy?

Under Section 1 of the 1995 Act a tenancy (whether oral or written) beginning on or after 1 September 1995 will be a farm business tenancy (FBT) provided that it satisfies the 'business' conditions and either the 'agriculture' or 'notice' condition.

The 'business' conditions require that at least part of the land must be farmed for the purposes of a trade or business and must have been so farmed since the beginning of the tenancy. 'Farming' is defined to include 'the carrying on in relation to land of any agricultural activity', and 'agriculture' has the same definition as in the Agricultural Holdings Act 1986.

There is a rebuttable presumption that if the land is farmed by way of a trade or business at the time the status of the tenancy is challenged it has been so farmed since the beginning of the tenancy. In other words, the burden of proof is on the party that claims that the condition is not fulfilled.

The 'agriculture' condition requires that the character of the tenancy is primarily or wholly agricultural. Unlike the 'business' conditions, the 'agriculture' condition needs only to be satisfied at the time of challenge to the tenancy's status.

The 'agriculture' condition can be avoided by compliance with the 'notice' conditions. These require that the Landlord and Tenant exchange notices on or before the date they enter into the tenancy agreement or, if earlier, the date the tenancy begins. The notices must identify the land to be comprised in the proposed tenancy and confirm the intention of the parties that the tenancy is to be and remain a farm business tenancy. The character of the tenancy must be wholly or primarily agricultural at the outset.

Two points arise from the 'notice' conditions. First, the notices must be exchanged; it is not good enough that one of the parties serves a notice on the other. Secondly, they must be exchanged on or before the earlier of the date of the agreement creating the tenancy or the date on which the tenancy begins (ie the date on which the tenant becomes entitled to enter into possession of the holding); the condition is not satisfied by a notice contained in the contract of tenancy itself.

If the 'business' conditions fail at any point in the term and the business use later recommences, the result (subject to what is said below) will be not a farm business tenancy but a tenancy protected by the Landlord & Tenant Act 1954, Part II.

Similarly, if neither the 'agriculture' nor the 'notice' conditions are fulfilled, the tenancy will not be a farm business tenancy. If the land is used for business purposes, it will be protected by Part II of the 1954 Act; if there is no business use, governance will revert to the common law.

In assessing the status of the tenancy, use in breach of covenant is disregarded, except where the landlord or a predecessor of his has consented to the changed use or the landlord personally has acquiesced in it. It is, therefore, advisable to import obligations as to user which will assist in maintaining the status of the tenancy as a farm business tenancy.

Termination of farm business tenancies

A farm business tenancy for a fixed term of two years or less expires automatically on the term date and therefore no notice need be served by either party to bring it to an end.

However, for a tenancy for a fixed term of more than two years to be terminated notice of between 12 and 24 months must be served. If neither party serves such a notice, the tenancy will continue as a tenancy from year to year.

A yearly tenancy, whether granted initially or arising after a fixed-term tenancy, can be terminated only by a notice of between 12 and 24 months.

Tenancies based on a period other than a year (eg weekly, monthly or quarterly tenancies) are terminated in accordance with common law rules by notice equating to one period of the tenancy (a week, a month or a quarter as the case may be) and expiring at the end of a period of the tenancy.

Break clauses

A break clause in a fixed-term tenancy for more than two years will operate only if notice of 12 and 24 months has first been served. A break clause in a fixed-term tenancy of two years or less can be operated on whatever period of notice the parties agree.

Compensation

The tenant is entitled to compensation for improvements that add to the letting value of the holding at the termination of the tenancy. Improvements are defined to include physical improvements and intangible advantages such as planning permission.

In order to be eligible for compensation the tenant must have obtained the written consent of his landlord or the arbitrator to make the improvement.

There are special provisions dealing with compensation where there are successive tenancies, and where the landlord has resumed possession of part or there has been a severance of the reversion.

Diversification by tenant under the 1995 Act

Clearly the effect of the various interrelated qualifying criteria for a farm business tenancy ('business', 'notice' and 'agriculture' conditions) is to create a multitude of possible scenarios for the actual status of a tenancy during its lifetime – dependent upon the activities being conducted on the holding at any particular time. Typically these would involve changes in either the 'business' nature of the holding or a move away from traditional 'agricultural' activities.

Indeed, provided the 'business' condition and the 'notice' condition are satisfied, the status of the tenancy would only change were the agricultural activity on the holding to amount to nothing more than *de minimis*. On the other hand if the 'notice' condition had not been satisfied, one would be relying upon the 'agriculture' condition requiring the holding to be 'primarily or wholly agricultural'.

Accordingly, farm business tenancies can often be used/retained when diversification/non-agricultural activities are planned on the holding.

This highlights one of the key, though often overlooked, advantages of farm business tenancies, namely their suitability to diversification: indeed, the 1995 Act was drafted with the changing nature of agriculture in England and Wales in mind. The fact that more use of its flexibility has not been made is not necessarily the fault of the 1995 Act itself but the lack of appreciation of its flexibility by professionals, tenants and landlords alike.

User clauses

As with the case of 1986 Act tenancies, the tenant should be familiar with the user covenants contained within the agreement. Any proposal that does not comply with such clauses will require the landlord's consent.

In particular, where the investment into a scheme is large it is imperative that the landlord is involved at an early stage.

The CLA have always advocated that landlords give serious consideration to tenants' proposals provided such proposals are well thought out and prepared. Similarly, tenants should be aware that even the most reasonable request for consent might be rejected on perfectly reasonable grounds.

Forms and precedents

The CLA publishes a number of detailed guides to agricultural tenancy legislation, and useful precedents for agreements. These include 'farm business tenancies', 'farm business tenancies for under two years' and 'grazing agreements'.

POSSIBLE REFORMS

In November 2002 the Tenancy Reform Industry Group (TRIG) was re-established. TRIG is a cross-industry group charged by DEFRA to look into possible areas of reform to both agricultural tenancy legislation and fiscal issues affecting the agricultural sector. It was first used to great effect in the formulation of the Agricultural Tenancies Act 1995.

Its re-establishment follows the 2002 study by the University of Plymouth into the 'Economic Evaluation of the Agricultural Tenancies Act 1995' as well as the Report of the Policy Commission on the Future of Food and Farming in January 2002. Both reports highlighted issues relating to diversification on tenanted holdings as well as other matters affecting agricultural tenancies.

Importantly, one one of the recommendations from the University of Plymouth report was that the usefulness of farm business tenancies was not fully appreciated and that DEFRA should seek to promote the awareness of the use of FBTs.

At the time of writing, TRIG is preparing its final report for ministers and as such it is difficult to say with any certainty which, if any, of its proposals will be adopted.

However, of all of TRIG's recommendations the one that would have the greatest impact, if implemented, is the proposal to introduce a Code of Good Practice in relation to tenants seeking their landlord's consent for diversification projects. It is envisaged that the Code would set out the procedural steps to be taken by each party including details of information to be disclosed. This would then create an environment in which both parties could give serious consideration to the proposal.

In addition to the Code, TRIG have proposed that a non-binding Ombudsman Scheme be established to deal with cases where consent has been refused or where, in the opinion of the tenant, unreasonable conditions have been imposed in return for consent being granted. The Ombudsman would then consider whether the refusal to grant consent, or indeed the conditions to be attached to consent, were reasonable in the circumstances.

It is hoped that the existence of such a Code of Good Practice will promote greater communication and co-operation between landlords and tenants.

References

Survey of Farm Landlords & CLA Data Analysis, National Farm Research Unit (April 2002)

An Economic Evaluation of the Agricultural Tenancies Act 1995, The University of Plymouth Department of Land Use and Rural Management (April 2002)

Compensation and Case B Notices to Quit, joint Guidance note: CLA, Tenant Farmers' Association, National Farmers' Union (October 1999)

Report of the Policy Commission on the Future of Food and Farming (January 2002), available from the Cabinet Office website: www.cabinet-office.gov.uk/farming

Agricultural Tenancies Act – Farm Business Tenancies, CLA advisory handbook CLA6 (1999)

Farm Business Tenancies for a Fixed Term of Two Years, CLA advisory handbook CLA18 (2000)

Grazing Agreements, CLA advisory handbook CLA13 (1999)

1.4 Capital gains tax and inheritance tax issues

Brian Castle, Senior Taxation Adviser, CLA

INTRODUCTION

The rural businessman/landowner faces a bewildering array of capital taxes on his assets and any transactions or disposals, or even a change of use, needs to take into account the likely impact on capital tax liabilities both current and future. In the case of diversification, it is important to consider how a change of use might affect reliefs accumulated by a previous business activity. It is important that a proposed change and its tax implications are fully understood before making a final commitment. Post mortem tax planning is usually unwelcome!

CAPITAL GAINS TAX

Capital gains tax is a tax on the increase in the value of an asset since it was acquired (or since March 1982, whichever is the latest) until the date of its disposal. Up until April 1998 the original cost of acquisition, or March 1982 base cost, would be augmented by the inclusion of indexation relief to reduce the impact of inflation over the period of ownership of the asset. However, as part of a package of reforms by the present Chancellor of the Exchequer to capital gains tax for non-corporate taxpayers, indexation relief has been frozen at its April 1998 level and retirement relief is being phased out. In their place is a new taper relief that reduces chargeable gains according to the length of time that the asset has been owned and the use to which it has been put. There are two rates of taper relief: business asset taper relief and non-business asset taper relief.

Business asset taper relief (BATR)

It is this relief that most rural businesses should aspire to retain as, at its maximum, it will reduce gains by up to 75 per cent after two years of appropriate business use of the asset. Business use of an asset will include the following:

☐ Assets used in an individual's trade;
☐ Shares in any unquoted trading company;
☐ Shares in a quoted trading company where the shareholder exercises at least 5 per cent of the voting rights;
☐ Shares held by an employee in a trading company;
☐ Shares held by an employee in a non-trading company by which he is employed, provided that he does not have an interest greater than 10 per cent in the company.

From April 2002 gains on business assets are tapered in accordance with the figures in Table 1.4.1.

Table 1.4.1 Business asset taper relief (BATR)

Number of complete years for which asset held	% of gain chargeable	Effective tax rate for higher-rate taxpayer %
0	100	40
1	50	20
2 or more	25	10

Thus, in the case of a rural business contemplating the diversification of its activities, the main consideration is that any underlying assets should retain their business asset status. Otherwise, the non-business asset rate of relief will apply and, as can be seen from the Table 1.4.2, the maximum rate of relief is 40 per cent but only after 10 years and with nothing for the first three years of ownership.

The rate of taper relief will thus depend on the current use of an asset. If there is a change of use, say, from farming to letting of the land this would potentially increase a future capital gains tax liability if the land was disposed of.

Rollover relief

It is possible to postpone a chargeable gain on the disposal of an

Table 1.4.2 Non-business asset taper relief

Number of complete years after April 1998 for which asset held	% of gain chargeable	Effective tax rate for higher-rate taxpayer %
0	100	40
1	100	40
2	100	40
3	95	38
4	90	36
5	85	34
6	80	32
7	75	30
8	70	28
9	65	26
10 or more	60	24

Assets held at 5 April 1998 qualify for a 'bonus' year of holding.

asset when the proceeds are re-invested into the acquisition of new assets. The main condition is that both the 'old assets' and the 'new assets' must be used for the purposes of a trade. Thus the disposal of, say, farmland and the purchase of a house to be rented out for residential purposes could not qualify for rollover relief. Relief would be equally denied if the first disposal was of the let property.

Retirement relief

Retirement relief was phased out in April 2003. The remaining amount of relief available for disposals relevant to the final tax year 2002/2003 is:

Gains up to £50,000   all gains exempt
Gains between £50,001 and £200,000   half the gains exempt

The conditions for retirement relief are quite complicated and beyond the scope of this book, and specialist advice needs to be taken before contemplating making a claim. Briefly, the relief is available on gains arising in either of the two following circumstances: disposal of a business; or cessation of a business and the disposal of chargeable assets used in that business within 12 months of the date of cessation.

In either case, the relief is only available to a person who is over the age of 50, or who is retiring from the business on the grounds of ill health.

Hold over relief

Owners of rural businesses could decide on a strategy to give away some business assets to other members of their family; in which case, if gains do arise on the disposal, the owner and the recipients might decide to hold over the gains until the new owner decides to dispose of the assets. Hold over relief is available on the gift of business assets or property that would qualify for agricultural property relief from inheritance tax (including let land).

Capital gains tax annual exemption and rates of tax

If, after considering all of the above reliefs, tax still has to be paid then the net gains can be further reduced by the annual exemption (currently £7,700) after which tax is charged on the gains as if the gains were the top slice of a person's income and charged at the following rates:

10% to starting rate limit	£1,920
20% to basic rate limit	£1,921–£29,900
40%	on balance of gains

INHERITANCE TAX

Introduction

Inheritance tax is a charge to tax on transfers made from an individual's estate at death and lifetime gifts made within seven years of death. The latter are known as 'potentially exempt transfers' on the basis that there is no immediate charge to tax upon making the gift, but if the transferor fails to survive the gift for seven years, or at least three years, then the gift is aggregated with the transferors estate at death and inheritance tax calculated accordingly. In the case of survival between four and seven years after the gift, the tax on the gift is tapered by 20 per cent for each year until full exemption is achieved after the seventh year. The charge to tax is at 40 per cent after deducting the nil rate band of £250,000. A full explanation of the workings of the tax is beyond the scope of this book and in any case specialist advice from a solicitor and/or tax specialist should be sought when drafting a will and deciding upon any inheritance tax planning. What is considered next is the impact of inheritance tax on a rural business.

Agricultural Property Relief and Business Property Relief

Governments have appreciated that if businesses are taxed heavily on death or on transfer then this can place additional burdens on those businesses, and may even place the survival of the business and jobs within it at risk. In order to avoid this there are two specific reliefs from inheritance tax: Agricultural Property Relief (APR); and Business property relief (BPR).

Both of these reliefs reduce the exposure of a business to inheritance tax to either 100 per cent or 50 per cent depending on certain conditions being met. These are now considered in turn.

Agricultural Property Relief

The scope of this relief is defined in Inheritance Tax Act 1984, sections 115–124. In order for property to qualify for APR, two prime conditions need to be satisfied in all cases.

☐ The property is occupied for the purposes of agriculture. This is satisfied either by the landowner occupying the land for two years prior to transfer or by owning the land for seven years and having it occupied for agricultural purposes by anybody during the seven years prior to transfer.

☐ The property is agricultural property as defined in IHTA 1984, section 115(2):

> '"agricultural property" means agricultural land or pasture and includes woodland and any building used in connection with the intensive rearing of livestock or fish if the woodland or building is occupied with agricultural land or pasture and the occupation is ancillary to that of the agricultural land or pasture; and also includes such cottages, farm buildings and farmhouses, together with the land occupied with them, as are of a character appropriate to the property.'

Relief is granted on the agricultural value of the agricultural property. This is not necessarily the market value of the property. The rate of relief is at either 100 per cent or 50 per cent depending on whether the transferor satisfies the conditions outlined below.

100 per cent APR

100 per cent relief applies to:

☐ Property where the transferor has the right to vacant possession or can obtain vacant possession within 12 months (or 24 months by extra statutory concession ESC F17);

☐ Property let on a tenancy that began on or after 1 September 1995 irrespective of the terms of that tenancy. Generally these are farm business tenancies (FBTs) under the provisions of the Agricultural Tenancies Act 1995.

☐ Let agricultural land that does not diminish the value of the land.

☐ Agricultural land owned prior to 10 March 1981 and which satisfies the previous conditions for 'working farmer' relief.

50 per cent APR

Relief at 50 per cent is given in any other circumstances in which the above conditions cannot be met. These would chiefly be agricultural tenancies in which the transferor could not get vacant possession of the land within 24 months.

Business Property Relief

Agricultural Property Relief takes priority over Business Property Relief. In any situation where both reliefs are available, then APR comes first and BPR second. The relief is provided for in the Inheritance Act 1984 sections 103 to 114.

Relief is available at 100 per cent in the following circumstances:

☐ a business carried on as a sole trader or a partner's interest in a business carried on in partnership;

☐ any unquoted shares in a company that does not carry on an excluded business*;

☐ unquoted securities (as opposed to shares) in a company that was controlled by the transferor before the transfer.

_____

* excluded business means a business: dealing in securities, stocks and shares; dealing in land or buildings; or making or holding investments.

50 per cent BPR is available in the following circumstances:

- ☐ shares or securities conferring control in a quoted company;
- ☐ land carried on by a partnership in which the transferor is a partner; or by a company (quoted or unquoted) in which he is a controlling shareholder;
- ☐ land, buildings and machinery used in a business in which the transferor had a life interest.

In the context of a rural business or an existing agricultural business that is proposing to diversify, the exclusions above from Business Property Relief have to be carefully considered. If a farmer decided to cease farming and let out redundant agricultural buildings for either commercial or residential lets then not only has the agricultural property ceased to be available, but no corresponding business property relief would be available, because the income would be in the form of rent and the rental business considered as being the making or holding of investments.

Other problem areas are businesses that are a mixture of activities such as farming with, perhaps, a caravan park or other investment activity. Recent case law has determined that the business has to be looked at in the round, and in certain circumstances where the investment activity is less than 20 per cent of the total activity of the business, viewed as a whole, business property relief remains available.

Table 1.4.3 is a summary of the various tax treatments of income in which rural businesses might be involved.

Table 1.4.3 Tax treatment of income from rural businesses

Activity	Income	Loss relief	CGT	IHT
Farming	Farming income Schedule D Case I	General but subject to hobby farming restrictions (eg s. 397 TA 1988).	All reliefs	100% APR[1]
Letting farms	Schedule A	Restricted but allowance for excess management expenses	Only hold-over relief	50% APR, but 100% APR on Farm Business Tenancies post 1/9/95
Furnished holiday lettings	Schedule A but deemed Schedule D Case I	Generally available	Deemed to qualify for all relief	100% BPR[2] may be available
Assured shorthold lettings	Schedule A	Fully restricted	No relief	Generally no reliefs but some farm cottages qualify for APR
Commercial woodlands	Not taxable	No relief	Standing timber is outside the scope; rollover relief on land	100% BPR if separate accounts maintained, otherwise special deferral under woodlands relief
Amenity woodlands	No general rule known: the 'Nelson's eye' approach		NONE	100% APR if ancillary to, and occupied with, agricultural land
Sporting rights	Normally Schedule A	Special rules within restrictions of Schedule A	NONE	None specific but some value may be included within agricultural land and hence qualify for APR
Houses open to public	If sufficiently like a business then Schedule D Case I	Full relief if treated as a trade	All relief on business element and possible exemption on private element	100% BPR on business element
Mineral royalties	50% income and 50% capital (subject to special rules)	Special rules apply	Special terminal loss relief only	No relief
Tipping	Normally capital		No relief specifically afforded but reliefs can be available based on additional use of land	
Ancillary businesses	Separate Trades under Schedule D Case I	Generally available	All reliefs	100% BPR
Recreation	Schedule A or Schedule D	Depends upon nature of income and facilities offered. Presumption towards no relief		

[1] APR = Agricultural Property Relief   [2] BPR = Business Property Relief

References

The CLA publishes a number of advisory handbooks covering taxation matters, currently including:

CGT Roll Over Relief (1999) CLA3
CGT Retirement Relief (1994) CLA4
Inheritance Tax Agricultural Property Relief (1995) CLA8
Taxation of Furnished Holiday Accommodation (2000) CLA20
Rating and Council Tax (2002) CLA31

Part Two:

The Operation of a Country Business

2.1 Business tenancies

Duncan Sigournay, Senior Legal Adviser, CLA

INTRODUCTION

In seeking to generate more income from rural property, there are often opportunities to let buildings (and indeed other land) for non-agricultural commercial uses. These opportunities may range from letting out a building to a farming contractor to store his machinery to a multi-million pound conversion of existing farm buildings to create a rural business park.

When considering such diversification, landowners must be careful not to fall foul of the regulations that govern the conversion and use of buildings. Similarly, they must also be aware of the legislation that governs such business lettings.

This chapter sets out the issues that must be considered in relation to such lettings and reviews the problems that can arise during the tenancy. In particular the following matters will be considered:

☐ The initial appraisal;
☐ The basic provisions of the Landlord and Tenant Act 1954;
☐ Termination of a business tenancy;
☐ Compensation issues;
☐ 'Contracting out' of the 1954 Act;
☐ Stamp duty;
☐ Registration;
☐ Alternative contractual arrangements – licences, tenancies at will.

THE INITIAL APPRAISAL

A building may become available for commercial letting in a number of ways: the farmer may have no further use for a building; an approach may be made by a commercial business; or, in a drive to generate more income within an existing business, management changes may result in the present activities being housed in fewer buildings, releasing space for other uses. Traditional buildings are often left unused because they are awkward, labour intensive and, perhaps, the livestock that used to occupy them may have disappeared. If in a sound condition, such buildings can be upgraded by conversion to provide useful commercial space.

Before embarking on a planning application or investing money to facilitate the letting, a detailed appraisal needs to be undertaken. It is important to assess the following factors at the outset:

☐ the nature of the uses to which the building may be put;
☐ the effect that any new activity will have on the farmhouse, on the enjoyment of the property and on the day-to-day running of the farm;
☐ the potential market for a tenancy of the building;
☐ the costs to be incurred in seeking planning permission and the project costs to repair and improve the building so that it is fit for its new use;
☐ the rental value that can reasonably be expected;
☐ the capital cost against the capital value of the scheme as completed.

If an analysis of these issues shows that there is relatively little impact on the existing business, that only a modest investment is required and that there is a reasonable prospect of letting and in due course re-letting the building, the owner may have confidence to proceed.

If an owner is a little uncertain but believes that there is a market for the building, it may be appropriate to go through the planning process to secure permission; thereafter the owner can look for a tenant and grant a lease on what is referred to (by surveyors) as a 'pre-let' basis: the tenancy is entered into – binding both parties – but its commencement, and the payment of rent, is delayed until the works are completed. This gives security to the owner before he invests in the conversion scheme.

If the cost of a conversion is substantial the owner should consider two issues: what effect that additional capital investment will have on his finances as the investment will have an effect on his balance sheet and perhaps his borrowings. Secondly the appraisal must take a very realistic approach to the rents that are likely to be achieved, including allowances for voids (periods when the property is empty) and bad debts. Unless there is a real prospect of a positive return and rental growth, owners should proceed with caution.

Professional advice

If a landowner wants to let to a new tenant he must consider what terms are appropriate for the letting including length of term, repairing obligations and rent. Where it is proposed that the letting is to be for a long term or it covers more than the odd barn or shed, it would be sensible to go to an agent or a solicitor to discuss the whole proposal. It may seem an unnecessary expense but in the context of the overall scheme and associated investment such a move may prove invaluable.

Some landowners may want to rely on their agents to provide suitable documents. It should be remembered, however, that it is an offence for a person who is not a solicitor or barrister to directly or indirectly prepare a lease for a term of over three years. However, no offence is committed if the document was drawn up without any fee, gain or reward.

In addition, the Agricultural Tenancies Act 1995 does allow certain accredited persons to draw up farm business tenancies in excess of three years. Such accredited persons include: a full member of the Central Association of Agricultural Valuers; an associate or Fellow of the Incorporated Society of Valuers and Auctioneers or of the Royal Institution of Chartered Surveyors.

Leases for a term less than or equal to three years do not have to be by deed to transfer the legal estate but those greater than three years do.

Code of Practice for Commercial Leases

When considering entering into a business lease, consideration should be given to the second edition of the Code of Practice for Commercial Leases in England and Wales (issued by the DTLR in 2002).

The Code sets out a number of recommendations that parties to commercial leases should consider, both at the lease negotiation stage and subsequently during the lease term itself.

THE LANDLORD AND TENANT ACT 1954, PART II

A person who is given, or in practice takes, exclusive possession of property will have a tenancy. Furthermore, if the property is to be used for business purposes it is likely that the tenancy will be governed by the Landlord and Tenant Act 1954 (the Act).

Business occupation

The Act 'applies to any tenancy where the property comprised in the tenancy is or includes premises which are occupied by the tenant and are so occupied for the purposes of a business carried on by him or for those and other purposes' – Section 23(1).

In the context of the Act 'business' is widely defined. It 'includes a trade, profession or employment and includes any activity carried on by – a body of persons whether corporate or unincorporate'.

The tenant does not have to occupy the whole premises to qualify for protection. Nor does he have to use the premises exclusively for business purposes. Premises used for mixed purposes are within the Act. So a cottage could be included with a workshop and the whole treated as business tenancy provided the occupation of the cottage is incidental to the business use and not a sham; in these circumstances the cottage would not be covered by the Housing Act 1988.

Indeed, for the purposes of the Act 'premises' can include bare land, for example gallops for training racehorses.

What is not a business tenancy?

The Act does not apply to:

- [ ] licences;
- [ ] incorporeal hereditaments (eg easements, profits);
- [ ] Agricultural Holdings Act tenancies;
- [ ] farm business tenancies governed by the Agricultural Tenancies Act 1995;
- [ ] mining leases;
- [ ] leases of licensed premises;
- [ ] service tenancies;
- [ ] short fixed-term tenancies of less than six months provided the tenancy does not contain provisions for renewing the term or

extending it beyond six months or the tenant and any predecessor in his business have not been in occupation for more
than 12 months in total.

TERMINATION OF A BUSINESS TENANCY

Termination of the tenancy by the landlord

Under the provisions of the Act a tenant of a business lease has
security of tenure so that the tenancy continues after the original
fixed term has expired unless the agreement is brought to an end in
accordance with the provisions of the Act. The only exception to
this is where the tenancy, or a superior tenancy, is forfeited under a
provision in the tenancy agreement.

In order to bring a tenancy to an end, the landlord must give
between six and twelve months' notice, expiring on or after the
contractual term date. The landlord's notice must be given on a
prescribed form stating the grounds on which he opposes the grant
of a new tenancy. As the time limits and procedures are strict, a
landlord should employ a solicitor, well versed in the law of
landlord and tenant, to act for him.

A tenant has two months from receipt of the landlord's notice in
which to serve a counter-notice stating that he is unwilling to give
up possession. If he does not serve the counter-notice then he will
have no right to apply for a new tenancy. His existing tenancy will
end on the date specified in the landlord's notice and he must leave.

After a tenant has served a counter-notice he must apply to the
Court for a grant of a new tenancy. The application must be made
between two and four months after the service of the landlord's
notice.

Termination of the tenancy by the tenant

The tenant can determine the tenancy by an ordinary Notice to
Quit if it is a periodic tenancy. A fixed-term tenancy can be brought
to an end by the tenant giving three months' notice in writing to
expire at the end of the term or on any quarter day thereafter. If the
tenancy includes break clauses, the tenant may serve notice and
end the agreement at such times as he chooses in accordance with
the tenancy agreement.

Alternatively, the tenant who wants a new tenancy to replace the existing one can serve on the landlord a request in statutory form for a new tenancy. This must specify a date for the start of the tenancy not less than six nor more than twelve months ahead. It must not be on a date before the existing tenancy would expire or could be determined. The tenant then has to apply to the court for the new tenancy not less than two nor more than four months after he has served the request on the landlord. The right to initiate a request for a new tenancy only exists where the tenant has a fixed-term tenancy exceeding a year or where the tenancy is for a certain term and then from year to year.

Grounds for opposing a new tenancy

Provided the landlord has specified one or more of the following grounds in the statutory notice to terminate the tenancy he can seek to prevent the grant of a new tenancy to the tenant. The grounds available to the landlord are:

☐ breach of the tenant's repairing obligations;
☐ persistent delays in paying rent;
☐ substantial breaches of the tenant's other obligations, or any other reason connected with the tenant's use or management of the premises;
☐ the provision of suitable alternative accommodation;
☐ where the current tenancy is a sub-letting of part only of the property comprised in a head-lease and the reversioner of that head-lease can demonstrate that the property could be let more economically as a whole;
☐ that the landlord intends to demolish, reconstruct or carry out substantial works of construction;
☐ that the landlord intends to occupy the premises for the purposes of a business carried on by himself (or of a company which he controls) or as his residence. This ground is not available to a landlord who has purchased his interest in the property within the preceding five years.

The new tenancy

If the landlord is not successful in his opposition to the grant of a new tenancy, the Court can grant a tenancy for a period not exceeding 14 years. The terms of the tenancy will be those agreed by the parties or in default of agreement those imposed by the Court. The Court will have regard to the terms of the former tenancy and all the relevant circumstances.

Once the order is made the tenant has 14 days in which to refuse to take the tenancy. The Court must then revoke the order. It has, however, discretion to order that the former tenancy shall continue for a period which will allow the landlord an opportunity to re-let.

The rent

The landlord and tenant can fix a market rent for the premises. A short lease may have no rent review provision but a well-drafted longer lease should contain a rent review clause which will operate at stated times throughout the lease. Where the original fixed term has expired or where there is a periodic term, the landlord may wish to increase the rent. In order to do so he must serve a notice to terminate the existing tenancy. This will set in motion the statutory renewal process, which will result in the tenant being granted a new tenancy at the current market rent.

Interim rent

Once a landlord has served a notice to terminate the existing tenancy (or a tenant has served a request for a new tenancy) a landlord can apply to the Court for the payment of an interim rent. Where the rent is expected to be higher than the existing rent it may be worth making an application, but the interim rent will be lower than the full market rent that will be charged under the new tenancy. The new rent will run from the date of the application or the date specified for the end of the former tenancy, whichever is later.

COMPENSATION ISSUES

Compensation – for disturbance of the tenant

The tenant is entitled to compensation where the Court refuses to grant a new tenancy on the grounds that the property could be let more profitably as a whole or that the landlord intends to develop the property or occupy it himself. These are all situations where there has been no fault on the part of the tenant. The tenancy is terminated for the benefit of the landlord.

The tenant is also entitled to compensation where the above grounds are specified in the landlord's notice and as a consequence the tenant does not make, or withdraws, his application for a new tenancy.

The landlord must pay the tenant a prescribed multiple of the rateable value. For most cases the multiplier is 1, making the compensation equal to the rateable value: where the business has been carried out in the premises for the whole of the 14 years preceding the termination of the current tenancy the compensation is twice the rateable value.

Compensation for improvements

By virtue of the Landlord and Tenant Act 1927 unless there is a covenant in the lease preventing the tenant from making improvements he may be able to claim compensation on the termination of his lease.

However, the Landlord and Tenant Act 1927 does not lay down a list of tenant's improvements for which the landlord must pay compensation at the end of the tenancy. As such, there is nothing in it to compare with the list of agricultural improvements for which compensation is payable under the Agricultural Holdings Act 1986. However, the following points should be noted:

- [ ] an improvement must add to the letting value of the holding;
- [ ] an improvement does not include any trade or other fixture which the tenant is by law entitled to remove. Generally, what is fixed to the property becomes part of it and cannot be removed. But trade fixtures (eg petrol pumps, partitions) can be removed provided it is not forbidden by the terms of the lease;
- [ ] an improvement must be 'reasonable and suitable to the character of the premises';
- [ ] an improvement should not diminish the value of any other property belonging to the same landlord;
- [ ] a claim cannot be made for an improvement made by the tenant where he has entered into a contract to make the improvements and received valuable consideration.

If a tenant is to be successful in a claim for compensation he must serve notice on his landlord of the intended improvement together with specification and plan. The landlord has three months to object.

If the landlord does not object the tenant can proceed with the improvement. If he does object the tenant can apply to the County Court or the Chancery Division of the High Court. The landlord can elect to do the improvement himself. If he does so he will not have to pay compensation to the tenant and he will be entitled to a reasonable increase in rent by agreement, or as determined by the Court. Where the tenant carries out the improvement, it must be made within the agreed time.

A tenant who has duly completed an improvement may require his landlord to give him a certificate to that effect. If the landlord does not give a certificate, then the tenant can apply to the Court.

Sometimes improvements have to be made to fulfil statutory requirements. The procedure described above will apply in such cases, except that the landlord cannot object to the improvement. Compensation is payable at the end of the tenancy for such improvements.

The claim for compensation must be made within three months of the first action taken to determine the tenancy, which may be the service of a Notice to Quit or under the Landlord and Tenant Act 1954, or be effected by forfeiture or re-entry. Where the tenancy expires at the end of a fixed term, the claim must be made not more than six nor less than three months before the termination. The claim must be in writing and signed by the tenant, his solicitor or agent and must give a description of the premises, the trade or business and a statement of the nature of the claim, the particulars of the improvement and date of completion, together with the cost and amount claimed.

Generally, a tenant must quit the premises to obtain compensation. Disputed cases have to be referred to the Court for settlement.

Section 1(1) of the Landlord and Tenant Act 1927 lays down the rules for assessing compensation. They are as follows: the sum must not exceed 1) the net addition to the value of the premises directly resulting from the improvement; or 2) the reasonable cost of carrying out the improvement at the termination of the tenancy less the cost of putting the works into a reasonable state of repair except so far as it is covered by the tenant's repairing liabilities.

Under point 1 above, account must be taken of the proposed use of the premises after termination of the tenancy, and if demolition, alteration or change of use is proposed, that is to be taken into account also. In these circumstances, an improvement can be worth nothing.

'CONTRACTING OUT' OF THE SECURITY OF TENURE PROVISIONS OF THE 1954 ACT

Notwithstanding the previous section regarding the tenant's ability to effectively demand a new tenancy at the end of the original contractual term, it is possible for the parties to 'contract out' of such provisions. Thus, at the end of the contractual term of a 'contracted out' business tenancy the tenant neither has the right to remain in possession nor indeed to activate the statutory procedure for a new tenancy.

'Contracting out' procedure

A joint application by the intended landlord and intended tenant must be made to the Court **before** the tenancy is granted. The security of tenure provisions of the 1954 Act will not be excluded if the lease or underlease is executed before the Court's authorisation is given, unless the grant is conditional on that authorisation being given.

The joint application is a relatively straightforward process and one that does not require personal attendance at court by either party.

Proposed reforms to the 'contracting out' procedure

Following a recent consultation exercise on modernising business lease legislation, a draft of the Regulatory Reform (Business Tenancies) (England and Wales) Order 2002 has been laid before Parliament.

The proposed amendments to the Landlord and Tenant Act 1954 seek to make the process of business lease renewal or termination quicker, easier, fairer and cheaper. Importantly, the proposed reforms do not seek to change the fundamental principle of security of tenure for business tenants.

One of the main provisions of the proposals is the removal of the necessity to obtain a Court order excluding the security of tenure provisions of the 1954 Act. Instead of the rather cumbersome and time consuming Court application, the landlord will be entitled to serve the tenant with a 'health warning' at least 14 days prior to the commencement of the lease stating that the lease is to be excluded from the security of tenure provisions of the 1954 Act. Where the requisite 14 days prior notice can not be given the tenant will be required to sign a statutory declaration stating that he has received the 'health warning' and is aware of its consequences.

At the time of publication these reforms have not yet come into force and consequently the existing joint application to the County Court is still required in order to 'contract out' of the security of tenure provisions of the 1954 Act.

STAMPING

Stamp duty may be payable on the grant of a lease depending on the amount of the premium, if any, the length of the term and the rent payable. The lease, which is the document signed by the landlord and held by the tenant, and counterpart, which is signed by the tenant, should be lodged for stamping with duty at the appropriate rate within 30 days of the grant. It is for the tenant to arrange for the stamping of the lease and he should be advised of his obligation. The landlord should stamp the counterpart. At the time of this publication it bears a fixed fee of £5.00.

Leases that are liable for stamp duty but have not been stamped cannot be produced in Court. It is possible for documents to be stamped late on the payment of a penalty. A new penalty regime was introduced by Finance Act 1999 for instruments on or after 1/10/1999. In summary:

☐ A penalty is levied on instruments not presented for stamping within 30 days of execution.

☐ Interest on unpaid stamp duty starts to run 30 days after the date of execution.

☐ If a lease is granted for seven years or more, it falls within Finance Act 1931, Section 28 and must be produced to the Inland Revenue in accordance with the requirements of that Section.

The rules on, and rates of, stamp duty change from time to time. The current position and more detailed advice should be obtained from the Office of the Controller of Stamps, Inland Revenue, South West Wing, Bush House, Strand, London WC2B 4QN.

REGISTRATION

If a lease is granted for over 21* years the title to the lease must be registered at HM Land Registry if the lessee is to secure legal title.

It must be stressed that it is important for both landlords and prospective tenants to be professionally advised where leases of this length are being prepared.

ALTERNATIVE CONTRACTUAL ARRANGEMENTS

Tenancies at will

Where a tenant is let into occupation pending the conclusion of a formal lease he will have a tenancy at will. For the avoidance of doubt as to the exact arrangement the agreement should be in writing. Provided that it is clearly understood that the tenant is let in under those conditions then the tenancy can be terminated by either party if the negotiations subsequently break down.

Given the inherent uncertainty of a tenancy at will, most tenants will be eager to formalise the main lease as a matter of priority.

As mentioned previously, a tenancy at will won't be protected by the Landlord and Tenant Act 1954 and therefore the 'contracting out' procedure highlighted earlier is not required; however, this does not remove the need for such a procedure prior to completion of the main tenancy agreement.

Licences

The essence of a licence is that the licensee (occupier) is not granted exclusive possession of the property. This contrasts with a tenancy that requires the tenant to have exclusive occupation of the premises. Accordingly, even if a document is called a licence, or indeed the parties intended it to be a licence, it is quite possible that

---

* When the Land Registration Act 2002 comes into force (anticipated date – autumn 2003) all leases granted for a term of greater than 7 years will become compulsory registrable – thus replacing the current 21 year threshold.

as a matter of law such an agreement (whether oral or in writing) will amount to a tenancy.

Typically, a licence can be used for property used for storage purposes. In such cases the licensee is granted the right to store specified goods within the building in a specified area which may vary from time to time. The owner remains in possession and control of the premises.

In order to create a licence the landowner must continue to use the property for his own purposes as well as giving the licensee certain rights. However, if the agreement amounts to nothing more than a 'sham', the courts will have little hesitation in declaring the agreement to be a tenancy.

Clearly such a situation has far reaching ramifications for the landlord since, if the property is used for business purposes, the tenancy will benefit from the security of tenure provisions of the Landlord and Tenant Act 1954.

Alternatively, where the storage is not for business purposes, the possible existence of a tenancy should not cause too many problems. The tenancy will be governed by common law and, as such, can be terminated by giving notice equivalent to a full rental period.

However, extreme caution should be taken when considering granting a licence since potentially the agreement may ultimately be held to be a tenancy subject to the provisions of the Landlord and Tenant Act 1954.

SUMMARY

Clearly, for those landlords familiar with agricultural tenancy legislation the provisions of the Landlord and Tenant Act 1954 can appear a little daunting. However, it must be remembered that the 1954 Act is considerably more flexible than the agricultural tenancy legislation in terms of freedom of contract – thus enabling the parties to adapt their agreements more closely to their particular circumstances.

References

Business Tenancies on Farms, CLA21 Handbook (June 2001)
Code of Practice for Commercial Leases (2nd Edition), DTLR (2002)
Model Storage Licence Agreement, CLA22 Handbook (June 2001)

2.2 Business licences and regulations

Jonathan Reuvid

INTRODUCTION

There is no general legal requirement to apply for a licence to carry on a specific business which the purchaser of a business or property, or someone entering into the tenancy of existing business premises, must undertake. Permitted business use is attached to specific premises as a part of the planning process described in some detail in Chapter 1.1.

Some occupations, notably the registered professions, require that practitioners are registered members of the relevant professional body, usually involving qualification by examination. However, there are activities in the professional domain which can be carried out by unqualified people, provided, of course, that they do not claim professional accreditation to which they are not entitled. For example, the conveyancing of real estate, traditionally a lucrative part of solicitors' services, can now be carried out on behalf of others by individuals who are not members of the legal profession.

Regulation is often achieved by other means. For example, in taking on the tenancy of or buying a public house, although the premises have been licensed for that purpose, the incoming landlord or landlady is required to apply for a personal licence to serve alcoholic beverages on the premises to which other responsibilities are attached, such as the observance of authorised opening hours and the maintenance of good order. In granting a licence the Magistrates are not looking for a formal qualification but are influenced primarily by the good character of the applicant, with previous experience playing a part.

One range of service activity, which has been subjected to welcome regulation during the past 15 years, is that of financial advice. With the establishment of the Financial Services Authority, all aspects of financial services from banking to insurance, pensions, dealing in securities and including general financial advice are under permanent scrutiny. Individuals wishing to practice as intermediaries in the provision of financial services to members of the public are required to apply for registration as financial intermediaries. Applicants are required to demonstrate prescribed levels of knowledge and qualification.

Many business and commercial activities do not require qualification. Running a village shop or a garden centre does not demand formal qualification. Neither do contract gardeners, painters and decorators nor, for that matter, property developers. Second-hand car salesmen are generally unqualified, although the franchise holders of specific marques of new vehicles may be required by the manufacturer to subject their sales staff to company training programmes.

Nevertheless, there are classes of tradespeople for whom membership of a trade association is a practical necessity in order to carry on and develop their businesses. In particular, those engaged in the building trades and in the provision of maintenance services, such as electrical engineers, plumbers, timber treatment specialists and thatchers would find it difficult to operate as more than 'odd job men' without a trade association affiliation for the reason that the providers of finance for home improvements will usually demand that the work be carried out by accredited tradesmen. Similarly, builders subcontracting their specialist work where warranties and indemnities are involved will need to satisfy their insurers' requirements. Membership of such trade associations may involve competence qualifications, but that is not invariably the case.

These occupational considerations will not be of more than passing interest to readers unless they are intending to set up their rural business in any of these fields. (Since there is a dearth of plumbers in many parts of the country, you might be tempted.)

However, there are other restrictions and regulations that apply to the use of land and buildings of which a general awareness is useful. Some regulations are of a specialist nature, such as the requirement under Section 11(6) of the Firearms Act 1968–1997 to approve a site for clay-pigeon shooting in order that a person may use a shotgun without a shotgun certificate on a designated area of land (see Chapter 4.6). Other regulations are of a more pervasive nature and this chapter provides overviews of employers' health and safety obligations, stemming from the Health and Safety at Work etc Act 1974, requirements under environmental law and the principles of the Data Protection Act 1984 to which all businesses are subject.

PERMISSION FOR CHANGE OF USE

Before turning to these three regulated areas, there is more to be said in respect of change of use, where an existing business with established use is purchased and the new owner wishes to extend the current use or conduct a quite different business on the premises without making any significant physical alteration to the premises themselves. The first question to resolve is whether or not you need to apply for planning permission.

Minor physical alterations

Planning permission is not always required. For example, changes to the inside of buildings or for small exterior alterations such as the installation of telephone connections and alarm boxes do not generally demand planning consent, although the listing authorities will need to approve most changes to listed buildings, particularly to Grade I and Grade II* listed buildings. Other small changes, such as the erection of fences and walls below a certain height, have general planning permission for which a specific application is unnecessary. To be safe, you can check informally with the council whether your proposed 'development' needs planning permission. More formally, you can also apply for a Lawful Development Certificate on payment of a fee. If a certificate is refused, you can then either apply for planning permission, or Appeal to the Secretary of State. The latter is likely to be a slower process.

Working from home

Working from home does not usually involve an application for planning permission. The key test is whether the overall character of the dwelling will change as a result of the business and permission probably will be needed if:

☐ your home will no longer be used mainly as a private residence;
☐ your business will result in a marked rise in traffic or people calling;

☐ your business will involve any activities unusual in a residential area;

☐ your business will disturb your neighbours at unreasonable hours or create other forms of nuisance such as noise or smells.

These issues involve value judgements and the first two are plainly a matter of degree. For example, at what point can it be said that the provision of bed and breakfast accommodation has changed a home into business premises ? The third and fourth manifestations of carrying on a business at home are the most likely to provoke neighbours' complaints and to drive business owners into making a planning application, if they have not already done so.

Changes of business use

Planning permission is not required when both the present and proposed uses fall within the same 'class' as defined in the Town and Country Planning (Use Classes) Order 1987. For example, a clothing shop may be changed to a greengrocer's without permission. It is also possible to change use between some classes without making an application. Details of the use classification system and the changes permitted by the Town and Country Planning (General Permitted Development) Order 1995 are summarised in Table 2.2.1.

Planning applications are also not required in cases of change of use from A1 to A1 plus a single flat above; and from A2 to A2 plus a single flat above. These changes are reversible without an application only if the part that is now a flat was, respectively, in either A1 or A2 use immediately before it became a flat. Conditions for the change from A1 or A2 are conditional upon there not being any change to the outside of the building and, if there is a display window at ground floor level, no incorporation of the ground floor into the flat.

Changes of use always requiring a planning application

Material changes of use involving any of the activities listed below always require planning permission:

☐ amusement centres;
☐ theatres;
☐ scrap yards;

Table 2.2.1 Use classes and changes not requiring a planning application

	Use classes	Permitted transfers to
A1	*Shops*	
	Shops, post offices, travel agents, hairdressers, funeral directors, dry cleaners	other A1
A2	*Financial and professional services*	
	Banks, building societies, betting offices, and other Financial and professional services	A1
	Sale of motor vehicles	A1
A3	*Food and drink*	
	Pubs, restaurants, cafes and food take-aways	A1, A2
B1	*Business*	
	Offices, research and development, light industry appropriate in a residential area	B8 (permission limited to 235 m^2 of floor space in the building)
B2	*General industrial*	
		B1, B8 (permission limited to 235 m^2 of floor space in the building)
B8	*Storage and distribution*	
	Including open air storage	B1 (permission limited to 235 m^2 of floor space in the building)
C1	*Hotels*	
	Hotels, boarding and guest houses where no significant element of care is provided	None
C2	*Residential institutions*	
	Residential care homes, hospitals, nursing homes, boarding schools, residential colleges and training centres	None
C3	*Dwelling houses*	
	Family houses, or houses occupied by up to six residents living together as a single household, including a household where care is provided for residents	None

- [ ] petrol filling stations;
- [ ] car showrooms (except for changes to Class A1 uses);
- [ ] taxi and car-hire businesses;
- [ ] hostels.

HEALTH AND SAFETY

It has to be acknowledged that the Health & Safety at Work etc Act 1974 is one statute among many which imposes duties upon a company or business and its directors or owners which must be obeyed but may not be in their strict commercial interests. Enforcement of the Act is carried out by the Health and Safety Executive (HSE) working with Local Authorities to uniform, rigorous standards.

Employers' obligations

The Act establishes a fundamental duty of care on the employer, which extends to providing safe systems of work, equipment and a totally safe and healthy workplace environment. Specific obligations include:

- [ ] Arrangements to ensure safe storage, handling and transport of all articles and substances.
- [ ] Effective communication with employees, supervision and training and adequate welfare provisions.
- [ ] Creation of a safety culture which prevents accident pyramids, where lack of precaution, ignorance, failure to report incidents and to react to minor accidents spirals into disasters.
- [ ] Where five or more people are employed, the drawing up of a health and safety policy, preferably within a health and safety handbook for staff use, which must contain the following:
  - general statement of H&S policy;
  - name of senior manager responsible for H&S and how responsibilities are allocated to individuals;
  - operation of any safety committee;
  - safety rules;
  - protective equipment;
  - fire regulations, drills and emergency procedures;
  - reference to other specialised documents (eg hazardous substances).

If this were not enough, the employer's duty of care is not confined to employees. It extends to customers in respect of product safety, subcontractors, visitors and general members of the public.

Satisfying these requirements is an onerous task and employers may choose to outsource their health and safety (H&S) management to a qualified H&S Officer. However, rural business owners and directors need to be aware that neither outsourcing nor the employment of an H&S professional will relieve them from legal responsibility.

Risk assessment

Employers are required to conduct a formal assessment of workplace H&S conditions and to make arrangements to determine what risks there are to employees that need to be addressed by the H&S policy. The necessary routines for the main stages in the process of assessing and controlling risks are:

☐ identifying hazards;
☐ designing, implementing and monitoring measures to eliminate or minimise risk;
☐ assessing risks (likelihood and severity) and prioritising action.

The items covered in a typical assessment would include:

☐ physical characteristics of the workplace;
☐ arrangements for maintenance and servicing of equipment;
☐ procedures for storage, transportation, use and disposal of hazardous substances;
☐ first aid provisions and facilities;
☐ smoking prohibition or restrictions;
☐ arrangements for visitors.

Law enforcement

While HSE inspectors deal mainly with factories, service industries, such as hotels, restaurants, offices and warehouses, are dealt with by local authority officers. It follows that most rural businesses will be subject to inspection by local authority H&S officers. Acting in that capacity, inspectors may enter premises without notice; examine books and documents; take statements, samples, measurements and photographs; and direct that work and equipment are left undisturbed.

Where contravention of a statutory provision is found, inspectors may issue either an improvement notice or a prohibition notice.

Employee obligations

Employees must co-operate in any changes relating to improving safety, must wear safety gear where required and must not be reckless. Failure to comply can result in lawful dismissal. In the event of a serious accident after wilfully ignoring safety warnings, employees may be prosecuted individually.

Criminal liability

An employer or a company and its directors may be prosecuted for corporate manslaughter, where it can be proven that a manager in charge had knowledge of the risks being taken which resulted in the death of an employee.

Occupational stress

In civil actions brought by employees, employers can be held responsible, in the context of H&S, for failure to contain workplace stress and are obliged to take reasonable steps to relieve workplace stress arising from any of the following:

- [ ] increase in work intensity;
- [ ] aggressive management styles;
- [ ] bullying or harassment;
- [ ] lack of guidance on how to do the job;
- [ ] over-exposure to customer demands;
- [ ] over-ambitious objectives;
- [ ] excessive computer work;
- [ ] even, over-promotion.

Other key H&S legislation

Control of Substances Hazardous to Health Regulations (COSHH) 1988
Obligations on employers using hazardous substances identified under COSHH 1988 in their businesses include:

- [ ] risk assessment at least every five years;
- [ ] introduction of systems to prevent or control risks and ensure that controls are monitored and recorded;

□ staff information of hazards, training in use of controls and health surveillance;
□ vigilance and reduction of risks by less hazardous materials and substances where possible.

The Reporting of Injuries, Diseases and Dangerous Occurrences Regulations (RIDDOR) 1995
Employers are required to keep records and report to the HSE instances of deaths and injuries, dangerous occurrences and violence by employees in the workplace.

Manual Handling Operations Regulations 1992
There are obligations on employers to train employees to lift loads in the correct way, provide lifting gear where applicable and consider whether automation of the lifting process is possible.

Rural business owners employing staff are also recommended to have an awareness of the following further legislation:

The Employers' Liability (Compulsory Insurance) Act 1969
The Health and Safety (Display Screen Equipment) Regulations 1992
The Personal Protective Equipment at Work Regulations 1992
The Provision and Use of Work Equipment Regulations 1992

ENVIRONMENTAL LAW

By definition environmental law applies mainly to manufacturing businesses, and rural businesses which are affected significantly will be in a minority. However, there are rural activities, like sawmills, for which there are environmental issues, and many service industries (eg agricultural machinery repair) are not immune.
The main issues covered by UK environmental law include:

□ emissions into the air (air pollution);
□ water quality and effluent;
□ solid waste (including toxic and radioactive waste);
□ dust emissions;
□ noise pollution;
□ litter;
□ waste disposal;
□ environmental labelling.

The main provisions on these topics are contained in the four following instruments of 'green legislation':

The Water Act 1989
The Town and Country Planning Act 1990
The Environment Protection Act 1990
The Environment Act 1995

Statutory powers are vested in the Environment Agency to regulate and control pollution, inspect premises and impose bans where operating methods or controls are found to need alteration to prevent or minimise pollution.

The owners of an unincorporated business are liable in civil law for environmental damage and liable in criminal law where statutory requirements have been infringed. Directors of companies are personally liable too where they connived or consented to offences or the offence was the caused by negligence.

Requirements

Businesses must be authorised before starting operations which use specified processes having an inherent risk of harm to the environment, and must operate according to the authorised conditions. They must monitor and adhere to emission limits, make adequate arrangements for the disposal of waste products and avoid causing 'statutory nuisance' from effluents. They must also be able to demonstrate that they have chosen the 'best practicable environmental option' for controlling identified pollution.

Sanctions

Where required authorisation has not been obtained or the conditions of authorisation are breached, the Environment Agency or a Local Environment Health Officer can issue:

either enforcement notices requiring immediate remedial action;

or prohibition notices suspending authorisation until remedial action has been taken.

Breach of an enforcement or prohibition notice is subject to an unlimited fine or imprisonment of up to two years.

Finally, the business's environmental management system may be independently assessed where the owners consider there is a benefit: for example, to facilitate due diligence when seeking external funding. The business may achieve ISO 4001 certification or registration under the Eco-Management and Audit Scheme of the European Commission.

DATA PROTECTION

The previous Data Protection Act 1984 applied only to data held on a computer. The more recent Data Protection Act 1998, which came into effect from 1 March 2000, also applies to manual records. The latter Act gives individuals, identified as 'data subjects', the right of access to personal data and requires data holders, identified as 'data controllers' and including employers, to be open about the use of information and follow certain principles in how it is obtained, used and stored.

In particular, employers should be mindful that employees have a right to any information held about them and must have given permission for such information to be held and processed. Sensitive personal data can only be held with the express consent, ideally in writing, of the employee concerned.

Monitoring of e-mails and telephone calls

Employers have the right to monitor telephone calls and e-mails sent by their staff, provided that they notify staff that they intend to do so. An appropriate clause in contracts of employment is recommended.

Compliance and future developments

Since this is a developing area of law, there are likely to be continuing amendments to current rules and changes of interpretation. Larger employers are recommended to have a written data protection policy which is included within the staff handbook.

Caveat

In matters concerned with all legislation and regulations referred to in this chapter, readers are counselled to take professional advice before applying for permissions, licences, approvals or authorisations to avoid errors which will damage their business case or expose themselves to further regulations or sanctions.

2.3 Self-employment and incorporation

Brian Castle, Senior Taxation Adviser, CLA

SUMMARY

Generally, most rural businesses operate as sole traders or partnerships and find that this enables them to operate their businesses without undue complication. However, the present Government has made a number of reductions in corporation tax and so the question then becomes 'which medium is more advantageous?' In order to answer this question it is necessary to consider a number of non-tax factors and then the tax advantages and disadvantages of incorporation.

NON-TAX FACTORS

Sole trader

The basic rural business is most likely to be a sole trader. This has the advantage of being easy to set up and run and is also free of formality. Unless the trader intends to register for VAT, there are few rules as to what records need to be kept. There are no auditing requirements of a sole trader's accounts, nor do these have to be filed at Companies House. The provision of capital for the business has to be provided either from the trader's own assets or from loans. However, there is no legal distinction between the sole trader and his personal property. Therefore, if the business fails, creditors can take into consideration the trader's possessions to settle any incurred debts.

Partnership

If more people are needed to help run a business then a partnership, perhaps of a husband and wife and/or other members of the family, or outsiders, can be considered in order to spread the workload and income round the partners in the business. Partnerships are in reality no more than a collection of sole traders and thus are in the same position regarding personal liabilities. The additional problem is that the actions of one partner, with or without the knowledge of the other partners, can bind those partners to the consequences of a bad decision. The legal framework governing partnerships is set out in the Partnership Act 1890; however, most partnerships are regulated by an agreement entered into by the partners in the form of a deed drafted by a solicitor. The agreement should, amongst other things, include:

☐ the name of the firm;
☐ the names of the partners and their duties;
☐ the partnership capital;
☐ partners' shares of profit and losses;
☐ what happens in the event of a partner leaving, retirement, death, dissolution etc.

The accounts of a partnership will be much the same as for a sole trader but will need further information in order to reflect the separate interests of the partners, such as separate capital and drawings accounts and the crediting of profit to the respective capital accounts.

Limited Liability Partnerships

A recent development has been the limited liability partnership (LLP), which is a new form of legal entity, introduced by the Limited Liability Partnership Act 2000. An LLP is a body corporate and exists as a legal person separate from its members. From the taxation angle there is no difference in the way that a Limited Liability Partnership will be taxed as compared with a general partnership. The following information has to be supplied to Companies House on an Incorporation Document (LLP2):

☐ the name of the Limited Liability Partnership;
☐ the location of the registered office;
☐ the name, address and date of birth of each member;
☐ which of the members is a designated member or whether all the members are designated members.

Designated members have certain duties such as signing off the accounts, arranging for the delivery of those accounts plus the annual return to Companies House and appointing auditors. In addition Companies House has to be kept informed of changes to the members of the Limited Liability Partnership, registered offices, etc. Much like a company, the name of an LLP needs to be displayed outside the place(s) of business. Correspondence should show the place of registration, registered office and registration number.

Incorporation

There comes a time when sole traders and partnerships wish to consider incorporation for some of the following reasons:

☐ savings in tax and national insurance (NI) liabilities by extracting profits in the form of dividends;

☐ better pension arrangements;

☐ a desire to reduce exposure to risk by adopting limited liability (but see also Limited Liability Partnership above);

☐ adopting a structure that enables shares to be distributed to family members and share incentive schemes for employees to be considered.

Reducing risk

A limited company is a separate legal entity and is solely liable for its debts and obligations. A shareholder will only be expected to contribute to the amount that they agreed to put in to the business. Thus the limited liability is an attraction to those who wish to invest in a risky venture but are not prepared to risk their entire personal wealth. The overall difficulty is that, despite the limited liability of the company, directors and shareholders may have to give security in the form of personal guarantee to major lenders, leasing companies and landlords.

Setting up a company

As in the case of forming a partnership, this is a job for a legal adviser or an accountant, although the adventurous entrepreneur could get a starter pack from Companies House. The company needs to be registered with the Registrar of Companies and the following needs to be included together with a registration fee of £20 (£80 if same day service is used):

☐ Memorandum of Association, which needs to state the name of the company, the intended location of the Registered Office and the company's objects.

☐ Articles of Association. A standard format can be taken from the Registrar of Companies and adopted or articles suitable for the new company can be drawn up.

☐ Form 10 stating names of directors, secretary of company and location of Registered Office.

☐ Form 12 – declaration of compliance – and Form 117 – certificate to commence trading.

Once a company has been set up there is an on going requirement to submit each year an annual return on form 363a (363s) plus an annual fee together with a copy of the audited accounts by the annual filing date. Failure to do so leads to penalties. The control of the behaviour of companies and their directors is governed by various Companies Acts but mainly Companies Act 1985.

TAXATION

Income tax on the profits of a sole trader or partner in a partnership currently cannot exceed 40 per cent and earnings will only be taxed once the individual's income exceeds the basic rate band of £29,900. The calculation of the break-even point after which incorporation is tax efficient rather depends on how the directors/shareholders extract the income.

The following example shows the break-even point between continuing as a sole trader and incorporating in 2002/03.

Harry Potter is a sole trader with taxable profits over £45,000 and is considering incorporation. The tax and NI position as a sole trader is as follows:

Profits	£45,010
Less personal relief	£4,615
Chargeable income	£40,395
Less	
Income tax	£10,546
Class 2 NIC	£104
Class 4 NIC	£1,806
	£12,456
Retained income	£32,554

If the same profits were earned within the newly incorporated company the tax and NI position would look like this:

Potter Ltd

Profits	£45,010
Less director's salary	£34,515
Class 1 NIC	£3,528
Taxable corporation tax	
(exempt 0%)	£6,967*

Mr Potter

Salary	£34,515
Less income tax	£6,348
Less Class 1 NIC	£2,580
Salary retained	£25,587*
Total Earnings retained*	£32,554

Thus in this example the break-even point for considering incorporation is profits in excess of £45,000.

However, even on earnings below £45,000 the picture may be altered by the possibility of paying the income out in the form of dividends. Consider the following example.

Mr Dumbledore a sole trader has profits of £10,000 in 2002/2003, which after tax and NI leaves him with retained income of £8,565.

If the business was to be carried on by a limited company and he drew remuneration of £6,800 (thus avoiding difficulties with minimum wage regulations and maximizing use of the personal tax allowance) the balance of the income could be paid in the form of dividends.

Dumbledore Ltd

Profits	£10,000
Less director's remuneration	£6,800
Less Class 1 NI	£258
Retained	£2,942

No corporation tax (exempt)

Mr Dumbledore

Remuneration	£6,800
Less income tax	
Less Class 1 NI	£469
Retained	£6,331

Thus if the retained profit in the company was paid in the form of a dividend the total amount receivable would be £9,273 with the dividend having a 10 per cent tax credit.

Pensions

The above example shows the current advantage of converting earned income into dividend income, particularly when the director is not a higher-rate taxpayer. In 2002/2003 a taxpayer with no other income could receive over £30,000 without any further income tax charge arising. However, one of the advantages of creating a limited company is the ability to establish a company pension scheme. The tax-deductible contributions from the director and the company will usually be in excess of the allowable premiums paid by the self-employed to personal pension schemes.

Benefits

On incorporation a formerly self-employed taxpayer will have to consider the impact of the stringent Schedule E benefits and expense rules, which cover such items as cars, use of assets, etc. The most important consideration is that where the company owns the director's main home this creates a liability to tax on the provision of beneficial accommodation. The ultimate sting is that directors are unable to escape such a charge by claiming exemption under ICTA 1988, Section 145, which provides exemption on the grounds that the accommodation has been provided for the better performance of an employee's duties or it is customary to provide such accommodation. Directors are specifically excluded from the scope of the exemption.

Losses

Companies have their own loss regime which is similar to sole traders and partnerships. However, trading losses are trapped within a company and so cannot be set against other income outside of the company.

Incorporation of an existing sole trader/partnership

It may well be that the owner(s) of an established business would decide to incorporate an existing business. Such a step leads to potential capital gains tax and stamp duty liabilities. Any business considering such a change should take professional advice in order to avoid unintended further tax bills.

Capital taxation

One of the reasons that most rural business do not incorporate are the potential disadvantages that exist on the capital tax side. The first is that business asset taper relief from capital gains tax only applies to unincorporated businesses. Chargeable gains within companies are still within the indexation regime. The most important aspect on the capital gains tax side is the inclusion of assets within a company that have the potential to increase in value, for example land and buildings. If these assets are sold by the company this can lead to a double charge to capital gains tax; firstly on the disposal of the asset by the company and then on the increased value of the shares in the hands of the shareholder, if the shares are subsequently disposed of.

Further information

Board of Inland Revenue
Somerset House
Strand
London WC2R 1LB
Tel: 020 7438 6692
Website: www.inlandrevenue.gov.uk

The Registrar of Companies
Companies House
Crown Way
Maindy
Cardiff CF14 3UZ
Tel: 0870 3333 636
Website: www.companies-house.gov.uk

2.4 Taxation issues

Brian Castle, Senior Taxation Adviser, CLA

INTRODUCTION

Around 24 million individual taxpayers and 200,000 taxpayer companies are required each year to contribute to the Chancellor of Exchequer and result in some £105 billion in income tax and £29 billion in corporation tax receipts. The determination and assessment of these liabilities creates an enormous workload on small businesses which, with or without assistance from accountants and tax advisers, has to be completed on an annual cycle.

The way that the tax system impacts on an individual business depends on the structure of the business. Is it run as a sole trader, partnership or limited company? Does the business have employees on whose behalf the business is required to operate PAYE in order to collect their income tax and National Insurance liabilities? Since the introduction of self assessment all of the responsibility falls on the taxpayer for informing the Inland Revenue of tax liabilities and there are potentially large penalties for failure to comply. The advice must be not to struggle with the system half-heartedly; otherwise, all your efforts in generating profits will be lost in ever-increasing problems with the Revenue authorities. The amounts paid to a good accountant or tax adviser to keep your tax affairs in order may be money well spent if it prevents extra payments of interest and penalties to the Inland Revenue.

INCOME TAX

Rural businesses trading as sole traders or partners within a partnership will pay income tax and National Insurance on the profits determined on what is known as the 'current year' basis. At the commencement of a business there are special rules to fit the business's accounting period in within the appropriate tax year. After that the tax liability is based on the profits for the accounting period which ends during the tax year. For example, if the accounts run from 1 July to 30 June then for the tax year 2003/2004 the relevant profits will be in the accounts to 30 June 2003. The easiest way is to have an accounting year that coincides with the fiscal year so that right from the start the profits naturally align with relevant tax year (fiscal year 6 April to the following 5 April or 1 April to 31 March). The computation of profit is based on the accounts prepared for the business and although a balance sheet is not strictly necessary, it can be a help. The profits may need to be adjusted in accordance with tax legislation, particularly with regards to personal expenditure and the treatment of depreciation of capital assets, in which case the depreciation has to be added back to the profits and capital allowances claimed instead. The self-assessment help notes for the self-employed, together with the return itself, provide a ready format for a small businesses accounts. If the turnover of the business is less than £15,000 then full accounts do not have to be provided to the Inspector of Taxes and a three-line analysis provided instead.

Business expenses

A business can claim and be allowed for tax purposes those items of expenditure that have been incurred 'wholly and exclusively' for the business. In addition, certain items where there is a mixed use, such as a private house used partly for the business, can have some of the expenditure set off against the taxable profits of the business. Furthermore, a business can claim capital allowances on certain items of working capital such as plant and machinery. Capital allowances are a statutory allowance given in place of depreciation that is normally included in the accounts of a business and added back as part of the adjustments to accounts.

Rates of tax and National Insurance

A sole trader and partner pay the normal rates of income tax. The rates for 2002/2003 are shown in Table 2.4.1.

Table 2.4.1 Rates of income tax 2002/2003

Band of Taxable income £	Band	Rate %	Tax
0–1,920	1,920	10	192
1,921–29,900	27,980	22	6,155.60
Over 29,900	–	40	–

A sole trader or partner pay two sets of National Insurance on the net profits. If the profits exceed £4,025 there is a payment of a fixed Class 2 contribution of £2 per week. A further Class 4 contribution of 7 per cent is also due on profits between £4,535 and the upper limit of £29,900.

Payment of the tax

The sole trader or partner will find that they have to make three payments of tax and national insurance in the annual cycle. Interim payments are made on 31 January and 31 July followed by a final payment/repayment on 31 January.

Losses

Losses from a rural business can be set against future profits of the same trade or other income or capital gains of the year of loss, or the year before. In the first four years of a business it is possible to set the losses against income of the three years prior to the commencement of the business.

Schedules

The present income tax system categorises income within what are known as schedules, and these have different rules as to how income and expenditure are dealt with and the availability of loss relief against other income. The current schedules are shown in Table 2.4.2.

Rural businesses

The common types of income that a rural business might receive would usually fall within either Schedule A or D (see Table 2.4.3).

Schedule A

Since 1995 Schedule A has taxed profits from UK land or property as if they were derived from a 'rental business'; the broad principle being that the profits are computed using the same principles as for a trade. The computation is based on normal accounting conventions and in particular that the accounts should be prepared on the 'earnings basis'. Allowable expenditure against the rents received is

Table 2.4.2 Income tax schedules

Schedule	Source	Basis of assessment
A	Profits from a business of letting land in the UK	Income of the current year of assessment
D Case I Case II Case III Case IV Case V Case VI	Profits of a trade in the UK Profits of a profession or vocation in the UK Interest, annuities and other annual payments Securities out of the UK Possessions out of the UK Annual profits or gains not falling within the above cases and not charged under any other schedule	Income of the accounting period ending in the tax year or income of the current year of assessment Income of the current year of assessment
E	Offices, employments and pensions	Income of the current year of assessment
F	Dividends and certain other distributions by companies	Income of the current year of assessment

Table 2.4.3 Schedules applicable to types of rural business income

Schedule	Type of income	Examples	Losses
A	Income from property	Agricultural tenancy, farm business tenancy etc Buildings let out to residential and commercial tenants	Only against other rental income
D (Case I)	Income from trade	Farming, trading activity such as bed and breakfast business, furnished holiday lettings (if satisfying certain criteria) Clay-pigeon shooting	Against other income in the same tax year or future year. Continuing losses from farming can be restricted after six years to future farming profits

determined under the same rule that determines allowable expenditure for trading income under ICTA 1988, Section 74. This provides that expenditure cannot be deducted unless it has been incurred 'wholly and exclusively' for business purposes. A detailed review of the rules of Schedule is beyond the scope of this book but those rural businesses that are letting or proposing to let property should certainly in the first instance read the Inland Revenue's own detailed booklet on this subject, *Taxation of Rents – A guide to property income IR150*. This should answer most questions.

Whilst the legislation talks about 'rental businesses,' this does not mean that the nature of the income has changed. The net profits cannot be treated as relevant earnings for the purposes of gaining relief on pension contributions and losses continue to be unavailable for set off against general income. Nor will the underlying assets qualify for the beneficial business asset treatment for capital gains tax purposes.

Trades and farming

Whether or not somebody is carrying on a trade is a matter of fact, but generally the term 'trade' suggests the undertaking of risk in exchanging goods and services for profit. If the business is a trade then the tax system under Case I Schedule D will treat the profits as earned income and thus losses, pension contributions, etc will be treated more favourably than if the income was from an unearned source, such as Schedule A described above. The underlying assets will also be treated as business assets for the purposes of the reliefs from capital gains tax.

The receipt of income from farming is brought within the charge to Case I Schedule D by specific legislation in the Taxes Acts. Generally, it can be assumed that the production of crops, the rearing of animals for consumption or for their products will give rise to receipts that are to be taxed as a trade. The conduct of farming can be directly by the farmer/landowner or via contract farming or share farming arrangements. All farming carried on in the United Kingdom by any particular person or partnership or body of persons is treated for tax purposes as one trade. Thus a change from one farming use or the cessation and commencement of another source of farming will not be a cessation for tax purposes.

If the landowner allows somebody else to undertake the trade and merely receives income from their occupation of the land then this receipt is unearned income in the form of rent and charged to tax under Schedule A.

Diversification

As a consequence of the impact of the foot and mouth crisis and the general downturn in the agricultural economy, most farmers and landowners are considering alternative sources of income. If diversification, or a change of business, takes place this will affect the way that the farmer/landowner is dealt with for tax purposes. A common assumption following Government's urging of farmers to diversify into horses is that such activity will be treated as a continuation of farming. Unfortunately, this is an instance where policies from two departments in the Government do not tie up: unless the horses are used in the farming business itself then they are not agricultural animals.

Common diversification projects are:

☐ furnished holiday lettings;
☐ bed and breakfast accommodation;
☐ letting redundant barns for residential/commercial purposes;
☐ horse livery and pony trekking establishments;
☐ Christmas tree plantations;
☐ clay-pigeon shooting;
☐ car-boot sales;
☐ landfill;
☐ mineral extraction.

Each of these activities would be treated differently for tax and VAT purposes and would require careful consideration of both tax and legal issues, such as seeking planning permission.

The income tax treatment of the income could have a bearing on the capital tax treatment of the underlying assets. (See Chapter 1.4 on capital gains tax and inheritance tax issues.) It is therefore important to weigh up the potential income that might be received from the new enterprise against the potential capital gains tax and inheritance liabilities that might be created in the future. As far as possible it is important not to lose the 'trading status' of the asset; otherwise this could increase the amount of capital gains tax ultimately payable on the disposal of the asset. The most obvious example is the cessation of farming and the letting of the farmland to somebody else under a farm business tenancy.

'Reform to perform'

Most farmers treat their farming enterprise as one economic unit; unfortunately the present UK tax system, based on Schedules, does not and thus requires an artificial division of the profits. The CLA have sought to reduce this complex and administratively costly method of tax calculation in its recent report 'Reform to Perform'.

CORPORATION TAX

Whereas income tax and capital gains tax are payable by sole traders and partners in a partnership, limited companies pay corporation tax. The determination of taxable profits is very much the same as for sole traders and partners and adopts the same schedule approach as income tax. The payment of corporation tax is on the actual profits of an accounting period. The rate of corporation tax is fixed each fiscal year and runs from 1 April to 31 March the following year. In the case of accounting periods that do not coincide with fiscal year the profits are time apportioned. If there has been an increase or decrease in the rate of corporation tax between two fiscal years the profits are charged at the relevant rate. Corporation tax is payable 9 months after the end of the company's accounting period. The remuneration paid to directors has to be dealt with under PAYE.

Losses

Losses can be deducted from company profits of a previous year or future profits or against any capital gains of the company.

Rates of corporation tax

The current rates of corporation tax for the financial year 2002 are:

Profits below £10,000	Nil
Between £10,000 and £50,000	23.75%

Small companies' rate

Profits between £50,000 and £300,000	19%
Between £300,000 and £1.5 million	32.75%
Full rate on profits in excess of £1.5 million	30%

PAYE AND NATIONAL INSURANCE

The operation of pay as you earn (PAYE) is a mandatory requirement on an employer where any employee earns more than £89 per week. A prospective employee should hand over a P45 at the commencement of their employment. If the employee fails to hand over a P45, then the employer has to complete a P46 informing the tax office of a new employee who requires a notice of coding in order to deduct the correct amount of tax. The employer then has to work out the tax and National Insurance contributions on a deductions working sheet on each pay day according to the tax and NI tables sent by the employer's tax office. The total tax and NI deductions are then sent each month to the Inland Revenue Accounts Office together with a paying-in slip. At the end of each tax year the employer has to complete and hand over a P60 to the employee by 31 May and forward copies plus a summary on P35 of all the tax and NI deductions made during the tax year. As always, there are penalties if an employer fails to comply with the obligations laid down in the regulations governing PAYE. Once a business takes on employees it needs to contact its own tax office to arrange for a PAYE scheme to be set up.

VALUE ADDED TAX (VAT)

Essentially VAT is a consumer tax collected by VAT registered traders on behalf of the Government. The tax is added at each stage of the business process and if a trader incurs VAT on supplies to his business then the 'input' tax can be deducted from the 'output' tax charged on the final customers and paid over to Customs and Excise. There are a number of VAT rates that can be applied to certain supplies and these range from 0 per cent to 17.5 per cent. The administration of the tax can be burdensome and, if that wasn't bad enough, Customs and Excise have a range of penalties for late payments and returns.

Registration

An important aspect of the VAT system is that it is persons who are registered rather than businesses and each registration covers all the business activities of that person. A person can be a sole trader, partnership or company. In the rural context it is quite possible for a farmer to be growing crops that will be zero rated and also be making standard rated supplies such as bed and breakfast accommodation and/or furnished holiday accommodation. If there is diversification away from farming activities, such as the letting of barns, then these could be a VAT exempt supply.

A trader needs to consider registration once their turnover exceeds the registration limit of £55,000. This is determined either by: sales in the previous year which exceeded the registration limit; or if sales in the next 30 days will exceed the registration limit

Should sales excluding VAT fall below the limit, a trader can ask for their registration to be cancelled. In those circumstances, the trader has to show that the sales will fall below the de-registration limit of £53,000. The registration and de-registration limits are increased each year in line with inflation. Failure to register when a person should do so can lead to penalties being imposed by Customs and Excise. The penalty can be 5 per cent of the tax due if registration is up to nine months overdue, 10 per cent up to 18 months and 15 per cent if longer than 18 months.

Voluntary registration

A trader can ask to be registered even if their sales are below the registration limits discussed above. The trader needs to satisfy Customs and Excise that he will be making taxable supplies in the course or furtherance of the business. A trader volunteering to register will gain from the recovery of input tax hitherto irrecoverable but will also increase the level of administration within the business and exposure to penalties and interest as already mentioned.

Record keeping

Customs and Excise expect VAT registered traders to keep meticulous records and to hold them for at least six years. The main records to be kept by a VAT registered business are:

☐   tax invoices;
☐   VAT account calculating the results for each tax period;

☐ VAT returns to Customs and Excise calculating the VAT payable or refundable.

Annual accounting

Generally most businesses will be making VAT returns every three months; however, small businesses can opt for annual accounting. The advantages of annual accounting are that the business can have a more predictable cash flow and less paperwork as only one annual VAT return needs to be sent in. The scheme is open to a business with a taxable turnover of less than £600,000 per annum, whose VAT returns are up to date and pays in more VAT than it reclaims. A business can continue within the annual accounting scheme until its taxable supplies exceed £750,000.

At commencement the trader and the VAT office agree on an estimate of VAT payable for the coming year. One-tenth of the amount is paid each month after the fourth month through to the twelfth month and a balancing payment or repayment is made on the basis of the annual VAT return. In the case of a business with a turnover of less than £100,000 only four payments of one-fifth of the previous year's payments need be made. If the VAT bill is less than £2,000 no interim payments have to be made and the trader pays any outstanding VAT along with the annual return.

Paying VAT

VAT payable by a trader should be paid over within one month of the quarterly accounting period or within two months of the annual period. Payment has to be made even if the business has not received payment from its own customers. Failure to pay the VAT will result in a warning. A surcharge liability notice will be issued, after which further late payments in the next 12 months will be penalised as follows:

☐ next late payment 2 per cent surcharge;
☐ second late payment 5 per cent surcharge;
☐ subsequent late payments 5 per cent for each payment to a maximum of 15 per cent.

Cash accounting scheme

Certain small businesses can pay their VAT on a cash accounting basis and only pay VAT due when the customer has paid the business and similarly only claim VAT back when a supplier has been paid. VAT does not have to be paid on bad debts. Traders are eligible to use this scheme if the following conditions are met:

☐ taxable turnover is less than £600,000;
☐ VAT outstanding is less than £5,000;
☐ VAT returns are up to date;
☐ no convictions for VAT offences or assessed for dishonest conduct.

SUMMARY

When considering the commencement of a new business or the diversification from an existing rural business it is important to consider the following:

☐ Sole trader is the simplest way to start a business.
☐ If more people are required to develop the business consider whether the flexibility of the partnership will suffice; otherwise consider a Limited Liability Partnership.
☐ Sole traders and partnerships have lower requirements in terms of accounts and returns. In the case of a partnership consider taking professional advice on the drafting of a partnership agreement.
☐ Limited companies have many advantages: limited liability, lower tax, and greater pension provision. Disadvantages are the greater costs of servicing and more 'red tape'.
☐ If changing the nature of the income being received by the business, consider the effect that such a change may have on the entitlement to capital tax reliefs.
☐ How the business will be treated for VAT purposes, for example changing from zero-rated farming to VAT exempt rental income.

Further information

Board of Inland Revenue
Somerset House
Strand
London WC2R 1LB
Tel: 020 7438 6692
Website: www.inlandrevenue.gov.uk

_____

HM Customs and Excise
New King's Beam House
22 Upper Ground
London SE1 9PJ
Tel: 020 7620 1313
Website: www.hmce.gov.uk

References

Reform to Perform – simplify taxes for small business units to increase enterprise, CLA (June 2002)

The CLA publishes a number of advisory handbooks on taxation matters, as follows:

CGT Roll Over Relief (1993) CLA3
CGT Retirement Relief (1994) CLA4
Inheritance Tax Agricultural Property Relief (1995) CLA8
Taxation of Furnished Holiday Accommodation (2000) CLA20
Rating and Council Tax (2002) CLA31

2.5 Accountancy and audit

John Skinner, Whitley Stimpson

BASIC BOOKKEEPING

Whether you run a business as a sole trader, a partnership or a limited company, you are legally obliged to maintain accounting books and records. For limited companies, the Companies Act requires that the accounting records 'shall be sufficient to show and explain the company's transactions', particularly containing 'entries from day to day of all sums of money received and expended'.

For unincorporated businesses, the rules of self-assessment taxation place a similar onus on the business owners and allow the Revenue to levy fines of up to £3,000 for 'inadequate records'.

On a more practical level, you should be looking to monitor your business from a financial perspective so that you know where you stand monetarily and what returns you are generating from your work.

If you have no particular liking for doing your bookkeeping, ask a local bookkeeper, or farm secretary, to do it for you. Money wisely spent here should limit the amount of work your accountant needs to carry out in producing your year end figures.

Otherwise, if you do your own bookkeeping, take a 'little and often' approach so it does not become daunting. The requirement to complete a VAT return each quarter (or monthly) should also provide enough stimulus for records to be regularly updated.

Your books and records need only be as sophisticated as the business that you run. A good stationer could provide you with a multi-column analysis book to record your income and expenditure under appropriate headings: equally this could be done on a computer spreadsheet.

At the other end of the spectrum, there are various accounting packages available, again increasing in complexity depending on your needs. These do however need training to be used effectively.

Ask for (and retain) invoices to support your expenditure wherever possible and where you have to raise an invoice, keep a copy. Look to establish a filing system for your invoices, whether alphabetical or chronological. You may even wish to cross reference invoices into your bookkeeping records to ease future locating.

At your financial year-end, you are also obliged to prepare and retain a valuation of your stock (ie goods you trade with). Stock must be valued at the price you paid for it or, if lower, its 'net realisable value', that is, what you can sell it for. It can be quite difficult to establish this value unless you actually sell the particular stock item after your year-end, in which case you would use that lower figure in your valuation.

It is also useful to maintain a register of your business's fixed assets (machinery, vehicles, etc), recording their purchase date and invoice cost. This would help the business safeguard its assets as well as providing a basis for the calculation of the depreciation of each asset. Also, on a practical level, a fixed asset register would prove very useful when it comes to insuring your business.

Again, this can be done manually or with computer spreadsheets, which are ideal for this sort of record keeping. Most computerised accounting packages include a fixed asset register program.

USE OF INFORMATION TECHNOLOGY

Having mentioned computer technology already, there is a range of business performance reports, not merely accounts, which can be readily generated through IT systems.

Admittedly, a reporting package can be integrated with an accounts package, or it could be a separate 'stand alone' system, but this could entail having to enter the same information twice.

Using a mixed farm business as an example, a management information system should be readily able to produce reports on:

- ☐ crop or field yield analysis;
- ☐ livestock gross margin;
- ☐ milk yields;
- ☐ cash flow management and budgeting;
- ☐ break-even analysis;
- ☐ overhead recovery analysis.

AUDIT ROUTINES

The company audit is often seen as 'the cost of incorporation'. A company is a separate legal entity from its shareholders – should the company be at fault, it is the company and not the shareholders that is sued.

The shareholders appoint a Board of Directors that is charged with the stewardship of the company's assets to provide a return on the shareholders' investment. The company's financial performance is reported in the annual accounts. With many companies, the directors are also often the controlling shareholders.

Under the Companies Act, only those limited companies with a turnover of more than £1 million, or a balance sheet with gross assets totaling more than £1.4 million, are obliged to have their accounts audited (with certain exceptions).

(As an aside, if you are concerned about the financial management of a company in which you own shares, where an audit is not statutorily required, provided that you (or a group of members) hold at least 10 per cent of any class of the company's issued share capital, you can request that the company has its accounts audited.)

Auditing has come under scrutiny recently with the collapse of various US-based global businesses where the auditors have appeared to be complicit in their financial mismanagement.

That aside, the Companies Act places the responsibility on a company's directors to prepare accounts that show a 'true and fair view'. In basic terms, an audit is an evidence-gathering exercise that allows the auditor to form an opinion as to whether he agrees that the accounts do give a 'true and fair view' of a company's affairs.

An audit is not designed specifically to detect fraud or error (nor is it designed to trip up the company's accounts staff) – not every transaction in a set of accounts is considered, as this would be excessively time-consuming. Given the selective nature of the items looked at during an audit, the auditor cannot say that a set of accounts is completely accurate, merely 'true and fair'.

'True and fair' has never been defined in law, as it is an ever-changing concept. Because of how the standards under which company accounts are drawn up evolve over time, what is considered 'true and fair' one year may not be 'true and fair' in subsequent years.

By convention, 'true' relates to the figures in the accounts, indicating that they are as accurate as possible and relevant to the reader's need for information. 'Fair' relates to how the figures are disclosed, indicating that they are understandable by the reader and free from bias.

Alternatively, a set of accounts would be said to be 'true and fair' if they were 'materially accurate'. An item is only material if it its inclusion or exclusion changes the reader's opinion of those accounts. £1 million could be immaterial in a multi-national company's accounts, but £5,000 could be material if it turns a profit into a loss.

An audit can be broken down into three basic stages: planning, fieldwork and completion. Planning is crucial to the audit process as it provides the auditor with an opportunity to assess the risk involved in the audit. Work needs to be designed to minimise the ultimate risk that the auditor will draw the wrong conclusion from his work and give an inappropriate audit opinion.

Planning is most easily carried out with a draft set of the company's accounts to hand, or at least a trial balance. This would enable the auditor to assess the company's performance compared to previous years and in comparison to other companies of a similar size in the same business sector. This can provide valuable initial evidence as to the reasonableness of the accounts.

The auditor will develop an initial understanding of the company and the industry in which it operates during the planning stage, and should be able to identify which areas of the accounts represent the most risk (ie where errors are likely to occur) and plan his fieldwork accordingly. This process becomes more efficient over the course of time as the auditor becomes more and more familiar with the company and its operations.

The plan would include specific details of what work will be carried out on the different areas of the accounts. The plan can be amended as the audit progresses for any issues that arise that were not apparent at the planning stage.

Another element of planning is for the auditor to set the 'materiality level' to be applied during the audit. There are various ways of setting materiality, but quite commonly it involves taking a combination of fixed percentages of key figures from the accounts, such as sales, net profit, gross and net assets.

Even after calculating materiality on a mathematical basis, the auditor may wish to apply his personal judgement given his own knowledge of the company and the risks involved. Materiality could be moved upwards or downwards as a result, consequently increasing or decreasing the workload.

Having calculated materiality, the auditor can then carry out his work effectively, paying little attention to any figures that fall below this level. Again, materiality can be reconsidered as the audit progresses for any new issues that come to light.

Also, a record should be kept of errors that the auditor does come across, because although individually an error may not be material, on a cumulative basis such errors may become material.

(As an aside, although an auditor may set himself a materiality figure, the Inland Revenue has no concept of materiality when it comes to inquiring into a company's affairs. This can be very frustrating for the company and the auditor.)

Certain figures in the accounts are material in nature, most notably transactions with the company's directors. By law, such transactions need to be disclosed in the accounts so that shareholders can see how directors may been benefiting from their position, not merely through their remuneration.

Some of the planning work needs to be carried out 'on site', such as obtaining an understanding of a company's accounting and internal control systems. Assessing these systems will allow the auditor to gauge their reliability, which can reduce the amount of work required to substantiate figures in the accounts.

Modern auditing tends to concentrate on looking at the figures contained on the company's balance sheet and gathering sufficient evidence to support each material amount. Enough evidence needs to be accumulated to support an item's:

☐ physical existence;
☐ completeness;
☐ disclosure in the accounts;
☐ valuation;
☐ occurrence;
☐ measurement;
☐ rights and obligations.

Different sources of evidence have different degrees of reliability, and a certain amount of 'professional scepticism' comes into play. This is not to say that auditors will automatically believe that a company will be misleading them, just that there may be some bias involved. After all, the auditor is giving an independent opinion in his audit report, so the more evidence he can amass from unbiased sources the better.

As a brief illustration of some of the routines that may be applied, for example for fixed assets, work could include physically verifying a selection of assets to the accounting records. A fixed asset register, as mentioned above, would make this exercise relatively simple, provided that the register is updated every time an asset is bought or sold.

A sample of additions in the year may be checked against supporting purchase invoices and depreciation for the year could be checked on a 'global' basis.

For stock, the auditor would want to attend the stocktake to assess the company's routines for counting its stock. As a separate exercise, a sample of stock lines could be selected to establish how they have been valued.

For debtors, the auditor would want to obtain confirmation from a selection of trade debtors acknowledging their indebtedness to the company. An alternative procedure would be to examine moneys received from debtors after the year end.

For bank balances, the auditor should write to the company's bank requesting confirmation of account balances at the year end, together with confirmation of overdraft facilities, assets held as security and so forth.

For creditors, the auditor may want to compare a selection of balances of trade creditors to supplier statements, as well as examining payments made after the year end to identify liabilities that may have existed at the year end. Auditing creditors can be more problematic than debtors, as there may be nothing in the accounts to suggest that a liability exists.

Share capital is usually quite a static figure on a company's balance sheet and can readily be confirmed by examining the company's statutory records and Annual Return.

The final routine in the course of an audit is the completion of the file and signing the audit report. The accounts have to be first signed by the directors before the auditor can sign his report. Prior to signing, the accounts are re-assessed to ensure that they are in line with evidence obtained by the auditor and that all the statutory disclosure requirements have been met.

Enquiries are made to ensure that no events have occurred since the year end that would have a material effect on the accounts, and the directors are asked to give written confirmation of any issues that the auditor has not been able to substantiate by any other means.

Also, the directors have to demonstrate that the company is a going concern (is able to operate for the foreseeable future) and the auditor must examine the assumptions the board has made.

Writing as an auditor, the whole audit process is eased by clients who are willing to co-operate in the process, such as by preparing schedules that substantiate the figures in their year-end balance sheet. You may regard your company audit as an expensive compliance exercise forced upon you by the Companies Act. As a firm, we use the auditing process to advise clients on how they can make their companies more efficient and how they are performing in comparison to their competitors.

2.6 Employees and employment law

Helen Shipsey, Senior Legal Adviser, CLA

INTRODUCTION

At the outset, the prospect of engaging an employee might appear daunting with the great volume of legislation that covers employment matters. However, preparation in advance and reference to a guide such as this will pre-empt many problems. This chapter can only provide an overview of the relevant legislation: in the event of specific problems legal advice will need to be sought.

INITIAL CONSIDERATIONS

Discrimination

From the beginning of the recruitment process, starting with advertising and interviewing, the prospective employer must be aware of the rules against discrimination: the Sex Discrimination Acts 1975 and 1986, the Race Relations Act 1976 and the Disability Discrimination Act 1995. These Acts make it unlawful for employers to discriminate against job applicants and workers because of their sex, race, marital status or disability. Discrimination can arise in advertisements for jobs, in the selection procedure, and in the way promotions are made.

The Equal Pay Act 1970 requires equal pay to be given to men and women. All part-time employees now qualify for statutory employment rights on the same basis as full-time employees. The regulations cover not just employees but workers in general.

Workers who consider they have been the subject of discrimination can refer the matter to an Employment Tribunal. There is no upper limit to the award that might be ordered and the Tribunal may recommend that the employer take action to remove or reduce the effect of the discrimination.

Employed or self-employed?

An employer may consider that it would be preferable to hire someone who is self-employed under a contract for services rather than a contract of service (contract of employment). Labels here are irrelevant and what will determine the status of the worker are the facts of the situation.

Various tests have been devised to help determine a worker's status. One test 'the personal service test' asks 'is it the case that the employee has undertaken to provide a personal service for his employer?' If the worker is able to send along a substitute, then this is probably enough to establish that the contract is not a contract of service and the worker is not an employee. Another test is the 'control test'. In general an employee can be said to be subject to greater control than an independent contractor, but that is not always the case.

Is the employee seen as part of the organisation or is he dependent on it? Can the employer require the individual to attend for work and can the individual require the employer to provide work? If yes to both it would be indicative of a contract of employment. It is important to establish with confidence what the status of the worker is as this will have a bearing on tax matters and whether certain legislation applies or not.

It is worth bearing in mind that much of the more recent legislation referred to in this chapter relates to 'workers' rather than 'employees' and so includes a wider group of people.

Insurance

An employer carrying on any business in Great Britain must insure and maintain insurance against liability for bodily injury or disease sustained by its employees arising out of and in the course of their employment in that business. It would also be prudent to determine what type of claims the employer might be vulnerable to from the acts of its employees and seek cover accordingly.

Health and safety at work

Under the 1974 Health and Safety at Work Act employers have a duty to ensure so far as is 'reasonably practicable' the health, safety and welfare at work of all employees. This involves the employer in maintaining safe premises, a safe system of work and the provision of information, training and supervision. An employer must comply with the Noise at Work Regulations 1989 along with a variety of regulations that may apply. A useful source of information on this subject is the Health and Safety Executive website at www.hse.gov.uk.

Employers of five or more employees must have a written statement of their health and safety policy. They must bring it to the attention of their employees.

Employers have a duty to run their businesses to ensure as far as 'reasonably practicable' that non-employees are not exposed to any risk to their health and safety. For instance, they should not allow dangerous animals to roam on public footpaths. Employees too must take reasonable care for themselves and their fellow workers who may be affected by their acts and omissions.

Contract of employment

Once an employee has been engaged they must be provided with a written statement of terms within 13 weeks of commencement of employment. All employees have a contract, whether it is in writing or not. The written statement is required by statute to cover certain terms:

☐ the parties;
☐ the date when the employment began;
☐ date of commencement of continuous employment;
☐ salary or the method of calculating remuneration;
☐ the intervals at which remuneration is to be paid;
☐ hours of work;
☐ holidays and holiday pay;
☐ job title or brief description of the work an employee is employed to do;
☐ place of work.

The following particulars must also be given but they may be given under another easily accessible document; it is sensible to attach this to the principal statement:

☐ Details of sickness provision. Whether provision will be made for pay during sickness and if so for how long. The Statutory Sick Pay Scheme makes provision for employers to pay sick pay for a maximum of 28 weeks in the year. These payments apply to agricultural workers as well as other workers and there are further obligations imposed by the Agricultural Wages Order.

☐ Pension provision. Most employers who employ five or more people have a legal obligation to offer a stakeholder pension with a payroll deduction facility to their employees. Employers will not have to make contributions on behalf of the employees but will need to ensure an appropriate scheme is set up.

☐ Notice. This must be at least the minimum set down in statute: one week from one month up to two years' employment, and thereafter one week for every full year worked up to a maximum of 12 weeks.

☐ Where the employment is not intended to be permanent, the period for which it is expected to continue or, if it is a fixed-term contract of employment, the date on which it is to end.

☐ Any collective agreements which directly affect the terms and conditions of the employment.

☐ Where the employee is required to work outside the United Kingdom for more than a month, details of that employment should be given, such as: the period that he is expected to work, the currency in which he is expected to be paid and any additional remuneration or any extra benefit provided by reason of the employee working outside the United Kingdom, as well as terms and conditions relating to the employee's return to the United Kingdom.

NB: where those particulars are not relevant, and not requirements of the contract of employment, that should be mentioned in the written statement.

In addition, there are terms that are implied into every contract of employment, such as – on the employee's part – to co-operate with the employer and a duty of faithful service and – on the employer's part – to pay wages and provide work. Further, it is possible that there are terms that become established with the custom and practice of the business.

Variation of terms and conditions

There is no arbitrary right to change an employee's terms and conditions of employment once they have been agreed. An employer must secure the consent of the employee if he does wish to bring about a change in terms. Failure to do so would create a situation where the employee might be able to resign and make a successful claim of constructive dismissal. This could happen where a Tribunal deemed that the change in terms had been a fundamental breach of contract. It is therefore imperative to consider carefully from the outset what the appropriate terms should be and allow for sufficient flexibility, for instance, in the hours to be worked.

Disciplinary procedures

Full details should be given of your company's disciplinary rules. Provisions in the Employment Act 2002 will come into effect at the end of 2003 or by Spring 2004, which means all contracts of employment will include a disciplinary and grievance procedure. It is currently a statutory requirement for employers of 20 or more employees to inform them of the applicable procedures. Those who employ fewer are required to identify the person to whom grievances should be addressed and how they should be made. A recent right has been introduced to allow workers in the United Kingdom to be accompanied in formal disciplinary or grievance hearings by a trade union official or a fellow worker. A refusal to allow such an accompaniment can result in an award of compensation of up to two weeks' pay against the employer. If an employee were to be dismissed following a refusal of accompaniment the chances of an unfair dismissal decision will be greatly increased. ACAS provides a Code of Practice on Disciplinary Practice and Procedures in Employment, which is available from your local ACAS office or from the website at www.acas.org.uk/publications/pdf/CP01.pdf and is the best document on which to base your rules.

Working hours

The Working Time Regulations 1998 sets down that there should be a maximum of 48 hours worked per week by a worker. There should be rest breaks during the day and daily rest periods of at least 11 hours. Weekly rest periods should be of at least 24 hours. There should be four weeks' paid holiday in each year, to which bank holidays may count. Additional protection must be provided for night workers and young workers. An individual worker may agree in writing that the limit shall not apply, by signing up to an opt-out agreement. A notice period (of up to three months) should be specified by which the agreement can be brought to an end.

National minimum wage (NMW)

A national minimum wage was introduced in April 1999. The current standard minimum rate is £4.20 for workers aged 22 and over (due to be increased to £4.50 in October 2003). Those who employ agricultural workers have been bound by the Agricultural Wages Board (AWB) order which sets out the basic rates of pay for those engaged in agricultural work. If the NMW at any time exceeds a certain level of the AWB or vice versa it is the higher level that must be paid. The DTI website at www.dti.gov.uk/ir/nmw is a good source of information on the NMW.

Provision of living accommodation

The provision of living accommodation by an employer may be taken into account on a limited basis. The value for a full week at present is £22.75. This means that where an employer wishes to accommodate his employee he must ensure that the employee is actually receiving a minimum of the NMW minus the limited amount for the benefit in kind.

Advice should be sought as to the most appropriate approach to accommodating an employee. Care must be taken in particular when accommodating an agricultural worker as the legislation provides the option for the employer not to give security of tenure, but certain steps must be taken in advance of accommodating the employee on the estate.

Sick pay for agricultural and non-agricultural workers

The Agricultural Wages Order provides for a special sick pay scheme to operate in respect of certain farm workers. All employers are responsible for paying Statutory Sick Pay (SSP). The Agricultural Workers Sick Pay Scheme (AWSP) and SSP operate together; if a payment is made under the SSP scheme this will count as part of any entitlement due under the AWSP scheme and vice versa. Comprehensive advice is available on the provisions of the

Agricultural Wages Board Order, which is issued annually from Nobel House, 17 Smith Square, London SW1P 3JR.

Maternity, paternity and adoption leave entitlement

New regulations apply to employees who are expecting a child on or after 6 April 2003, or adopting one. Ordinary maternity leave will now be 26 weeks. Additional maternity leave will run from the end of ordinary maternity leave for 26 weeks. An employee will qualify for additional maternity leave if she has been continuously employed for at least 26 weeks at the beginning of the fourteenth week before the expected week of childbirth (e.w.c.).

In respect of paternity leave eligible employees will be entitled to choose to take either one week or two consecutive weeks' paid paternity leave (not odd days). Statutory Paternity Pay (SPP) is at the same rate as SMP. Employees will be required to inform their employers of their intention to take paternity leave by the fifteenth week before the baby is expected, unless this is not reasonably practicable.

Adoption leave and pay is available from April 2003 to individuals who adopt, and one member of a couple where they adopt jointly. The partner of an individual or the other of the couple may be entitled to paternity leave and pay.

If a pregnant employee is dismissed for any reason connected with her pregnancy or because she took maternity leave she can make a complaint to an employment tribunal. Dismissing a woman in connection with her pregnancy is automatically unfair, no matter how long her service has been. During the period of leave in connection with these entitlements, all contractual rights other than remuneration must be maintained. During additional maternity leave the employment contract continues but in a restricted form. The employee will be entitled in general to return to the same job.

The DTI website at www.dti.gov.uk/er/regs.htm is a good source of information about these entitlements.

Employers' recovery of payments

Employers are able to claim back at least 92 per cent of the payments they make, with those eligible for small employers' relief able to claim back 100 per cent plus an additional amount in compensation for the employer's portion of National Insurance contributions paid on SMP and SPP.

In addition, under the new arrangements, employers who need to can get funding in advance for payments of SMP from the Inland Revenue.

Parental leave

Employees who have a baby or adopt a child on or after 15 December 1999 and have been employed for one year are entitled to take unpaid leave to look after a child or make arrangements for the child's welfare. Thirteen weeks are available for each child, to be taken by its fifth birthday (if disabled, up to the eighteenth birthday and for an adopted child, five years from adoption). Again more detailed guidance is provided on the DTI website as above.

Time off for dependants

There is statutory provision for an employee to take limited time off to deal with urgent problems concerning a dependant of the employee or someone who lives with the employee as part of their family. The right does not include a statutory right to pay and so this is a matter for the employer's discretion.

Right to request flexible working time

This new legislation gives employees the right to ask their employers to consider their case for a restructuring of their work. The legislation provides the framework of how to make such an application and how the employer must deal with it. The employer is not obliged to accede to such a request but it must be able to justify its decision on business grounds. See the DTI website.

Pensions

An employer with five or more employees must introduce a stakeholder pension scheme for relevant employees. There are some exceptions, such as where there is a qualifying scheme provided for staff.

BRINGING A CONTRACT OF EMPLOYMENT TO AN END

Dismissal

Before one can look at whether a dismissal is fair or unfair it is necessary to look at what is meant by the word 'dismissal'.
A dismissal is defined as the termination of employment by:

☐ The employer with or without notice.

☐ The expiry of a fixed-term contract without its renewal.

☐ The employee's resignation with or without notice, where the employee has resigned because the employer, by its conduct in breaching the contract of employment, has shown an intention not to be bound by the contract. This is known as constructive dismissal. It should be noted that it is not enough to leave merely because the employer has acted unreasonably. The employer's conduct must amount to a very serious breach of the contract of employment.

☐ The employer's refusal to allow an employee to return to work after the birth of her baby where she has a legal right to do so.

Notice of dismissal

There is no statutory requirement for notice of dismissal to be given in writing. It is compulsory however to produce a written statement of reasons if requested by an employee of at least one year's continuous service. The written reasons must be supplied within 14 days of the request. It is generally good practice to provide written reasons and make it clear why the employee is being dismissed.

Termination of the contract

Where an employee is dismissed he is entitled to the statutory or contractual period of notice unless he is dismissed without notice for serious misconduct. The statutory minimum periods of notice are:

☐ one week's notice after at least four weeks' service;
☐ at least two weeks' notice for two years' continuous service;
☐ at least three weeks' notice for three years' continuous service and so on up to twelve weeks;

☐ at least twelve weeks' notice for twelve or more years' continuous service.

The parties can of course agree to longer terms of notice in the contract of employment.

Complaint of unfair dismissal

It is only employees who may complain of unfair dismissal. The legislation applies to all who have been employed continuously for one year, whether full- or part-time, by the employer. There are some special situations where the one year's service is not required, for example where there is a dismissal arising from health and safety matters or maternity rights or sex and race discrimination, or membership of a trade union or non-membership.

Those who have reached retirement age – and if there is no normal retirement age then the age of 65 will apply to all employees – are not entitled to claim unfair dismissal under the current legislation. However, there has been a successful case brought on the basis that the relevant legislation – the Employment Rights Act 1996 which sets the upper qualifying age limit – has a disproportionate impact on men since more men than women work past their retirement age and is thus unlawful. Therefore at present there is a degree of uncertainty as to what employers are able to do in respect of employees who wish to continue to work.

There are a few other categories of people who are not entitled to bring a claim for unfair dismissal.

Fair reason for dismissal

A dismissal may be fair if the reason is:

☐ Related to the employee's capability or qualification for the job.
☐ Related to the employee's conduct.
☐ That the employee has been made redundant. You need to ensure that the method of selection was fair in the first place.
☐ That a statutory duty or restriction on either the employer or the employee prevents the employment being continued.
☐ Some other substantial reason which justifies the dismissal of an employee holding the position which he held, such as where the employee was taken on as a temporary replacement for a worker who has returned after being absent for medical

reasons (provided of course that it had been explained to the employee in question that his employment was only to be temporary).

Even if the employer can show that the reason for the dismissal falls within one of the potentially fair reasons for dismissal it will still have to be prepared to satisfy, if necessary, an Employment Tribunal that it acted reasonably in the circumstances in treating it as a sufficient reason for dismissing the employee. It will also have to show that as the employer it has followed a fair dismissal procedure. This will only be the case if:

☐ the firm's disciplinary procedure has been followed;
☐ the employee has been given a chance to improve work performance or conduct;
☐ the employee has been given a chance to explain his conduct;
☐ the employee has been allowed to exercise his right of appeal.

The employer's size and administrative resources will be taken into account.

Remedies

An employee who believes he has been unfairly dismissed has three months in which to bring a claim to the Employment Tribunal. The Tribunal can award three types of remedy:

☐ Reinstatement: this requires the employer to treat the employee as if he had never been dismissed. Any arrears of pay or other benefits must be paid up.
☐ Re-engagement: the employee is employed in a new job, which is comparable to the old or otherwise suitable.
☐ Compensation: the basic award is calculated according to the formula described below.

An employee gets one and a half weeks' pay for each year of employment over the age of 41; one week's pay for each year of employment between the ages of 22 and 40, and a half week's pay for each year under the age of 22. The award is reduced by one-twelfth for each month the employee is over 64. A maximum of 20 years' service is taken into account. The statutory maximum amount of a week's pay is currently £260. It is generally reviewed annually in February.

The award may be reduced where employees have caused or contributed to the dismissal, or their conduct before dismissal warrants a reduction. In addition, the employee may be entitled to a compensatory award. The current maximum is £53,500.

Redundancy

An employer who is considering making someone redundant must first ensure that there is a genuine redundancy situation. The Employment Rights Act 1996 sets out the situations where there might be a dismissal by way of redundancy. Section 139 of the Act provides that an employee is dismissed for redundancy where the dismissal is attributable wholly or mainly to:

a) the fact that his employer has ceased, or intends to cease, to carry on the business for the purposes of which the employee was employed by him, or has ceased, or intends to cease, to carry on that business in the place where the employee was so employed; or

b) the fact that the requirements of that business for employees to carry out work of a particular kind, or for employees to carry out work of a particular kind in the place where he was so employed, have ceased or diminished or are expected to cease or diminish.

Selection for redundancy

It is imperative, once having decided that there is a redundancy situation, to select the most appropriate candidate, using criteria that can be determined objectively. In a business with a large workforce it is good practice to have a selection procedure determined in advance of having to consider making any redundancies. If the employee believes he has been unfairly selected he may bring a claim for unfair dismissal. The criteria that might be applied include length of service, record of attendance, experience and capability. The key is to ensure that these factors can be verified by reference to records kept by the estate and that they are applied consistently across the workplace.

Consultation with employees

Good industrial relations practice and the law (when 20 or more employees are to be made redundant) require consultation with employees for dismissal by redundancy. Consultation or a warning is essential even with a small business. The size of the undertaking may well affect the nature or formality of the consultation but it cannot excuse the lack of any consultation at all.

It is essential that in addition to following the correct procedure for redundancy, adequate consultation has taken place between the employer and employee and with his trade union where appropriate, otherwise the employee's dismissal will be deemed to be unfair.

Rights of redundant employees

Where an employee is made redundant, that person has certain rights:

☐ the right to paid time off work to look for another job or to arrange for training;
☐ the right to redundancy pay;
☐ the right to notice, as per normal dismissal requirements;
☐ where alternative work is available, the right to a trial period without jeopardising his redundancy pay.

Redundancy payments

Only employees have the right to claim a redundancy payment. Self-employed workers do not qualify. Neither do employees who have been employed for less than two years. The payment is calculated in the same way as the basic award for compensation for dismissal save that service under the age of 18 does not count.

When the payment is made the employer must provide a written statement to show how the redundancy payment was calculated. There is a financial penalty for failing to do this.

A redundancy payment will not be required if the employee is offered further employment by the same employer or an associated one on the same terms as before, and accepts the offer. There is also the scenario where the employee is offered work by the same employer on different terms or in a different place and accepts the offer. Here the employee is allowed a trial period of four weeks in the new job to see whether or not it is suitable. If he decides it is not he may terminate the new contract and be treated as though he had been dismissed on the date when his old contract ended. If he has behaved reasonably he will be entitled to his redundancy payment.

THE TRANSFER OF UNDERTAKING REGULATIONS 1981, AS AMENDED

Where consideration is being given to taking on an existing business, extreme care must be taken and advice sought to ensure that in so doing unexpected obligations are not taken on. Where a person transfers a commercial or non-commercial undertaking or part of it to another person these regulations apply. This means that employees of the business before the transfer will not have their contracts terminated by the transfer: instead they will continue as though they had been made between the employees and the new owner. If an employee is dismissed because of a relevant transfer, that dismissal will be unfair unless an employment tribunal decides that an economic, technical or organisational reason entailing changes in the workforce was the main cause of the dismissal and that the employer acted reasonably in the circumstances. The new owner takes on all the rights and responsibilities appertaining to those employment contracts except criminal liabilities and employees' occupational pension rights.

Further reading

The CLA publishes a number of advisory handbooks covering employment law, including:

The Provision of Living Accommodation to Employees (1994) CLA17 and *Employment Law* (2000) CLA17. Members have access to free guidance on employment issues which can be downloaded from the members' area of the CLA website. Current guidance notes include:

☐ Employment law update GN12-03
☐ Right to request flexible working GN09-03

2.7 Liability in tort and contract

Karen Jones, Chief Legal Adviser, CLA

OVERVIEW

Businesses in the countryside are highly diverse, ranging from traditional farms through to factory units and holiday lets. Specific regulations exist controlling many business activities (eg fire and furnishing regulations where premises are let) and over the past years, health and safety legislation has expanded to protect the interests of employees and others against dangers inherent in certain business operations (see Chapters 2.2 and 2.6). However, such businesses also have a background liability stemming from the law of tort and contract.

The first section of this chapter concentrates on the most relevant torts (civil wrongs) that can impact upon the liability of those running businesses from a rural setting: negligence, occupiers' liability and nuisance. The second section examines the principles of contract law, an understanding of which is essential to the efficient running of a business, and gives useful tips on how to avoid common pitfalls.

TORT AND OWNERSHIP OF PROPERTY

Introduction

Occupiers have to consider the safety of visitors and others on their premises from hazards deriving from things done on the land or from the state of the premises. This is within the realm of negligence and occupiers' liability. Where things done on the premises affect other property owners, this is within the province of nuisance; changing the use of land can impact on neighbours and others in the local environment and this has to be considered to avoid the potential for complaint and dispute.

Negligence

Many tortious obligations derive from statute (see below). However, there is also a common law duty to take reasonable care to avoid acts or omissions that you can reasonably foresee would be likely to injure other persons. Failure to have regard to this duty can result in a negligence claim if damage results either in the form of physical damage to property or personal injury.

So what is expected to avoid such liability? First, there needs to be sufficient proximity between parties for a duty to be owed. As a generality the degree of care required must be commensurate with the risk measured by the likelihood and potential gravity of harm. The risk has to be balanced against the practicalities associated with minimising or overcoming it.

In practice, the steps necessary to discharge any duty of care have to be decided on a case-by-case basis, turning on these principles. However, satisfaction of statutory obligations, for example health and safety regulations, or even adherence to codes of practice or guidance covering a particular activity will help to protect against a successful negligence claim.

Occupiers' liability

The main statutes covering liability of occupiers of premises for damage to others are the Occupiers' Liability Acts 1957 and 1984. The 1957 Act covers the duty of care owed by the occupier to people lawfully on the premises (that is visitors who are people expressly or impliedly invited onto the land, such as the postman) and the 1984 statute covers all other types of entrants (including, but not restricted to, trespassers).

Occupiers owe visitors a duty to take such care as, in all the circumstances of the case, is reasonable to see that the visitor will be reasonably safe in using the premises for the purposes for which he is there.

In practice what does this mean? Although the steps necessary to discharge the duty are fact dependent, it is certainly the case that an occupier is not required to protect the visitor against every potential source of harm: reasonableness is the order of the day. If visitors are adults, an occupier is allowed to assume that visitors will take reasonable care of themselves (the Act specifically requires occupiers to expect children to be less careful than adults). Often simply giving an adequate warning can discharge a duty.

In addition, where the visitor is an independent contractor (eg an electrician or roofer) the occupier need not protect him against the dangers that are part of the work. Finally, liability for problems caused by the work of such a contractor generally lies with that contractor provided that it was reasonable for the occupier to assume a competent job had been done.

For non-visitors (usually trespassers but can include others, for example users of a shared access), a duty of care is owed by the occupier to those entrants if he knows or has reasonable grounds to believe that they are in the vicinity of risks on his land and it is reasonable for him to offer some protection. Again, the steps necessary to discharge the duty are, in practice, very fact dependent. However, signs giving adequate warning of the danger can be used, but fencing or the closing off of a hazard may be necessary where it is a particular danger. In assessing the risk, the cases indicate that the law is very protective of children and makes clear that occupiers need to recognise the attraction of youngsters to hazardous situations and places and to act accordingly.

Who's liable? Who is the occupier?

There is no statutory definition of 'occupier' for the purposes of the Occupiers' Liability Acts. It is really only a convenient term to denote a person who has sufficient control over the premises to put him under a duty of care to entrants.

Generally in a tenancy situation, liability for dangers on the premises lies with the tenant (the landlord having given over control of the premises). However, this is not the end of the story for the landlord if he is liable for maintenance and repairs under the tenancy. In such a case, under the Defective Premises Act 1972, if the landlord knew or ought to have known of a defect he is required to take reasonable care to protect the tenant and all persons who might reasonably be expected to be affected by those defects.

Further, many arrangements for use of the land fall short of a tenancy. Although 'let', there is not the exclusive possession necessary for a true tenancy and the arrangement amounts to a licence (common examples would include the 'letting' of land for sporting events). In these cases it should be remembered that it is the person who retains practical control such that he could deal with a potential hazard that bears the liability and in practice there can be more than one 'occupier'. In deciding who is the occupier, the terms of the licence are important in outlining relevant rights and obligations. Further, when granting such licences, consideration should be given within the agreement to occupiers' liability and the need for indemnities and obligatory public liability insurance.

Exemption clauses

Many occupiers seek to exclude liability to visitors by use of exclusion or limitation clauses. Such clauses are discussed in some detail below in the contract section of this chapter. However, a practical problem in use of these clauses is that to be effective they must be seen by the entrant. As such, where notices are used to convey the term these must be placed in a prominent position, usually at the entrance to the property.

In addition, for businesses the Unfair Contracts Terms Act 1977 (UCTA) applies to clauses that seek to exclude or restrict liability. UCTA prohibits any attempt to exclude or restrict liability for death or personal injury caused by negligence (which includes breach of duty under the 1957 Act). Any clause purporting to have this effect is unenforceable. Other clauses limiting or excluding liability for other damage are subject to a test of reasonableness.

For trespassers, it is particularly difficult to argue knowledge of any exclusion of limitation notice. In addition, although UCTA does not expressly apply to the duty to non-visitors, there is an argument that similar considerations would apply to exclusion/limitation of the trespasser duty as apply to the visitor duty.

Given the technical difficulties discussed above, where reliance is to be placed on exemption clauses, it is highly advisable to seek advice from a solicitor on the drafting of the clauses.

Insurance

Although few claims are made against occupiers, when they are made they can be significant and it is highly advisable to maintain public liability insurance. Such insurance is usually inexpensive but costs have been increasing recently. The cost will in part depend on the nature of the premises and the hazards associated with activities on the land; an insurance broker will be able to advise on appropriate cover. It is important that the insurance cover includes legal expenses, as these can exceed any damages recovered.

Nuisance

A claim to nuisance can be made where there is an unreasonable use of land that adversely affects others. If the nuisance affects a section of the public, the Attorney General or local authority can bring a claim in public nuisance. Public nuisance is a crime and cases can only be brought by individuals where they have suffered extra damage over and above that suffered by the general population. In practice, such claims are rare, the more important consideration for the rural business being claims of statutory or private nuisance.

Out of these latter two areas, there is no doubt that with regard to 'environmental' nuisances the statutory nuisance procedure is most often used. The reason is that it is the local authority rather than private individuals who generally bring the case and bear the costs, and thus the system is less onerous on individuals than pursuing an action for private nuisance.

Statutory nuisance

Section 79 of the Environmental Protection Act 1990, lists a series of statutory nuisances. Broadly a statutory nuisance is likely to occur where the premises are in themselves in such a state as to be prejudicial to health or a nuisance, or if noise, dust, smell, effluvia, smoke or fumes are emitted in such a way as to be prejudicial to health or a nuisance.

The enforcing body is the local authority through the Environmental Health Officer (EHO). If a complaint is made to the EHO it must be investigated, and this can lead to service of an abatement notice. The norm is for the EHO to discuss the matter with the occupier. This may lead to service of a draft notice and steps being taken to resolve the situation without service of a formal notice.

If a formal notice is served, an appeal can be made within 21 days to the magistrates' court. The grounds for appeal cover procedural errors in the nature or service of the notice or that the requirements of the notice are unreasonable in character or extent, or unnec-essary. A further and important ground of appeal for certain nuisances arising on trade, industrial or business premises is that the 'best practicable means' were used to prevent or counteract the effects of the nuisance. This ground of appeal is also a defence if matters do proceed to court.

If served with a notice, the occupier is left with a choice whether to comply with the terms or to appeal. If nothing is done, it is an offence not to comply with a notice, with significant fines particu-larly for statutory nuisances committed on industrial trade or business premises. The local authority also has a power to deal with the nuisance and recover its expenses.

Private nuisance

A private nuisance arises when there is an unlawful interference with a person's enjoyment of land or some right over or in connection with it. In reality a nuisance arises where use of land unreasonably inter-feres with a neighbour's enjoyment of his own property. Typical examples would include development affecting the natural drainage thereby causing flooding of neighbouring property or unreasonable interference with a neighbour's use of a shared access.

So how do the courts decide whether use is unreasonable? The cases indicate that the degree of interference and the character of the locality as a whole are likely to be taken into account; uses of land reasonable in the city may be thought unreasonable in a rural setting. However, if a complaint arises because of a special sensi-tivity (for example some medical condition that renders the complainant sensitive to noise which others would find acceptable), the claim will be unsuccessful.

If a nuisance can be established the normal remedy is an injunction to prevent a continuing nuisance and/or for damages for loss already suffered (both pecuniary and non-pecuniary).

How to avoid conflict

The discussion above highlights that for any business in the rural environment, consideration has to be given to how use of the land impacts on neighbours. This is particularly the case where a signif-icant change in use of land is proposed. It is advisable to discuss plans with local people and be amenable to taking steps to deal with their concerns. In the end it is far better and cost effective to avoid conflict and take steps to lessen the negative impact of a business upon neighbours, than to end up in dispute.

ESSENTIALS OF CONTRACT LAW

Introduction

The formation and execution of contracts is an essential element of every business. However, frequently, when a dispute arises between the parties, there is confusion as to whether the parties are really contractually bound, and the extent and meaning of the terms and the entitlement of each party on breach. The aim of this section is to give a fundamental overview of contract law to assist in avoiding common pitfalls.

The essentials of a contract

There are three essential ingredients for the creation of a binding contract:

☐ agreement;
☐ intention to create legal relations;
☐ consideration.

Although it is advisable for a contract to be in writing (see below), generally this is not essential (notable exceptions are contracts transferring land). The belief held by many that oral agreements, which have not been reduced to writing, are not binding is, on this basis, simply wrong.

Negotiating an agreement

For a binding agreement an offer from one party has to be accepted by another. In addition, the agreement has to be complete and there has to be certainty of terms; it is no use if only essential matters of principle are resolved leaving important points unsettled.

Offer and acceptance

The offer needs to be a definite promise to be bound provided that certain terms are satisfied. Where cautious words are used such as 'he may be prepared to sell...' this will not amount to an offer, just an invitation to treat (enter into negotiations). Notable examples of invitations to treat are requests for tender, and advertisements.

An acceptance is a final unqualified assent to all the terms of the offer. Often this does not occur following the first offer, as counter-offers are made. It is only at the stage where there is clear acceptance of all of the terms of the last counter-offer that an agreement is formed.

In practice, problems often occur where businesses contract on their own standard forms. An example is where a firm places an order for goods on its own purchase form, which is accepted by the seller on its own sales form, and the standard terms and conditions on the forms differ. It is advisable to avoid this situation and the potential for dispute, and make clear the agreed terms at the outset.

Acceptance can be written or oral or implied by conduct unless the offer expressly stipulates otherwise. Generally, the acceptance has to be communicated to the offeror. Prior to acceptance the offer can be withdrawn as long as this is communicated to the offeree.

Intention to be legally bound

This is rarely a point of contention, as the presumption in commercial and business agreements is that the parties intend to create legal relations.

Consideration

Consideration is the price paid to enforce the promise under the contract – each party gives something to the other, which need not be money. Promises for gifts are unenforceable.

Although there must be some consideration, the courts will not refuse to enforce a contract on the basis that the consideration from one party is commercially inadequate; it is up to the contracting parties to negotiate their own deal. However, the consideration must have some value. As an example, a promise to perform an existing contractual duty or a duty imposed by the law will have no value in the eyes of the law. That being said, the cases do show that the Courts strive to find consideration in order to allow enforcement of a contract, particularly where the terms of the agreement have been fulfilled by one party.

The terms of the contract

It is often said that, with contract, what you see is what you get. This, on many occasions, is not true.

Where all the agreed terms are written down, some may not be enforceable (see below). However, a common practical problem is that entirely oral contracts give rise to evidential problems in establishing the agreed terms when the parties are in dispute. It is far better to submit an agreement to writing to avoid this complication at a later date. In addition, the process of writing down the terms can highlight any areas where agreement has yet to be reached, or misunderstandings in what has been agreed.

Even in the case of a contract reduced to writing, terms can be implied into the agreement, for example where necessary to give business efficacy (or meaning) to the contract or by statute.

Statutory intervention is of particular importance. Undertakings as to the quality, fitness for purpose and correspondence with description or sample are implied into contracts for the sale or supply of goods or hire-purchase agreements. In addition suppliers of services are required to exercise reasonable skill and care in performing those services.

Are some terms more important than others?

Some terms go to the heart of the agreement between the parties. Breach of such terms (conditions) gives rise to the right not only to damages but to treat the contract as at an end. Other terms of lesser importance (warranties) merely give a party the right to damages if there is a breach by the other side but the contract with the existing rights and obligations continues. (Damages are aimed at placing the claimant in the position as if the contract had been performed correctly.)

Clearly, it is important to know which terms are conditions and which are warranties; in the event of breach of a warranty, if the 'innocent' party treats this as the end of the contract this in itself will be a breach and damages will flow.

Some terms are conditions or warranties by statute (see examples in the Sale of Goods Act 1979). However, at the negotiating stage, parties can generally agree which terms are conditions and make clear the results of breach. This can then avoid the difficulties in trying to establish whether it is safe to treat the contract as at an end in the event of a breach.

Exemption clauses

These are clauses, frequently seen in standard terms and conditions, which seek to exclude or limit liability. To be binding such clauses must be brought to the attention of the parties in some way. If a document containing the clause is signed, this is sufficient. In the case of unsigned documents or oral dealings, it is a question of fact whether reasonable notice of the term was given. In practice, it is prudent for the party seeking to rely on the clause to take overt steps to draw the contracting party's attention to the clause.

Unfair Contract Terms Act 1977 (UCTA)

This Act controls the use of exemption clauses to limit the liability of businesses. The effect of the Act is that some clauses are void and thus have no effect, others are subject to a test of reasonableness. Table 2.7.1 summarises the main effects of the Act, with the relevant section of the Act given in parentheses.

Table 2.7.1 The main effects of the Unfair Contract Terms Act 1977

Clauses are void	Clauses valid only if reasonable
Excluding/limiting liability for death or personal injury caused by negligence (Section 2)	Excluding/limiting liability for other loss or damage caused by negligence (Section 2)
Manufacturers' guarantees excluding/limiting liability for loss or damage caused by defective consumer goods in consumer use where the defect results from the negligence of the manufacturer (Section 5)	In a consumer contract or in standard written terms excluding/limiting liability for breach of contract or purporting to render a performance substantially different from that which was reasonably expected or to render no performance at all (Section 3)
In contracts for the sale or supply of goods or hire-purchase, excluding statutory guarantees of title (Sections 6 and 7)	
In contracts with consumers for the sale or supply of goods or hire-purchase excluding/limiting statutorily implied terms as to conformity with description or sample, quality or fitness for purpose (Sections 6 and 7)	In non-consumer contracts for the sale or supply of goods or hire-purchase, excluding/limiting statutory guarantees as to description, quality and fitness for purpose (Sections 6 and 7)

The reasonableness test

It is for the person who seeks to rely on the exemption clause to prove that it is reasonable.

Guidance is given within UCTA in that the reasonableness of a contract term is to be adjudged according to the circumstances which were, or ought reasonably to have been, known to or in the contemplation of the parties when the contract was made. Further, where a person seeks to limit liability to a specified amount of money, regard has to be given to his resources to meet any liability and his ability to obtain insurance.

Schedule 2 of UCTA lists factors to consider in application of the reasonableness test to exemption clauses in contracts for the sale and supply of goods or hire purchase (Sections 6 and 7). It is clear that these guidelines will be looked at in other types of contracts. The factors to consider are:

☐ the relative bargaining positions of the parties;
☐ whether the customer received an inducement to enter into the term;
☐ whether the customer knew or ought to have known of the existence and extent of the term;
☐ where the term excludes or restricts liability if some condition is not complied with, whether it was reasonable at the time of the contract to expect that compliance with the condition would be practicable;
☐ whether the goods were manufactured, processed or adapted to the special order of the customer.

Unfair Terms in Consumer Contracts Regulations 1999

These regulations protect consumers against unfair standard terms in contracts. They require standard terms to be expressed in plain language, for consumers to be dealt with fairly and any term must take account of the interests and rights of the consumer. However, the regulations do not apply to contracts between businesses or between private individuals. They only apply to contracts between a seller and consumer. A breach of these regulations may be referred to the Director of Fair Trading for investigation. The contact telephone number is 020 7211 8470.

Misrepresentation

Statements of fact are often made by one side during contractual negotiations that fall short of being terms but which induce the other side to enter into the contract. A misrepresentation occurs when such a statement proves to be false. This can happen fraudulently, but most often the incorrect statement is at worst negligently made and often innocently. However, this still entitles the party to whom the statement was made to treat the contract as void and/or claim damages.

Non-disclosure of facts is rarely deemed a misrepresentation save on rare occasions such as a failure to reveal material facts in contracts of insurance. Opinions and mere 'sales puff' are not misrepresentations, unless the person making the statement knows that it contravenes the true facts. However, given the serious implications of a misrepresentation being made, care needs to be exercised in pre-contractual negotiations to ensure that any statement which is material to the choice whether to enter the contract or not, is correct.

Commercial debts

The late payment of commercial debts (interest) Act 1998 introduces a statutory right for businesses to claim interest on late payment of commercial debt. From 1 November 2002 all businesses and the public sector may claim interest from all other businesses and the public sector on outstanding debts. A payment is deemed late when it is outside the agreed credit limit or if the contract remains silent 30 days after the goods are delivered. The rate of interest is 8 per cent above bank rate.

Tips to avoid conflict

The following are some helpful tips:

☐ Reducing an agreement to writing helps to avoid confusion.
☐ Ideally both parties should sign a written document. Alternatively, clear written evidence that both parties agree to the terms should exist.
☐ All the essential terms should be agreed.
☐ If the parties wish to be able to terminate the contract on breach of a certain term, they should say so in the contract.

☐ Remember that terms can be implied – this will happen in contracts for the sale of goods or supply of services and hire-purchase agreements.

☐ Professional drafting of exemption clauses may be necessary if reliance is to be placed on them.

☐ There are significant limitations when dealing with consumers.

☐ Seek professional advice when drafting standard terms and conditions for your business, or drafting contracts of significant value.

Further reading

The CLA publishes a range of advisory handbooks covering liability in tort and contract. These include:

Law Relating to Livestock and Domestic Animals (2001) CLA27
Environmental Protection Act (1995) CLA7
Employment Law (2000) CLA17

CLA members also have access to a whole range of Guidance Notes in the secure members' area of the CLA website.

2.8 Litigation

Jeffrey Hansen, former Legal Adviser, CLA

PRELIMINARY ISSUES

When considering litigation, it is necessary to gauge the possible success or viability of a potential claim. The prospective claimant will have to think about a number of issues and take early action to enhance his prospects of success.

From the outset, it will be necessary to identify the prospective defendant and his whereabouts. Checks should be made on whether the potential claim is within the limitation period. If an action is begun outside the limitation period then normally it will be impossible to proceed with it. The limitation periods are as follows:

Action	Limitation
Contract (excluding personal injury)	Six years from the breach of the contractual term
Personal injury	Three years from the date of accident or the date of knowledge of the extent of the injury
Tort (excluding personal injury and latent damage)	Six years from when damage occurs
Latent damage (where damage occurs through negligence but not personal injury)	Six years from date of breach or three years from the date of knowledge if this occurs after the original six years has expired, with a long stop limitation of 15 years

It is vital too, to consider the defendant's solvency. It may not be worthwhile to proceed against an individual or company on the verge of bankruptcy, as any judgement obtained may be difficult to enforce. It is important to consider whether there is any alternative way of obtaining the remedy that is sought, as a balance must be struck between the costs of pursuing the case and the prospects of obtaining a successful outcome. Costs can often be prohibitive.

The following practical steps must also be taken:

☐ Relevant documents and other tangible evidence should be retained.

☐ Photographs may also support a potential claim.

☐ Contact should be made with witnesses to ask whether they are prepared to give evidence at any forthcoming hearing.

☐ Where relevant, thought should be given to obtaining expert evidence to support the case.

Negotiations with the other side, on a without prejudice basis, should continue throughout this preliminary stage with a view to reaching settlement, as resorting to litigation can often be a costly exercise.

However, if it is not possible to negotiate settlement and it is concluded that litigation is the only way forward then, if it has not already been sent, details of the claim should be communicated to the prospective defendant, prior to embarking upon proceedings. This is by way of a 'letter before action'. This formal letter should:

☐ outline the factual circumstances of the case;

☐ detail any losses or damage;

☐ invite settlement proposals within a specific time period;

☐ warn of intended Court proceedings in the event that those settlement proposals are not forthcoming.

If the other party fails to respond positively to this letter, then litigation is the likely outcome.

VENUE

Most claims will begin within the County Court. Claims with a value of £5,000 or less (£1,000 or less for personal injury matters) will issue (start) in the County Court and will be allocated to what is known as the Small Claims procedure. Even if successful, it is extremely rare to obtain costs for legal representation for a small claim; so most claimants will act in person. The Small Claims procedure is relatively straightforward and informal and is said to be 'user friendly' for those who decide to represent themselves. Free, helpful leaflets, explaining the procedure and how to progress a claim can be obtained from any local County Court office.

The procedure for claims which exceed the small claims limit is similar, as these claims will also issue in the County Court but they will later be allocated by the Court to a different procedure or what is known as a 'track', depending upon the value and complexity of the claim. A claim with a value of more than £5,000 but not exceeding £15,000 will be allocated to the fast track and a claim exceeding £15,000 will be allocated to the multi-track. These hearings will be less straightforward and will be heard in open court where members of the public can attend. Unlike small claims, where it is rare to obtain reimbursement for legal representation, if a case falls within either the fast track or multi-track it may be possible to recover some of these costs from the other side, in the event that the claim is successful. It is recommended, therefore, that claimants engage a solicitor to prepare and conduct their claim, if it appears that it will exceed the small claims limit.

COMMENCING PROCEEDINGS

To commence proceedings, it is necessary to complete a claim form, form N1. If the claimant is representing himself then the form can be obtained from the County Court office, free of charge. It can also be accessed and down loaded from the Court service website www.courtservice.gov.uk. The form is accompanied by helpful notes on how to complete it, but claimants who experience difficulty may ask County Court office staff for help (although court staff cannot give legal advice) or they can attend their local citizens' advice bureau for assistance. It is also possible to initiate a claim on the Internet at www.moneyclaim.gov.uk, which is supported by a help desk should a claimant need any further assistance.

The claim form should set out details of the claim and the remedy that is sought. There is a fee payable to issue the claim form, which will relate to the value of the claim. Details of the amount to be paid can be obtained from the County Court office or from the free leaflet available from the Court office from 1 April 2003 entitled *Guide to County Court Fees*.

A claimant may also charge interest upon a debt. This should be included within the claim form. It should be quantified on a daily basis, which is easily done by calculating 0.00022 multiplied by the amount that is claimed. This will give the daily amount of the interest which must then be calculated from the day it fell due until the day on which the proceedings were issued.

The claim form is issued when it is sealed by the Court and given a case number. It must be served upon the defendant within four months from the date of issue.

Normally, the Court will serve the form through the post but the claimant can arrange to serve it upon the defendant himself.

DEFENDING PROCEEDINGS

The claim form is sent to the defendant along with other papers that the defendant is required to complete and return to the Court office within 14 days from the date of receipt. This response pack permits the defendant to respond to the claim either by admitting all of it or part of it, or the defendant may defend the claim and formulate a claim himself, by way of a counterclaim. The time for response may be extended by the defendant to 28 days if he returns the acknowledgement of service form (contained within the response pack) within 14 days of receipt. Once a defence has been returned, the claim will usually be transferred automatically to the defendant's local Court, which will be the venue for the final hearing.

The defendant needs to act quickly, as ignoring the form will allow the claimant to apply to the Court for judgement and then the defendant will be ordered to pay the amount of the claim and costs. Again, if the claim is for £5,000 or less (£1,000 or less in a personal injury matter) the defendant may decide to represent himself as, even if successful, he will not be able to recover the costs of his legal representation. If the claim appears to exceed this limit then it is recommended that the defendant consult with a solicitor to conduct his case.

The claimant can also apply to the Court for judgement if he believes that the defendant has not entered an effective defence. A defendant, therefore, should take care in drafting his defence, ensuring that he answers each part of the claim.

If judgement has been entered by the Court in the absence of a response from the defendant within the requisite time period, he can still make an application to the Court seeking to overturn that judgement if he can prove that his application has been made expeditiously and that there are merits to his defence. If he is able to prove this he may be permitted by the Court to enter his defence at this later stage, although such permission will probably be accompanied by an order for costs.

An application to Court can be made, requesting that the Court deal with the matter, without the need for a hearing. It is a matter for the Court to decide whether it is prepared to deal with it in this way, but if it believes it to be straightforward and expedites the situation then it is more than likely that it will be dealt with in the absence of the parties.

ALLOCATION OF THE MATTER

If a partial admission or defence is returned to the Court then the Court will wish to allocate the matter to a track. An allocation questionnaire will be received by the claimant and the defendant who will then be required to complete it and return it within a specified time, indicating amongst other things the value of the claim, the number of witnesses and an estimate of the time it will take for the forthcoming hearing and whether negotiations with the other side are continuing and whether further time is required for possible settlement. Both the claimant and defendant should co-operate with each other in completing the questionnaires. The forms should then be forwarded to the Court. The claimant will have to pay a further fee, as will the defendant in the event of a counterclaim. Details of the fee levels can be obtained from the County Court office.

Once the allocation questionnaires are received by the Court, their contents will be considered by the judge who will allocate the matter to a ' track '. If more information is required then it will be requested. Alternatively, the district judge may order an allocation hearing where both parties have to attend. Directions will be issued along with a timetable, relating to obtaining evidence and disclosing it to the other party, thus preparing the matter for a final hearing or trial.

The trial of a small claims matter will be informal and will be heard before a district judge in his chambers. The final hearing for a fast track or multi-track matter will be more complex and it is therefore recommended that legal representation be obtained.

ENFORCEMENT

If a defendant fails to respond to a judgement order then it will fall to the claimant to seek to enforce it. Again, there is a helpful, free leaflet available from the County Court office entitled *I have a judgement but the defendant hasn't paid – what can I do?* which explains the procedures available for enforcing judgements. These include involving a court bailiff under a warrant of execution, an attachment of earnings order, a third-party debt order or a charging order. Fees will be payable when the Court becomes involved with enforcement. Advice should be sought from a solicitor or from the citizens' advice bureau as to the best method of enforcement.

ALTERNATIVE DISPUTE RESOLUTION

If a consumer has a dispute with a supplier of goods or services which cannot be settled through negotiation then it may be possible to consider alternative dispute resolution (ADR). These schemes are designed to involve a third party, such as a mediator, arbitrator or ombudsman, to assist the parties in arriving at a satisfactory outcome.

It is recommended that anyone who is considering this course of action should discuss the matter with a solicitor as some of the schemes are legally binding and it will therefore be impossible to refer the matter to Court, if there is dissatisfaction with the final decision.

However, there are advantages to dispute resolution schemes. They are cheap and less formal than progressing a matter to Court. It may be worthwhile to proceed with a non-binding scheme for, if there is a negative outcome, the matter can still be referred to Court.

Alternative dispute resolution for consumer disputes is most often provided by trade associations, such as The Association of British Travel Agents (ABTA), for travel agents. If the consumer has a dispute with a supplier they should first establish whether the supplier is a member of the trade association and then contact that body to formulate a complaint.

Conciliation is usually the first stage in a consumer dispute. The conciliator will often be a member of the particular trade association and will ask for written representations from both parties. The decision of the conciliator is non-binding and the matter can still be referred to Court.

Arbitration involves the use of an arbitrator who will usually be a member of the Chartered Institute of Arbitrators and both the consumer and supplier will agree that any decision that is reached will be legally binding. If the outcome is unsatisfactory it will be impossible to refer the matter to Court unless it is necessary to enforce an award made by the arbitrator.

Mediation involves a third party who will meet with both the supplier and consumer and attempt to assist the parties to reach an agreement. If an agreement is reached then the terms of the agreement will be set out in a document which will usually be legally binding and it will not be possible to refer the matter to a Court, except for the purpose of enforcement.

Many service providers will also have an ombudsman scheme. This is true of insurers, the banking industry and estate agents. If a referral is made, the ombudsman will consider any evidence and make a recommendation but this will not be legally binding and the matter can still be referred to Court.

It may be true that a consumer has little to lose if he refers a matter for alternative dispute resolution, when it is non-binding. If the scheme is legally binding then a solicitor should be consulted to discuss the advantages and disadvantages of proceeding with such a complaint, rather than taking the matter to Court.

The CLA has promoted an alternative dispute resolutions scheme, jointly with the RICS, for use in disputes over statutory compensation in relation to Compulsory Acquisition. Details can be found in the CLA advisory handbook, *The Lands Tribunal* (2001) CLA24.

2.9 Insurance issues

Stuart Rootham, RK Harrison

INTRODUCTION

When contemplating diversification in any form, as part of the planning process you will almost certainly prepare a detailed budget and if setting up in business yourself prepare a detailed business plan. Either way, insurance will be an important consideration for your new venture and needs to be included in the early stages of any planning process.

It is best to seek the advice of a professional broker that has experience in dealing with rural businesses before you even contemplate budgeting for your proposed business or property development. It could have serious ramifications on your finances if it is not properly researched. It could be that the cover you are looking for is extremely costly or in some cases cover may not be available at any cost and could ruin all your plans.

Some of the considerations when purchasing insurance remain the same for most policies:

☐ Has your adviser properly explained the different types of cover available to you?

☐ Have you considered fully the scope of cover required and taken the time to ensure you have set the correct sums insured and limits of indemnity required?

☐ Have the key terms, conditions and exceptions been properly explained to you?

☐ Has your adviser offered a professional service, and are you satisfied that they will continue to do so?

☐ How strong is the financial position of the insurer your broker has recommended?

From an insurance perspective the considerations are best broken down into two distinct types of diversification: property renovation followed by onward sale or rental to third parties; and development of your own start-up business.

We have supplied some simple guidelines for you to consider before embarking upon your new venture.

PROPERTY DEVELOPMENT

If you have outbuildings, an unused barn or an old commercial building that you are planning to renovate for commercial or residential usage, there are many costs that will need to be taken into account when budgeting. The extent of insurance cover that you will need to consider will depend upon the nature of the development work to be undertaken and where professional builders are being used, the contract terms entered into with them. The insurance issues fall into three specific areas:

☐ If developing existing buildings on your land, you need to ensure that the existing structures are properly insured during the construction period.

☐ Cover will need to be arranged on the 'contract works', covering both material costs and labour costs that would be incurred to reinstate work.

☐ Making sure that adequate employers' liability and public liability covers are in force. If using a firm of builders don't make the mistake of assuming that they have proper cover in place – check!

Looking at these individually you can see that insurance alone needs planning and co-ordinating nearly as much as the building work.

Property insurance

Unless the project is a new build, insurance will be needed for the existing building structure. If the existing structure is already insured it is vital that you inform your insurers that building work is due to be carried out and provide them with full details of the development. Failure to do so could invalidate your cover in the event of damage occurring during the building work. The reason for this is that the presence of contractors working on the building increases the risk of damage arising considerably and insurers deem this to be a material change in risk. Once notified your insurer will confirm any terms that they wish to apply during the construction period.

Your existing structure should be insured for as wide a range of perils as possible. These perils include fire, damage by aircraft or falling debris, lightning, explosion, storm damage, flood, malicious damage and many more. Depending on the current state of repair of the structure insurers may only offer selected perils on your property but it is best to talk to your adviser about the extent of cover available and any policy warranties that apply during the building work.

Contract works insurance

This covers loss or damage to the building works (both labour and materials) during the contract period. Normally cover is arranged on an 'all risks' basis covering a wide range of perils with the sum insured under the policy equivalent to the total value of the contract, plus an allowance for fees and debris removal costs. This ensures that if a total-loss fire occurs the day before work is due to be completed, the policy will cover the cost of reinstating the works.

If you are entering into a formal contract with a firm of builders, it is important to check the contract terms as to who has responsibility for insuring the contract works. If possible, use an insurance adviser that has experience in this type of insurance and who can review the building contract conditions on your behalf to ensure that the insurance in place is in line with your contractual obligations.

Employers' and Public Liability Insurance

If you are employing a firm of builders to complete the project on your behalf, you should establish the extent of their liability insurance cover and request evidence that such cover is in force. They should hold Employers' Liability insurance with a limit of indemnity of no less than £10 million and Public Liability with a limit of indemnity of at least £2 million.

Where you are managing the project yourself, employing labour as needed, you will need to purchase your own liability covers at similar levels.

Again your insurance adviser will be able to advise you fully on these covers and what you should be looking for.

When the work is complete

Once the project nears completion, you will need to prepare cover on the new soon-to-be-completed structure. Remember that the existing property policy is only covering the original structure for its re-build in its previous condition/state and Contract Works insurance expires as soon as the building work is complete.

A Property Owner's Policy will provide the exact cover you are looking for on your new completed building(s), whether it be for the short term, until your property is sold, or for the coming years whilst leasing the properties to businesses or to individuals as homes. This class of insurance is extremely attractive to insurers, with most major insurers offering their own products specifically designed to provide comprehensive cover for the property owner. You should ensure that your adviser is sourcing all available markets to give you competitive premium terms and quality cover.

Your premium will be affected by a number of variations and you should also consider these when you are looking at the future cost of leasing a property to tenants:

☐ The insurers will rate your policy on the location of the development, for example, 'Is the area susceptible to flooding?'
☐ They will consider the construction of the property; properties with timber floors and wooden barns will attract higher premium rates.
☐ Who will be the tenants of the property? Fireworks manufacturer vs. an accountant's office for a commercial property, and the moral hazard presented by any residential tenants.

Within a Property Owner's Policy you will be able to insure the structure for the cost of re-building, protect your liability as the property owner and insure against loss of rental income you receive from the leaseholders following damage to the buildings.

Many property owners pass all or a proportion of the cost of the insurance onto the tenants as part of the monthly rental costs. This would be written into the lease agreement and is clearly in the interests of the property owner, as you attempt to keep overheads to a minimum.

STARTING YOUR OWN BUSINESS

All banks or finance brokers will most certainly ask for a CV and comprehensive business plan when you are attempting to raise finance for your business venture and you will need to show that you have made provisions for insurance in this plan. But how much do you need to put aside?

The figures regarding new businesses failure in their first year are extremely high and this has been assigned to a lack of forward thinking and research into the business you choose. Some will ask their accountant whilst others will rely on the advice of friends when setting aside a figure for insurance, but the obvious place to start is with an experienced insurance adviser.

Having come up with a brilliant idea for a new business venture you need to get an indication of insurance availability and likely cost at an early stage. It is quite possible that your brilliant idea is perceived by insurers as being extremely high risk and attracts very high premium terms that would make your plan completely unviable before you've even started.

The above scenario is the exception rather than the norm. Most insurers are keen to write small commercial businesses, so for most businesses obtaining a quotation will not prove difficult.

There are many different classes of insurance that a business can buy. Getting advice as to what is right for your business is important. To illustrate the range of covers to consider we have split them down into four separate categories:

☐ protecting the physical assets;
☐ protecting your liabilities;
☐ protecting you and your staff;
☐ protecting your balance sheet.

Within each of these categories there is further separation as we break it down into the cover you can get under each of these headings. The following are either sections of an insurance policy or are policies in their own right; you must consider what cover you need:

Protecting your physical assets
Buildings
Contents
Business Interruption
Money
Goods in Transit
Motor

Protecting your liabilities
Employer's Liability
Public Liability
Products Liability
Professional Indemnity

Protecting your balance sheet
Directors & Officers Liability
Employment Practice Liability
Legal Expenses Insurance
Fidelity Guarantee (Theft by
    Employees)

Protecting you and your staff
Personal Accident
Travel Insurance (inc. business
    trips)
Employment Benefits
Private Medical Insurance

To obtain quotations for your business you will need to provide financial projections in terms of wages and turnover, projected profits, and asset values, etc.

In the current economic climate, insurers are more determined than ever to achieve underwriting profits. This means that they are much more selective about which customers they take on. It is important that you can demonstrate that your business takes risk management seriously. Insurers will be interested in:

☐ The quality of physical security in place at your business premises to prevent theft. Whilst alarm protection is important, for a rural business, its value is lessened if the police are some distance away and unable to respond in a short enough time period It is more important to make your premises difficult to get into in the first place.

☐ Fire safety at your premises. Do you have adequate fire extinguishers in place? Do you have smoke alarms fitted? Are fire exits kept clear at all times? Have you carried out a Fire Risk Assessment? Do you allow smoking on the premises? Do you keep your premises tidy and take waste off the premises regularly?

☐ Health & Safety. Are you aware of your obligations to employees under law? Does your business have a written Health & Safety Policy? Have you carried out workplace risks assessments?

Your insurance adviser should be able to help you in all of the above areas. Most insurers will carry out a survey of your premises when they go on cover so it is best to be prepared and make sure your business is in good management shape from day one.

The buying of insurance is usually a very straightforward process. For most small businesses the insurance requirements can be discussed over the telephone as it may not be financially viable for the insurance adviser to visit on site. The key is to ensure that a written detailed quotation is provided and, if you have any doubts, to request a copy of the policy wording before purchasing. Keep copies of any correspondence as this can help avoid any potential disputes at a later date.

Ideally you should speak to an insurance adviser that is involved in rural business and understands your insurance needs. They should also be able to source all of the policies mentioned in this chapter themselves.

_____

2.10 Marketing and promoting the business

Roderick Millar and Jonathan Reuvid

There is much confusion about marketing. This stems from two sources. Firstly, the definition of 'marketing' requires clarification. And secondly, the amount of resources a small business should allocate to it needs to be addressed.

The definition is simple to deal with. To marketing professionals and academics marketing can be summed up as 'offering what you can sell'. To the public it is more usually thought of as 'selling what you can offer'. If you are to run a successful business, the first definition is the better one to be guided by, and so a more holistic approach is necessary, involving what those in the trade refer to as the four Ps: product, price, place and promotion. To this the Public Relations industry also adds a fifth 'P', perception.

The amount of resources you can and should allocate to marketing is much more subjective. There is no empirical test to tell you what you must spend in both time and money in order to achieve any specific level of return. The marketing industry in all its many forms, from advertising sales people and trade show organisers to copywriters and PR agents, will all make cogent arguments why you should use their services. And being sales people they will often make you worry that you will be left behind if you do not use them. The bottom line should never be 'can you afford *not* to', but always 'will the marketing return justify the costs'. No doubt everyone would like to take full-page colour spreads in the weekend supplements backed up by TV and billboard campaigns – but clearly that is not an option to those on a limited budget. This chapter will try to indicate some of the options available to those on a small business budget.

MARKET RESEARCH

The beginning of your marketing process should be in place long before you start trading your new product or service. This applies as much to Microsoft's latest software as to the new hairdressing salon on the high street. They must both establish if there is a market demand for a new product and what exactly the demand is for; they must conduct market research. The difference is that Microsoft has rather larger marketing resources than the hairdresser does.

Established businesses have a huge advantage over start-up businesses in carrying out market research. They have exposure to market sentiment and everyday reactions through their current business activities. Added to this is their database of past and present customers that they ought to be able to analyse and, should they wish, contact for views and opinions. This information can also form the basis for extrapolating their current data to build up likely market information for different geographic areas or market sectors.

The brand-new start-up business is unlikely to have any of these resources readily available to it, and while discussion amongst like-minded competitors is often a lot more open than you may expect, you will not be handed databases and customer views by your future competition. Therefore, the prospective businessman must try to build a picture of what the market for his product or service is currently like and whether there is sufficient demand for his concept and its benefits. Gathering this information can be done either by collecting brand new data direct from the marketplace specifically for your own purposes (primary data) or from data already gathered by others that you can shape for your own use (secondary data). Obviously, primary data will be more relevant and more up to date; you can assess how reliable it will be because you know how it was collected and collated. Secondary data may well require you to make some assumptions as to how and where it was gathered and how reliable it is; it may be slightly out of date and also is likely to be only partially relevant to your product or service. However, it will be very much cheaper to acquire.

In today's economy there is no shortage of available information. The trick is to sift out the wheat from the chaff. Identifying the correct questions to ask is important. You must think carefully about what factors you need in order to sell your product or service successfully. This will include the profile of your potential customers (age, spending power, where they live, family status, sex) a profile of the market (Is it growing or shrinking? Which sectors of the market are doing best and why? What is the long-term trend?), and some marketing research (What are your competitors doing to sell their products? What is working and what is not?).

If you have a rural business selling locally, then your market research can be done more on a primary than on a secondary basis. You can go out and speak to potential customers; you can observe the competition. The more disparate your potential customer base the more difficult it will be for you to track them down and have a useful dialogue with them. In this case secondary data collection will become more important and, for tracking sector trends, will be your only option. The following are possible sources of information:

☐ Trade magazines and financial press will offer some information but probably unsystematically – that is, it will be pot luck what you find.

☐ The background information you seek will most likely be somewhere on the Internet, but sourcing can be tiresome and assessing its reliability and how up-to-date it may be, is often a problem.

☐ Larger libraries will have a range of market research books that can give you useful information.

☐ In addition to these sources you may find that your local authority business advice unit will have current information available to you about local business and markets, as will the local Chamber of Commerce and Business Link office.

Most of these sources of information will be either free or inexpensive to access. If you still require more information then you can purchase market information from market research and business information companies. The British Market Research Association will be able to provide a list (www.bmra.org.uk).

SEGMENTATION AND STRATEGY

Having gathered the relevant market information for your business concept's sector, your next marketing task is to identify where exactly your product or service fits within the sector. The most basic segmentation is to know if you want to sell to business or consumers. Consumers are more numerous and normally will pay higher prices, but they are more difficult to reach (they do not list themselves like companies do in trade directories and magazines, or in the Yellow Pages with contact names and numbers), more fickle (most companies will not change their suppliers just because a new one comes along), and purchase in smaller quantities less regularly.

As a small business you will need to focus on specific segments of the market since you will be unable to offer all things to all comers. Are you going for high-end users willing to pay for quality and/or uniqueness, or are you trying to provide a service locally where none currently exists? What is your 'unique selling point' – or USP in marketing jargon – that sets you apart from the competition?

With your sector knowledge and your segment identified you must now design your marketing strategy and thence plan. The information gained will indicate what is the best way to reach your potential customers:

- ☐ trade magazines;
- ☐ local press;
- ☐ national press;
- ☐ local radio;
- ☐ bus advertising;
- ☐ promotions;
- ☐ trade shows;
- ☐ leafleting;
- ☐ direct mail;
- ☐ inserts.

You will have an idea of how generous or frugal your marketing budget can be so you will have a feel for how much advertising and PR you will be able to afford. The research you have carried out to this point in identifying your gap in the market, who you should be selling to and what in particular it is they want will provide a clear indication as to what type of media you should be using.

If your target market is well-paid young individuals who purchase goods for their image and lifestyle associations rather than pure value-for-money, then your advertising must be in media that projects image and lifestyle. While this is obvious from the unpressurised standpoint of writing the business plan, when you are in the thick of trying to get some media exposure you can easily start to lose control of the original plan. For even the smallest business will be approached occasionally by sales departments wanting you to spend your business's money on promoting yourself in their publications, on their products or at their shows. It is for this reason that it is very important to design a clear marketing strategy that you can refer to and keep as a controlling influence over the media offers that will come your way. Amend and update the strategy as an ongoing project certainly, but in your own time – not because someone else tells you to!

The strategy you build is like a road map – it will show you where you are and where you want to get to. It will also show the preferred route for getting there and the most comprehensive strategic plans will also show you how to get back on track if you lose your way or are detoured by events beyond your control. The first task is to set your targets – 'where you want to go' – whether that is to increase sales of an existing business by 15 per cent or generate sales for a new business to a minimum level. Then plan a timetable of marketing 'events'; these can be any marketing action such as a press release, placing of adverts, leafleting your local area, trade show or whatever you choose – all of them will be chosen because they reach out specifically to your target market and you believe they will bring in more added sales value than they cost.

Critical to all these 'events' is the evaluation process that you must go through after each one of them. Especially for a new business where the response to any event is fairly unpredictable, it is vital to know which marketing tactics produce results and then work out why. The simplest way to track the success of events is to note down all responses you get from potential customers from the event and how many positive sales this leads to. It is very easy *not* to ask customers enquiring about your product where they heard about you, but it is also very foolish. Nobody will mind being asked, it gives an impression of a well-organised company and, vitally, it provides you with critical information on which to base future marketing events.

IMAGE

Part of the marketing function is to build the image of your business and your products. As a small business you will have very limited resources to address to this area of marketing. You should be focusing your product trading on a homogenous sector of the market and your goal should be to present as coherent an image for your business, as possible across all its aspects. Essentially, all companies do this – if we look at the Ford Motor Company, their

Ford branded cars are placed so as to be attractive and affordable to the mass market, but Ford also owns Jaguar and Aston Martin, executive and super-luxury cars, which they keep very distinct from the Ford name in their marketing, although it is well known that many components are shared between the different cars in the group range.

It is therefore important to consider the impact that every marketing event you undertake will have on your entire range of products or services, not just the single item you are promoting. The quality of the material used in your advertising or promotion will underscore the message you want to get across. That your business's reputation takes years to build but can be destroyed in moments is no less true for being a well-worn cliché.

DIRECT MARKETING

Direct mail is often considered to be the black sheep of the marketing toolbox. However, it is really a victim of its own success. If the response rate to direct mail was not so high, in terms of cost in relation to increased sales, then it would not be as prevalent as it is currently. It is this prevalence that leads to the problem of 'junk mail' piling up behind your door every morning.

The advantage of direct mail to the marketer is that it is very flexible. You can choose your recipients' geographic area, their income level, their leisure preferences and so on. You can also choose how much you wish to spend on any given mailout with great flexibility. The drawbacks are in choosing to whom the mailout should be sent, the expense and the legal implications. For the start-up business, purchasing a list can be relatively expensive, and also requires a degree of specialist knowledge in selecting your list broker and the criteria by which the particular list is built up. It is worth researching the use of direct marketing carefully if you intend to spend a significant percentage of your marketing budget on it. The British Direct Marketing Association (www.dma.org.uk, 020 7291 3300) can provide much useful information. For overseas information, Kogan Page annually publishes *The Directory of International Direct and E-Marketing*.

If your business is well established you are likely to have built up a database of past customers' details. If your business is not of the type where you collect your customers' details as a matter of course, it is worth considering methods by which you might be able to gather such information through a loyalty card, notification of sales offers or similar schemes. When you have a list of customers you are in a position where not only can you re-contact them but you *may* be able to trade your list with other companies in your area. However, there are increasingly strict data protection laws governing notification of customers (at the time of taking their details) if you wish to share their details, in any way, with other bodies. Again the DMA can guide you with this.

ADVERTISING AND PUBLIC RELATIONS

It should be so simple to get your message across. You know your product or service inside out, you understand the benefits and you recognise the quality. What is more frustrating is you also know that people will enjoy using your product – all you have to do is persuade them to try it. And that is the problem.

The situation is difficult because all your competitors are trying to gain the consumer's attention as well. There is a lot of 'noise' out there in the market place and your job is to make sure you are heard above everyone else. Advertising and public relations (PR) are your routes to doing this, but be aware that markets in the United Kingdom are very sophisticated and it will take a fair amount of expertise to make your business stand out. This chapter is not able to cover the vast range of skills and advice needed to ensure that your advert or press release is eye-catching. The basic principles are simple enough, although the details are where the difference is made.

☐ ABC – accuracy, brevity, clarity – make good copy.
☐ Avoid jargon and formality.
☐ Never bend the truth (this includes phrases like 'once in a lifetime chance' if it's not); it cheapens the message and damages your reputation.
☐ Keep it interesting and relevant (if you are writing a press release, open with an idea that will work as a headline).

The ability to write good adverts and press releases is more experience than natural skill. If you have the time to learn about it then it will be time well spent; if not it may well pay to find an expert to help you out. If you have any contacts in the media they may well be able to help draft the copy for you and show you what makes the difference. If this route is not available and you feel your attempts with only a book to help you are uninspiring, then it may be time to use professional help – the PR agent.

The problem with PR agencies is that you have to pay them! That in itself is not surprising, but quantifying their success is awkward. Most agencies will be keen to get you on a monthly retainer. If your marketing budget can afford this, then it will probably serve you to sign up to a limited term contract as you will then be able to set out exactly what you expect them to provide over what time period and discuss with them what they hope to achieve in this period in terms of copy placed or extra sales achieved.

The advantages of PR agencies, beyond their ability to write compelling copy, is that they should have a good selection of media contacts through which they can get your message heard. Your business is to produce and sell a successful product; often this will not give you much space to build relationships with the media, and your PR agent is there to overcome this barrier. Their business is based on their ability to get their client's messages into the media, be it local press, national press, radio or any other medium you feel would work, through an established network of contacts.

In choosing an agent or agency you must therefore make sure of a number of key points:

☐ The most important is that you trust them; this means that you should get hold of references from their existing clients and see what they have done for them.

☐ You should also feel completely comfortable working with them. Do you have a rapport? Do they understand your business implicitly? Do they have time for your business? How quickly do they return your initial calls?

☐ Beyond your relationship with them you need to know how effective they are. What are their copywriting skills like? They are not all as good as each other by any means. What are their media contacts like – especially in the area of the media you are interested in?

☐ Get a limited-term contract written up, which sets out your requirements and budget.

☐ Keep a very tight rein on costs – often the retainer fee will be small while the 'extras' can mount up quickly.

Towards the end of the limited-term contract (you may need six months before any real progress can be judged) evaluate what difference to your profit margins the PR agency has made. If you feel that it is negligible then discuss this with them and, if needs be, be prepared to leave them.

DAMAGE LIMITATION

An area often overlooked in small businesses is a damage limitation or crisis management plan. PR agents should be good at helping develop these, but they are essentially straightforward and you should be able to create a plan yourself.

No business wants a crisis but, inevitably, they will appear from time to time, in varying degrees of severity. If you have taken time to consider what you should best do in various disaster scenarios before they occur you will be very much better placed to deal with them should the scenario become reality. Not only will the plan give you a clear idea of how to progress, but its very existence should reassure you and give a sense of calm. Crisis management falls into two parts. The first is how to deal with the practical side of the problem, whether it may be power or machine failure that stops production, transport problems that prevent distribution to customers, accident or injury to personnel or, perhaps the most business critical, a problem with the product or service that causes illness, injury or significant financial problems to the customer. Your plan will identify each different scenario and then follow it through certain stages: action to stop further damage and action to restore service. The second element is the communications side. There should be clear procedures to inform your customers what the problem is, how long it will continue, what measures are being taken to rectify the problem and what measures are being taken to ensure it does not occur again. With health and safety issues you will also need procedures to notify relatives of injury or, heaven forbid, fatality. You will also need to have a plan for dealing with the press. This is, from a marketing point of view, where the plan comes into its own. The reputation of your business will rely on a single, coherent message being put out about the crisis. A single senior person, essentially the owner or chairman, should be the spokesman. They should unambiguously give out all the known facts, avoid any conjecture, indicate how the problem is being contained and ensure that any essential safety information is clearly provided. The silver lining to crises is that the media attention can be turned to the business's advantage if it is correctly handled. The eradication of panic and chaotic reaction will go along way to doing this.

THE INTERNET

The limitations of the Internet as a transforming marketing tool have been clearly seen in the last three years. The reality that the Internet will not instantly create an endless stream of cheap sales has been clearly, if belatedly, understood. With hindsight, it is becoming clearer that the Internet is good as a very effective means of providing information about businesses. It is not so good at directly selling products or services. In a way this is good news for the small business. It is relatively cheap to establish a simple website for your business, but expensive to set up a transactional site. A simple website should provide as much information as possible, without running the risk of becoming quickly out of date. So give a brief description of what your business does as a necessary opening requirement, and take the opportunity to show where the business originated from and why, as this draws the reader in. Include a clear list of what products or services you offer, with greater detail available if possible. Given that your website is primarily an information rather than a dialogue portal, it is important to provide a postal address and telephone contact numbers. It is also useful to provide a guide to 'who is who' in the business so that the appropriate person can be contacted.

The expensive element of the Internet is if you wish to conduct sales over the net. This requires a much greater investment in computer hardware and software, which will need a substantial volume of transactions to make it profitable. Many companies are now realising that the consumer primarily wants information from the website and is happier to make purchases by traditional means. Clearly this does not apply to all products and businesses and there will be many successful Internet sales businesses in the future, but unless you intend to be an Internet specialist you must cost carefully the investment required (and time involved developing and maintaining the software and equipment) against your expected return.

Fortunately, there is an enormous amount of detailed information on Internet marketing, both freely available on the Internet itself and in printed form.

TRADE SHOWS AND EXHIBITIONS

Trade fairs and exhibitions may offer great opportunities to showcase your business and increase your sales, but like all other parts of the marketing equation you have to know why you are there and what you want to get out of it. Just turning up and 'being there' will be an unrewarding experience. Therefore you must go through the now, hopefully, familiar routine of asking yourself what your objectives are from being at a trade fair; to launch a new product or service; heighten your profile in a particular geographic area; or increase sales to a specialist sector. Evaluate a realistic target for the exhibition: get 200 new potential customer names; sell £10,000 of product; get a profile in the local press and so on.

Having identified your specific objectives it will be much easier to decide whether or not the trade fair is appropriate. Ask for the media pack from the organisers to see who goes, where they are from and what you can expect them to spend. Time and money invested in an unsuccessful trade show can be easily avoided by a little research at this point. For rural businesses, trade fairs and exhibitions that draw in potential customers and are focused on your catchment area may be few and far between. Many do not provide an effective channel to market.

Once at the exhibition hall, as with other advertising, you must make yourself stand out from the crowd. A little money invested in bright and clear display materials will pay dividends quickly if the alternative is an amateurish look. Probably the most important task is to make sure that your staff is enthusiastic and knowledgeable. An upbeat and animated person on the stand will be more successful than a bored and embarrassed person regardless of the product or quality of display materials.

Finally, the post-exhibition follow-up is vital. Throughout your marketing process any lead that is not followed up is a lost lead, and is therefore money wasted. With trade shows you should plan your follow-up procedure *before* you go to the show so that you can get it dealt with swiftly afterwards. This avoids the risk that you delay it too long so that it never happens, or happens too late, and also ensures that your follow up, whether it be an enquiry form or telephone call, gets to the customer before anyone else's.

SUMMARY

A checklist for marketing

1. Do you 'offer what you can sell' or try to 'sell what you can offer'?
2. How carefully do you collect your sales data and analyse it?
3. What are the key research objectives you need to answer? Have you carried out any primary research? How objective have you made it?
4. What is your ideal customer profile? Does it exist in your area?
5. Have you clearly identified your USP? What sort of potential market does this direct you to? Does it exist in your area?
6. Have you considered all potential markets in your area? Are you going for the most accessible and/or lucrative? If not, are you happy why this is the case?
7. How can you best reach your customers? Do you have any experience with this form of media? Do you know how best to utilise it?
8. Are you confident your cost of marketing for any 'event' is less than its minimum likely return? If not, do you know why you are spending money on it?
9. Does your product or service lend itself to direct marketing? If not, are you sure there is not an angle you are missing?
10. Have you considered investing in a PR agent? If so, do you have a mutually agreed list of targets and a timetable for achieving them?
11. Are you maximising your profitable exposure to the Internet? This can mean are you spending too much on it as well as not enough.

2.11 ICT and broadband for rural business usage

Sean Johnson, Senior IT Analyst and Charles Trotman, Rural Economy Adviser, CLA

INTRODUCTION

When we talk about Information Communication Technology (ICT) we tend to think mainly of computers but, whilst they are part of ICT albeit the major part, ICT covers all aspects of Information and Communications.

We have seen a colossal rise in the amount of technology we use to communicate. Since Alexander Graham Bell spoke the first words into the 'harmonic telephone' for Thomas Watson to hear on the 3 June 1875, we have seen telephones become a necessity. With it came other technologies, some now virtually obsolete and some that will undoubtedly become obsolete.

Telex has been replaced by fax, and fax will be replaced by e-mail. With the first mobile phones we could never have envisaged that the most used part of mobile phone technology would be SMS messaging and of course we now see a computer on virtually every desk in every office.

With any technology, normally the by-products and innovative thinking of entrepreneurs gives us other methods of communication that we hadn't even thought we needed but now rely on.

ICT is seen by many to be fundamental to the growth and success of businesses, especially in rural areas. Internet access and e-mail has changed the way we work and broadband is seen by many to be the vital component for businesses, especially in rural areas.

This chapter covers the main issues raised by ICT and sets out the advantages and disadvantages of broadband for rural business. It also attempts to de-mystify the subject with layman's guides to the different types of networks and broadband on offer. It is, however, not a substitute for professional advice.

THE TYPES AND USES OF ICT

ICT is now an integral part of modern business. From the time we pick up the telephone to speak to a customer to sending the invoice for goods, most if not all the processes are covered by ICT.

In very broad terms we can split ICT into two main areas: voice and data.

Voice communication

Voice communication plays a major role in ICT and, whether we like it or not, we are now all tied to our phones virtually every minute of the day. With this amount of voice traffic we are seeing more and more companies using voicemail and automated switchboards to enable them to satisfy their customers' needs.

Data technologies

From the introduction of the computer into businesses in the late 1950s we have seen prices drop and technologies advance at an alarming rate; a few years ago, a small business would have started down the road to computerisation with one computer, after a while another is added, for another employee or to perform a dedicated task such as the accounts. This is normally where problems start to occur. Printing is the first potentially problematic issue; you can save the files you want printing to a floppy disk and then take this to the computer that is attached to the printer, but this is time consuming and we are starting to see modern machines being supplied without floppy disk drives.

Once you reach this stage you need to start thinking about networks. There are two main types of network: peer to peer and server based. These are reviewed in more detail in the final section of this chapter.

THE IMPACT OF ICT ON RURAL BUSINESS

Because of the location of many rural businesses, the impact of ICT on them is far greater than the impact of ICT on businesses located in urban areas. Urban businesses have the advantage of localised specialised industries and transport links that are not normally available to rural businesses.

ICT can enable rural businesses to compete in today's fast-moving market place. It can break down the barriers traditionally associated with rural areas. With effective use of ICT there is no longer a barrier for national or international trade based upon the location of the business. Because of this, rural businesses would be more likely to attract and retain highly-skilled employees and enable them to work in the villages and towns that they grew up in; this in turn supplies the other services that benefit from localised workforces.

Mobile phone technology is another area where businesses can react to customers' needs not based on the location of their employees. Unfortunately, however, we still see less coverage in rural areas than in urban areas.

With the new videophones that are starting to emerge a whole new plethora of applications and opportunities may evolve.

In major cities we are now seeing wireless hotspots being installed: small areas where wireless-enabled devices such as laptops and PDAs can access the Internet at high speed. These innovations can be as useful in rural areas as in urban areas.

BROADBAND

What is broadband?

Broadband is the term used to describe faster access to the Internet and is available through a number of different means. These are explained in more detail below.

Essentially, there are five different types of broadband:

☐ ADSL (Asymmetric Digital Subscriber Line);
☐ cable modem;
☐ leased lines;
☐ satellite;
☐ wireless.

The main advantage of broadband over a standard (narrowband) connection is speed. To give an example, a PC (personal computer) using a standard phone connection can download 56,000 'bits' of information (approximately 7,000 characters) a second. Broadband however, allows a PC to download information at a rate between 512,000 and 2,000,000 'bits' per second, some 40 times faster than a standard connection.

Other advantages of broadband are that it is always connected and it is a flat rate price, meaning that the user is charged a standard price per month or year, regardless of the amount of time spent on the Internet.

ADSL

ADSL runs on the current telephone line system. In order to be able to use broadband, telephone exchanges have to be ADSL enabled, which can cost as much as £250,000 each. Out of some 5,500 exchanges, only approximately 1,200 have so far been enabled.

One of the main problems with ADSL is that it requires the recipient to live within 3.5 km of an enabled telephone exchange, or within 5.5 km if using RADSL (Rate Adaptive Digital Subscriber Line), although the speed of service could still be reduced. Outside of these areas, ADSL/RADSL will not be available. The recipient must also have a BT telephone line in order to receive ADSL. Another problem is that if there are poor voice connections on the telephone line, it is unlikely that broadband could be installed. Finally, BT may not enable some exchanges because of a lack of demand.

Cable

Cable is effectively a cable that runs underground that is used for cable TV and is only available through a limited number of cable companies, such as Cable and Wireless. It also requires a special cable modem or network card that connects the computer to the cable infrastructure and then sends electronic information to the Internet Service Provider (ISP) and then onto the Internet.

There will be a sizeable infrastructure cost in order for the cables to be laid. In addition, the cable operator must be operating in the applicable area. Many of the cable companies are heavily in debt.

_____

Satellite

Satellite broadband (see Figure 2.11.1) requires the setting up of a reception dish (like satellite TV) which has to be positioned externally so that it can see the satellite in its line of sight. A request for information is relayed from the computer to the satellite dish. This is then sent to the satellite, then to the ISP and then to the Internet. Information is retrieved and is then relayed back to the computer through the same process, but in the opposite direction.

One of the major constraints of satellite is cost. There is also a problem that satellites can be affected by adverse weather conditions. Moreover, if the dish is knocked out of position this can affect or disrupt the signal. Finally, there is a problem over something known as 'latency'. To give an analogy: a television interview over a long distance will use satellite. However, it is noticeable that after a question is asked, there can be a delay before the question is heard at the other end.

Leased lines

Leased lines are ones that are put in by BT and are for the use of a single user or company only. The main advantages of leased lines are:

☐ There is no contention (ie sharing of the infrastructure with other users) which could slow down access.
☐ Leased lines have a guaranteed bandwidth.
☐ There is a high level of availability and service through Service Level Agreements, which are not available with the other types of broadband.

The main disadvantage, however, is that it can be far more expensive than the other options. Before leased lines are laid, BT will carry out a survey as to practicability and cost, and it could be that the latter will make leased lines uneconomic for many users.

Wireless

Wireless broadband – essentially a system where there are no wires – is based on a network of a central transmitter and a series of receivers. The clear advantage of wireless broadband is that of speed: at 11 Mbps, it is far faster than other forms of broadband.

However, it does have a number of disadvantages. Firstly, the technology in the United Kingdom is still very much in its infancy

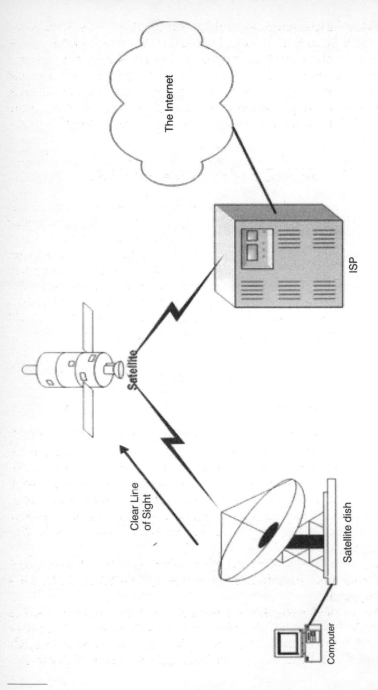

The Internet

ISP

Satellite

Clear Line
of Sight

Satellite dish

Computer

Figure 2.11.1 Satellite broadband network

and is at the trial stage. Secondly, speed can drop or the connection can fail if there is no clear line of sight in the same way as mobile phone signals can be lost. Thirdly, the hardware costs per recipient tend to be more expensive, with each having to have individual receivers (although, it appears costs are less than satellite). Despite these issues, it has to be recognised the wireless broadband is more than likely to be the way forward for broadband technology in the future.

SERVICE LEVEL AGREEMENTS

A service level agreement (SLA) is an agreement between a user (consumer) and a supplier (provider) that states the levels of service that can be expected. For example, if a phone line fails, the SLA will state how long it can be out of service before an engineer will begin looking for the problem. For ISPs and phone companies, they also provide guarantees of 'uptime' (the length of time the service is available); these are normally expressed in percentages such as 99.9 per cent. If the ISP doesn't fulfil this uptime guarantee, the user will generally be given compensation in the form of a refund.

NETWORKS

Peer to peer networks

A peer to peer network is a group of user-oriented PCs that basi-cally operate as equals. Each PC is called a *peer*. The peers share resources, such as files and printers, but no specialised servers exist. Each peer is responsible for its own security, and, in a sense, each peer is both a client (because it requests services from the other peers) and a server (because it offers services to the other peers). Small networks – usually under 10 machines – may work well in this configuration.

Each computer on the network can share an Internet connection, files and most peripherals (eg printers, CD-ROM, DVD, Tape backup, etc).

Peer to peer networks are not able to share applications. For example, if you have Microsoft Word installed on one computer, other computers can not run the application. Each computer needs the application program installed on each system wishing to run

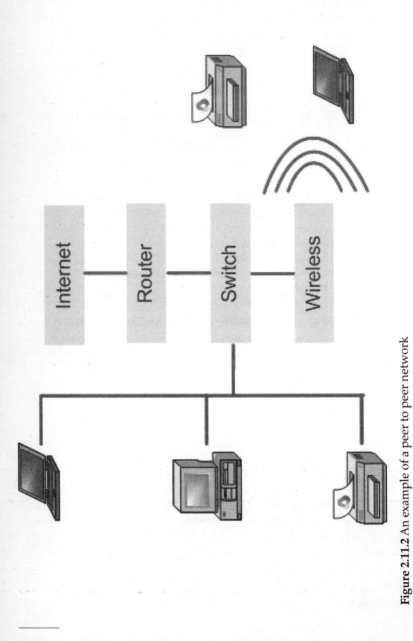

Figure 2.11.2 An example of a peer to peer network

that application. If one user has the 'rights' to a file located on another system and has the application program (such as Microsoft Word) by which the file was created installed on their local machine, they can load, change and save that file on the network computer.

The computers are each connected to an Access Point through a network card and CAT 5 (an international standard for computer wiring) wiring or wireless. The speed at which data moves across the network ranges from 10 Mbps to 1 Gbps (a normal Internet dial-up connection runs at 56 Kbps, which is 178 times slower that the slowest network speeds of 10 Mbps). The required bandwidth is determined by the applications and Internet access.

Shared Internet access can be accomplished by connecting an Internet access device (Analog Modem, ADSL or Cable Modem) to a Router. The Router acts as a gateway to the Internet for devices on the network. The connection speed is dictated by the external Internet device and is not limited by your internal network.

This peer to peer model has all the elements of the client server model, except for the server. If future software requires a server-type model then one can be simply added into the network.

All the software needed to connect computers over this physical network is included in Microsoft's Windows operating systems and other operating systems such as Linux and Apple Mac OS. Additional software is needed for the Internet gateway to insure 'Firewall' protection against hacking and other unwanted outside intrusion.

Server-based networks

In a server-based network environment, resources are located on a central server or group of servers. A server is a computer that is specifically designated to provide services for the other computers on the network. A network client is a computer that accesses the resources available on the server.

The server-based network model is more efficient for all but the smallest networks because hardware resources can be concentrated on relatively few highly-utilised network servers; client computers can be designed with minimal hardware configurations. A basic network client machine, for instance, might have a Pentium processor and 64–128 megabytes of RAM. A typical server might have 2 gigabytes of RAM (or more) and many gigabytes of file storage capacity.

Humans often specialise so that they become very good at one type of task. This approach has benefits for network servers as well. By dedicating a server to providing a specific set of services, it becomes possible to carefully tailor the computer to the requirements for that service, which results in optimal performance, simpler troubleshooting and enhanced scalability. Both Exchange Server (Microsoft's Mail and Groupware product) and SQL Server (Microsoft's Database Server), for instance, are very resource-intensive services, and running these on a server that also provides file and print services can often result in decreased performance. Dedicating a single server to SQL Server, while expensive, greatly improves overall access to both the SQL databases and normal file and print requests.

A file server is a server that stores files on the network for users (see Figure 2.11.3). A user at a client machine can save a file to a hard

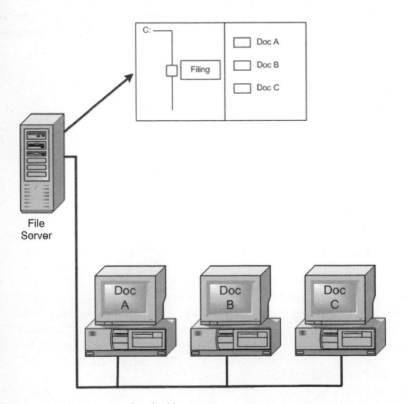

Figure 2.11.3 An example of a file server

drive located on the file server. If users want to access the file later, they can access it from the client machine through a network connection to the file server. Maintaining a central location for file storage on the server makes it easier to provide a backup copy of important files and implement a fault-tolerance system, such as the RAID (Redundant Array of Inexpensive Disks) systems. A file server stores files for users on other network machines.

A print server manages access to network printing resources, thus enabling several client machines to use the same printer (see figure 2.11.4). Because files and printers are so basic and so important to most networks, file and print services are very basic components of most network operating systems, and a single machine commonly acts (or is able to act) as both a file server and a print server. A print server manages access to a shared printer, making it accessible to users at other network machines.

An application server is a server that actually runs an application (or part of an application) for the client (see Figure 2.11.5). Whereas

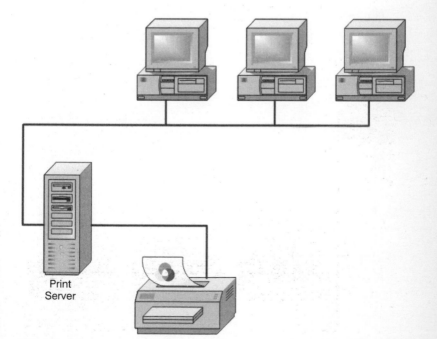

Figure 2.11.4 An example of a print server

a file server simply holds data (in the form of a file) that is then retrieved and processed at the client, an application server performs all or part of the processing on the server end. An application server might search through a large database to provide a requested record for a client. Or an application server might be part of a client/server application, in which both the client and the server perform some of the processing.

An application server runs all or part of an application on behalf of the client and then transmits the result to the client for further processing.

Once a company has decided to install a network they then have what is commonly referred to as a local area network (LAN), ie a group of computers and network communication devices interconnected within a geographically limited area, such as a building or campus. An LAN tends to use only one type of transmission medium; that is cabling.

LANs are characterised by the following:

☐   They transfer data at high speeds.
☐   They exist in a limited geographical area.
☐   Their technology is generally less expensive.

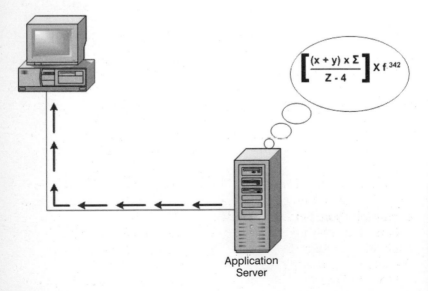

$$\left[\frac{(x + y) \times \Sigma}{Z - 4} \right] X f^{342}$$

Application
Server

Figure 2.11.5 An example of an application server

Larger organisations or some rural organisations that are diversely spread may need to also install a wide area network (WAN), which interconnects LANs. A WAN may be located entirely within a county or country, or it may be interconnected around the world.

WANs are characterised by the following:

☐ They exist in an unlimited geographical area.
☐ They are more susceptible to errors due to the distances data travels.
☐ They interconnect multiple LANs.
☐ They are more sophisticated and complex than LANs.
☐ Their technology is expensive.

WANs can be further classified into two categories: enterprise WANs and global WANs. An enterprise WAN is a WAN that connects the widely separated computer resources of a single organisation. An organisation with computer operations at several distant sites can employ an enterprise WAN to interconnect the sites. An enterprise WAN can use a combination of private and commercial network services but is dedicated to the needs of a particular organisation. A global WAN interconnects networks of several corporations or organisations. An example of a global WAN is the Internet.

WANs are often a natural outgrowth of the need to connect geographically separate LANs into a single network. For instance, a company might have several branch offices in different cities. Every branch would have its own LAN so that branch employees could share files and other resources, and all the branches together would be part of a WAN, a greater network that enables the exchange of files, messages and application services between cities.

Much of the complexity and expense of operating a WAN is caused by the great distances that the signal must travel to reach the interconnected locations. WAN links are often slower and typically depend on a public transmission medium leased from a communications service provider.

One of the reasons broadband is so important for smaller diverse companies or an organisation such as the CLA is that you can use the Internet as a cost efficient way of implementing a WAN.

Details of the CLA campaign for better access to broadband can be found at www.cla.org.uk/campaigns.

GLOSSARY

ADSL Asymmetric Digital Subscriber Line. (**NB:** with ADSL you can also use your phone to make normal voice calls when you are connected to the Internet.)

Analogue Sound waves.

Bandwidth Bandwidth is a generic term for the size (56,000 bits etc) of the connection to the Internet. Broadband is actually 'Broad Bandwidth'.

Cable modem A device that either goes inside your computer or connects to the outside of your computer and allows your computer to connect to the cable infrastructure of your cable provider.

Contention ratios With ADSL, cable and satellite broadband the connection to the Internet is shared by other people from the exchange to your ISP. Typically with a single-user home system it can be shared with up to 50 other people and with a business package the bandwidth will be shared with up to 20 other businesses.

e-mail e-mail (electronic mail) has grown from the original messages that were sent round the forefather of the Internet, the Advanced Research Projects Agency Network (ARPANET) of the US Department of Defence.

IP address This is a unique number that every computer on the Internet has to have to enable them to communicate.

ISP Internet Service Providers are companies that provide access to the Internet (eg BTInternet, Demon, Pipex).

Network card A device that fits inside your computer and connects it to other computers.

RADSL Rate Adaptive Digital Subscriber Line. When connecting, the RADSL modem will adjust the upstream bandwidth to allow for a wider downstream frequency band. As a result the connection will be more tolerant towards errors caused by line noise (interference).

World Wide Web (www)   The Internet is the physical infrastructure and the World Wide Web is one of the applications that run over this infrastructure.

Part Three:

Financial Management and Funding

3.1 Finance and funding

Philip Coysh, Farming & Agricultural Finance Ltd

Developing your new rural enterprise will undoubtedly require a full review of your finances. Even during periods of agricultural recession many farming and agricultural businesses have managed to survive simply on a long-term mortgage secured on the land plus a working capital overdraft. Whilst financial restructuring has always taken place in the industry during and following each period of agricultural recession, the main clearing banks have always seen farms and agricultural property as 'a good bet'. The reasons for this are two-fold: firstly, land values have traditionally remained high even during times of low farming income; and, secondly, bad debts in agriculture have historically been minimal due to a very strong asset base. The rural sector has been categorised as being asset rich and cash poor!

However, lenders will not necessarily view a new diversified business in the same light. There may be less security available, the business will not have a track record and the owners are likely to be inexperienced in this new area of business. It is therefore essential that a detailed business plan be produced, which will cover such areas as overall business strategy, research undertaken and demand for the product, local competition and the effect that the new enterprise will have on your existing business. The business plan will need to include two to three years' cashflows/projections and should be drawn up with the assistance of professional consultants who know the sector well.

Only when you have clearly thought out your strategy and are armed with your professional business plan should you approach lending institutions. It is probably best to talk initially to your own bank; you will have a track record with them and, hopefully, a good existing relationship. But you should also approach other lenders, perhaps a specialist in the sector or a competitor bank. For whilst you may consider your existing bank manager to be the best in the agricultural sector, for instance, he may not be as knowledgeable or understanding of your new venture. Likewise your existing bank may be keen to lend in one sector but, at the moment in time when you approach them, they may feel overexposed in your new sector or their model may, for whatever reason, have a problem with some aspect of your business plan.

But what sort of finance facilities should you be seeking and what are the options and sources of finance available for a new rural development project? Traditionally, the rural sector has been financed by long-term mortgages of up to 40 years combined with working capital overdrafts. Often capital development and purchases of land have been placed on overdrafts and consolidated onto long-term loans at a later date. But it is undoubtedly more sensible to structure your debt according to the anticipated life expectancy of the capital item being purchased.

LONG-TERM MORTGAGES

Long-term mortgages are available from banks and specialist commercial and residential lenders, usually for periods of between 10 and 25 years. The lender will normally insist on a first charge security on property – and perhaps a first or second charge on the proprietor's home for a new start-up business.

In most business sectors there is a clear distinction between the commercial premises from which the business trades and the family home where the proprietor lives. In the agricultural and rural sector this distinction becomes somewhat blurred. A farmhouse, for example, forms part of the farm and may be extremely close to the buildings that are being developed for the new enterprise. Likewise, a successful businessman may own a fine home in the country with farmland and buildings that are used for equestrian purposes. He is clearly not a farmer but may run his own non-rural business from the 'farm' or a rural enterprise from the buildings adjoining his 'country home'. In these circumstances it becomes extremely difficult to segment such properties into 'business' or 'residential' categories.

It is therefore beneficial to talk to various lenders to see whether a residential or commercial mortgage is the best 'fit'. Residential mortgages tend to be cheaper and more flexible than commercial mortgages although it may be more difficult to justify allocating the loan interest as a business expense. High street residential lenders will also wish to split off the house from the commercial aspects of the property and this could result in increased legal fees. They also will normally wish to see evidence of historic income and may not be so willing to lend against a business plan. However, if there is sufficient equity in your own domestic property to fund the new enterprise a residential mortgage may be your cheapest option.

Commercial mortgages are available from most high street banks – although some may wish to limit the loan period to a maximum of 20 years – and specialist commercial mortgage lenders, some of who will be operating exclusively in the agricultural or rural markets.

The main clearing banks will undoubtedly wish for you to transfer all your banking to them, rather than simply operating a transactional mortgage facility. For new limited company start-ups they are likely to also require directors' guarantees, supported by first or second mortgages on the family homes. These guarantees are designed to ensure that the founders of the company have a tangible incentive to ensure the success of the business.

On the plus side, the banks will be able to offer you all your borrowing requirements – both long term and short term – as well as other services too. Most banks will provide you with a business manager with whom you can develop an ongoing relationship. Ideally you should find out how long they have been in the role and how long they are likely to remain there.

Whilst it is often convenient to have one financial source who can provide all your financial needs, it is not always the best option. For one thing it limits your options if there is a change of credit policy on the bank's part. It also means that you do not necessarily always obtain the most competitive rates and terms. Increasingly, businesses in the rural sector are allocating their financial facilities across a number of different lenders; this enables them to obtain competitive quotes as well as ensuring that not all their eggs are in one basket.

Agriculture has traditionally been served by a small number of specialist long-term lenders, mostly owned by major financial institutions but operating under specific sector brandings; some of these have branched out to provide facilities for diversified and non-farm rural enterprises whilst others have stuck primarily to farming. It is worth seeking out these lenders as they do offer competitive 'stand alone' long-term facilities and can be very flexible. One of their advantages is that they understand the rural economy; another is that, after an initial setting-up fee, they do not charge ongoing fees or seek annual reviews. A third advantage is that they will often structure repayments on a seasonal basis especially if the income stream for the business is seasonal. This not only applies to farming but also to such enterprises as holiday lets or tourist activities where the main income is likely to be in the summer months.

Interest rate margins for long-term loans to agriculture have traditionally been much lower than in other business sectors, largely due to the low risk of loss and the relatively high and stable value of farmland. Margins of between 1 per cent and 2 per cent over base rate have been standard, with rates sometimes falling below 1 per cent for quality businesses. However, farmers who are diversifying into other enterprises should not expect rates as fine as they have been used to for commercial farming. Risks will be higher, the business will be unproven and the business premises may not be as attractive as farmland to potential purchasers. Mark Twain famously said of land, 'They ain't making it anymore!' For this reason, if no other, farmland is always likely to be attractive to buyers at the right price whereas a purchaser for the converted farm building may be more difficult to find. This means that lenders will be looking for an interest rate premium for mortgages where the security is other than bare land. For this reason you are likely to be able to negotiate a finer interest rate margin if the main security offered is a mixture of land and residential property, rather than, for example, a former barn being converted into office accommodation.

Usually both variable and fixed rates are available, although some lenders are reluctant to lend on a long-term fixed-rate basis and will offer variable-rate lending as a matter of course. The mortgage can usually be fixed for any period from 1 to 25 years, with appropriate breaks if required when a decision can be made to either stick with the new fixed rate or transfer to a variable rate.

It is also important to structure the term of the mortgage to the life of the property. It is not appropriate, for example, to fund a poultry shed over 25 years when it's useful life may only be 15 years. As a rule of thumb the loan period should be no longer than the expected useful life of the property before it needs refurbishing.

_____

Some people simply take the longest loan term available – usually 25 years – because this reduces monthly payments and eases cash flow but they may fail to remember that the longer the term the more interest is paid to the lender as the balance of the mortgage remains higher for longer. The same, of course, applies to interest-only loans. Most commercial lenders will agree to a one or two year capital repayment holiday whilst the new enterprise is being established; some may even agree to roll the interest up for 12 months. But, whilst interest-only mortgages have become commonplace in the residential mortgage market – some would argue this is a worrying trend as it simply stokes up trouble for the future – it is certainly unwise to take out a long-term interest-only mortgage for a commercial venture. The whole point of a long-term mortgage is to discipline oneself to structure regular repayments over a longer period in order to clear the loan within the chosen time frame.

PRIVATE LOANS

Medium- to long-term private loans are commonplace in the rural sector, especially with parents assisting children to continue working in the countryside and maintain the family farm. Private funding, however, has its downsides as well as benefits and all parties should be aware of the risks.

For the recipient a private loan is usually a cheap and easy way of raising capital but many family frictions have occurred because of misunderstandings about the terms of the loan, often because no documentation has ever been drawn up.

The best plan is to get a solicitor or accountant to draw up an agreement which should cover the terms of the loan – the rate of interest, repayment terms and the circumstances in which it can be withdrawn. It is also beneficial to all parties to make it clear in the document whether the lender is to have any control in the running or management of the business or any entitlement to share in the profits.

A private loan may well be a real boon for someone starting a new business enterprise but the fact that family funds are available should not detract from the hard work of preparing a professional business plan and undertaking the necessary market research and competitor analysis that is required to help secure the success of the new venture.

BANK LOANS

A variable-rate Flexible Business Loan from the local bank is the favourite means of business funding in both Germany and Spain; 70 per cent of German businesses are funded through variable-rate business loans and in Spain it's as high as 80 per cent. However, in Britain it is fixed-rate Business Development Loans that have proved popular.

Both variable- and fixed-rate bank loans tend to be for medium-term requirements, usually between 5 and 20 years, and can be for a wide range of business requirements, such as the purchase of machinery, property or vehicles. Again the term of the loan will reflect the value and expected life of the asset. Repayments will usually be made monthly or quarterly on a capital and interest repayment basis, although capital repayment holidays of up to two years may be available.

These loans may be offered on a secured or unsecured basis depending upon the strength of the proposition. However, rates for unsecured lending will be significantly higher than secured loans – typically 1.5 per cent to 2 per cent higher – but even secured Business Loans will be tend to be higher than long-term secured commercial mortgages. Again, a bank will require you to maintain a current account if you take up a business loan with them.

ASSET-BASED FINANCE

Leasing and Lease Purchase schemes are a popular way of financing machinery and vehicles. The major feature of asset finance is that the finance company looks to the value of the asset as security rather than to the strength of the balance sheet of the business. This means that it is extremely useful for new start-ups and also means that any available deed security is used to fund long-term capital requirements rather than machinery and vehicles.

Lease Purchase is a flexible hire purchase scheme that enables you to own the asset at the end of the repayment term. Usually you would need to put down a deposit of approximately 20 per cent of the cost price and then repay the capital and interest over a term of between two and seven years, depending upon the life of the asset. At the end of the term the asset becomes your property.

Finance Leasing is similar to Lease Purchase except that it is a rental scheme rather than a purchasing scheme and therefore enables you to claim higher tax allowances. It is particularly useful where there is no requirement to own the asset at the end of the agreement, for example, a car or computer that may well be out of date in a few years time. Depending on your tax and VAT position, certain leasing structures may be more advantageous than bank loans but you will need to consult your accountant for advice on this.

All the major banks have their own in-house leasing and HP companies but there are also specialists working in the agricultural and rural sectors who may be able to fund specialist equipment that a standard leasing company would not be attracted to.

FACTORING

For many businesses unpaid invoices are one of the largest assets. Factoring used to be the preserve of the struggling business but today it is another finance option, particularly useful for smaller companies undergoing fairly rapid growth, typically with a turnover of between £50,000 and £300,000 per year.

Factoring immediately releases a percentage of outstanding invoices (usually around 80 per cent) and frees you up from the job of chasing debt so you can concentrate on managing the rest of the business. The funding is more flexible than bank debt and is available more quickly than an overdraft facility as factoring companies will look forward to the strength of the balance sheet, rather than back to past trading performance.

Many start-up businesses are restricted in their growth by the lack of working capital and factoring can often be the solution, although it is important to guard against over-trading or growing too rapidly. Factoring is usually more expensive than bank borrowing, but the advantages of providing cover against bad debts and reducing administration may outweigh this extra cost.

BANK OVERDRAFT

During the early 1990s nearly 60 per cent of lending to small businesses in the United Kingdom took the form of an overdraft facility. Since that time banks have sought to reduce dependence on overdrafts and this percentage has fallen fast.

In the agricultural sector overdrafts have historically been used to fund everything from a whole farm purchase to a new combine. Fortunately, the use of the overdraft as the sole means of borrowing money is a thing of the past but small business owners in the rural economy still naturally veer towards the overdraft when considering new investment for their business.

Sticking with an overdraft through thick and thin is a bit like using only the first gear in a car – great for going up steep hills but not such a good idea once you hit the motorway. But, having said that, the overdraft remains a useful tool especially for new start-ups and for getting to grips with cash flow problems.

An overdraft is beautifully elastic – as small or as big as you want – and you only pay for what you use. The problems start when you get into the habit of using your overdraft to make large capital purchases or to fund growth. An overdraft facility should simply fund your normal trading fluctuations and no more. Of course, to know what level of overdraft you actually need requires careful financial planning and the use of cash flows to see where your peaks and troughs are.

Remember that the bank will constantly monitor the level of the overdraft and will expect it to fluctuate, including the account going into credit periodically. If this does not happen and a 'hard core' of borrowing is identified, then the bank will wish to convert part of the overdraft into a short-term loan with a structured repayment programme. One important aspect for you to remember is that overdraft facilities are usually granted 'on demand' which means that the bank can demand instant repayment at any time, although some banks now have agreed to a 12 month guaranteed overdraft facility which does give some security for the borrower.

Interest rates for overdrafts will vary depending upon the perceived strength of the business and whether the facility is secured or unsecured. Of course, all overdrafts are granted on a variable-rate basis. Again, as with other facilities, rates as low as 1 per cent over base rate for secured overdrafts, which have historically been available to good agricultural businesses, will not be available to businesses diversifying away from commercial farming. You should expect your bank to quote margins of between 1.5 per cent and 3 per cent for fully-secured overdrafts and over 4 per cent for a start-up company with no track record.

GOVERNMENT GRANTS

Finally, we must look at the cheapest of all forms of funding – cheapest but certainly not the easiest or simplest. There are a large number of government grants available to rural businesses. However, the schemes are becoming more complex as funding now comes from a variety of different sources and more government agencies are involved. Further, whereas subsidy payments to farmers used to be given as of right, modern-day grants are usually project-based, collaborative and competitive – and there are different schemes for different parts of the country.

If you are about to embark on a new rural diversification, it is imperative that you take professional advice as to whether any grants can be applied for. You will need to undertake research, obtain planning consent, provide quotations, consider both environmental and health and safety aspects, be prepared for a mass of paperwork (including a business plan) and compete with other applicants – and there will no guarantee of success.

3.2 Equity alternatives

Jonathan Reuvid

INTRODUCTION

The various forms of debt finance available to individuals seeking funds to start up rural businesses, either as sole traders, in partnership or through a limited company were identified and discussed in Chapter 3.1. The alternative to debt finance is equity funding; selling a proportion of the share capital in the company established to run the business to outside investors. By definition, equity finance is only applicable to businesses that are incorporated. However, a sole trader or partnership can always reform the business into a limited company in order to attract investors, although this will necessarily affect the taxation of the business and the personal taxation status of the owners.

Debt and equity finance are not mutually exclusive alternatives and, for every company, a number of funding solutions are possible involving different combinations of debt and equity. At the upper end of the scale, companies that are considering public flotation are likely to adopt a funding package in which equity is the main element. For readers of this book public flotation is unlikely to be more than a remote future possibility and, in the present depressed state of equity markets, as unlikely as winning the National Lottery. This chapter focuses, therefore, on the forms of equity finance that are realistic for the owners of rural businesses and ignores or makes passing reference only to those that are not.

PRIVATE PLACING

A company can raise finance from outside investors without any commitment to an ultimate independent public offering (IPO). Generally, professional investors and investment funds will have little interest in buying shares in a company unless there is a clear exit route, for example, the possibility of selling the company in the future to another company in the same trade or another group of investors. One exception to this rule is biotech and other high technology businesses, which can raise money from investors knowledgeable in their sector. They may be confident that if the technology proves successful, the rewards will be substantial whichever exit route is chosen. Of the case histories included in Part Four of this book only the energy renewal business described in Chapter 4.5 would qualify.

For rural businesses generally, the most likely private investors are relatives, friends and wealthy individuals living locally, who have an interest in supporting the original owners personally or a business of which they approve 'on the doorstep' where they can hopefully enjoy contributing to the creation of a flourishing enterprise.

Even if the new investors are a small group of family or friends, it is important that they are treated as investors at arm's length and that some form of investment memorandum is prepared which gives full details of the company and an accurate description of the business, its history and the directors' aims and objectives for its future development. If the business is established, audited accounts should be included in appendix. If the business is a start-up, that will not be possible. No formal profit forecast is necessary in either case, but an outline business plan for a new business should be included.

It is important that investors should have clear expectations; if you do not intend to pay dividends, you should say so. All too often private investors are persuaded, or persuade themselves, to buy shares in a company of which the directors are known to them with expectations that are totally unrealistic. Inevitably, disillusionment follows and in the consequent bickering family feuds are born and friendships falter.

In the case of one or two private investors taking a substantial stake in the company, perhaps as much as 25 per cent or more, a more hard-headed approach is usually taken by the investor. Often a seat on the board of the company is demanded and it is normal for the original and new shareholders to enter into a shareholders' agreement that defines how the affairs of the company shall be conducted. For example, the shareholders' agreement may specify that decisions to increase the borrowings of the company, to issue more shares or to purchase or sell significant assets above a certain value may only be taken with the unanimous consent of the shareholders. Such agreements supplement the provisions of the company's Articles of Association, which may also be strengthened, typically in respect of the pre-emptive rights of shareholders to purchase each other's shares in the event of sale.

The law provides that a small group of investors (in simple terms less than 50 persons) can invest on the basis of a private placing memorandum. This is classified as an investment advertisement and, as such, must be approved by a person authorised under the Financial Service and Markets Act 2000. The person approving the document must ensure that the document is correct in all material respects and does not mislead the reader in any way whatever. For this purpose, the directors of the company inviting investment should appoint an authorised Financial Services Intermediary – most likely a local chartered accountant or solicitor.

At the next level of investment, an offer to the public (which, in simple terms, is to more than 50 persons) must be made in the form of a prospectus. The prospectus must conform to The Public Offer of Securities Regulations 1995 ('the POS Regs'), a statutory instrument that defines an offer of securities to the public and specifies the form and content of the document which must be published when it has been decided to make such an offer. The POS Regs contains most of the information found in an AiM admission document or listing particulars.

PRIVATE EQUITY AND VENTURE CAPITAL

The venture capital industry in the United Kingdom thrived until the 2002 investment slump. According to the British Venture Capital Association ('BVCA'), the UK venture capital, or private equity industry, was the largest in Europe, accounting for 38 per cent of private equity investment in Europe in 2000 and second in size only to that of the United States. The UK private equity industry had invested over £43 billion (£35 billion in the United Kingdom) in close to 20,500 companies since 1983. Of this, 50 per cent is used for expansion or development, the rest for management buy-outs and other transactions.

Colin Aaronson of Grant Thornton points out in *Going Public* (Kogan Page, 2002), that venture capital (VC) is something of a misnomer.

'Although around one hundred firms are listed by the BVCA as being interested in funding early stage businesses, most VC money is used to provide development capital of MBO finance.

VCs will provide a mixture of debt and equity, calculated to earn them the desired rate of return, which will usually fall between 30 per cent and 40 per cent per annum on an investment. This level of return can only be achieved through growth, and is required to compensate the VC firm for the high degree of risk and the high level of resources it must commit to each investment. The greatest risk in any investment is that the VC will not be able to find a suitable exit route.'

For this reason, only a limited number of rural businesses are likely to attract VC funds. Of the businesses profiled in Part Four, probably only the Barn Brasserie (Chapter 4.4), A Day in the Country (Chapter 4.6) and the York Auction Centre (4.7) would be eligible, and then only in relation to aggressive development plans. Smaller rural businesses should look to the alternative source of private equity, described as business angels, in the next section of this chapter.

Companies looking for private equity can contact the BVCA to identify potential investors. All VC firms have stated sets of investment criteria, based principally on industry sector, geographical location and the stage of a company's development. Colin Aaronson of Grant Thornton identifies as an alternative route the appointment of a financial adviser, possibly your local firm of accountants, to introduce a suitable VC firm. The adviser will know which VC firms are investing in a particular sector at any one time, and which are likely to be interested in funding your company. 'Using an adviser can save time, and should avoid the company unnecessarily hawking its business around the market. Indeed there are many VC firms who either prefer or expect to deal with an intermediary.'

On first contact, the VC firm will require a business plan including thorough information on the company and detailed financial forecasts. The VC will review the business plan and meet with management on several occasions before it decides to proceed with verification (the 'due diligence' process) as a pre-condition to investment in a business. Rather depressingly, Colin Aaronson quotes estimates that no more than 2 per cent of business plans gain funding.

After a VC decides, in principle, to make an investment in a business there is normally an interval of three to four months before funds are received by the company. During this period, extensive due diligence is undertaken (at the expense of the company), involving accountants reporting on the operations of the business and on the integrity of the financial forecasts, industry experts reporting on the commercial operations of the business and on the assumptions underlying the financial forecasts, and lawyers reviewing contracts, questions of title to tangible assets and intellectual property and various other legal matters.

Most VCs will insist on a non-executive being appointed to the board and some become more involved in the management issues of the companies in which they have invested. There is a cost to this involvement, but many companies welcome the experience and advice that these non-executive directors bring to the company.

BUSINESS ANGELS

Business angels are successful and experienced businesspeople who want to become involved with a young growing business and have funds to invest. Some of the potential local investors described earlier in this chapter for private placings may be classified as business angels. However, business angels generally become actively involved in the companies they invest in; so being able to work with one is crucial to the success of the relationship, and you need to be sure that you are comfortable with such an investor before making a commitment. Research indicates that angels place greater emphasis on location rather than industry sector, with most looking to invest in businesses located within an hour's drive from home.

Because of the confidential nature of the investment, it is only possible to approximate the size of the business angel market. Research suggests that there are approximately 20,000 business angels in the United Kingdom, investing around £500 million a year in 3,500 businesses in amounts from £25,000 to £1 million, and occasionally more. Individually, angels rarely commit more than £50,000 to a single investment; amounts greater than that are usually provided by syndicates of angels.

Being a business angel is a high-risk, high-reward activity. It is estimated that one third of all investee companies fail; at the other end of the spectrum, around 20 per cent generate returns of greater than 50 per cent per annum for their angel investors.

The most common outcome for business angel investments, at around 40 per cent, is some form of insolvency. However, about half of all investments are sold either to other shareholders, management, a third party or to another business through a trade sale, and around 10 per cent through some form of flotation.

Business angels will require much the same information during negotiations as VCs but are more likely to carry out parts of the due diligence themselves, particularly the reviews of commercial operations and the underlying business plan assumptions.

EQUITY vs. DEBT FINANCE

There is a natural inclination on the part of most business owners to avoid introducing outside shareholders. On the one hand, the idea of having to satisfy shareholders' expectations and answer to them at meetings seems likely to be an irritation; on the other hand sharing the capital value of a growing business with investors who are not family may be deeply distasteful.

For rural businesses, asset backed by substantial farmland and buildings, the ability to raise long-term finance through secured loans may be greater than for other small businesses, so that there is no compulsion to look for equity funding. The argument for debt finance is strengthened further by the current low rates of interest. Nevertheless, business owners should be mindful of the impact of increasing interest rates on cash flow and profits wherever the interest payable on loans is related to base rate.

There is a general expectation that interest rates will start to rise during the second half of 2003 and through 2004, and for those starting-up or expanding businesses now it may be wise to be prudent about their levels of borrowing. The risk that accompanies heavy debt, even when the asset cover is strong, is often forgotten, and there is sufficient risk for private companies now in the current business environment without further hostages to fortune. If additional debt also entails the giving of personal guarantees, the risk is greatly heightened.

In this climate, provided that commitments to incoming investors to provide an exit from the business within a specified time can be avoided – particularly where the location of the business premises and your living accommodation are inseparable – equity investment, if on offer, should not be turned down lightly.

3.3 Buying and selling the business

Jonathan Reuvid

BUYING vs. SELLING

This chapter is intended primarily for readers who are considering buying into country living by purchasing an established business that someone else has developed. It is also relevant for those at the other end of the investment continuum who have built up a rural business, probably over a period of many years, and have reached a point or time in life when they are contemplating a sale.

At first sight, it would be tempting to think that entrance is the converse of exit and that the criteria which an astute, well-advised purchaser will apply to buying a business will be matched by a seller who recognises prospective purchasers' requirements and structures his or her offering accordingly. However, there is one essential difference between buyer and seller which overrides all other factors and imposes its own logic on their mindsets and on the pattern of most negotiations: whereas the prospective purchaser can walk away from the transaction up to the point that contracts are signed, the prospective seller can't abdicate from the business he is trying to sell.

The purchaser can abort in the negotiations stage at any time if he decides that he doesn't like the terms of purchase, if he changes his mind about the attractiveness of the business or if he loses confidence in his post-completion business plan. No doubt, there are many alternative business propositions that he can evaluate – plenty more 'fish in the sea' for the frustrated suitor. The vendor's situation is quite different: he too can abort the transaction up to the moment of signature, but he can't walk away from the business he is trying to sell. He can look for another purchaser but that may not be too easy in a buyer's market when investment opportunities are plentiful but private investors are thin on the ground. To adopt a racing analogy, the seller can change riders but he can't change horses. The purchaser, in the role of the rider, can always look for another mount.

For this reason alone, the vendor of a business needs to prepare for sale carefully by presenting the business clearly and intelligibly in an attractive light, but without misrepresentation. The owner will be well advised to take professional advice before putting their business on the market. The role of advisers is discussed in some detail towards the end of the chapter.

Certainly, the vendor needs to understand in advance the information that the prospective purchaser will demand, the concerns to which he is likely to attach the most importance and, not least, the purchaser's mindset. In order to examine these issues and how to manage them, this chapter addresses the elements of buying and selling a business, first from the standpoint of a well-prepared and well-advised purchaser; and then from the standpoint of a vendor, selling a business for the first time.

THE PURCHASER'S POSITION

Before investigating any specific opportunity to purchase, the prospective investor is advised to define his business objectives and to establish the ground rules that he will follow in review and negotiation. This will save considerable time and self-questioning later and help to avoid the temptation of adapting principles to circumstances in the face of an attractive but over-priced or otherwise unsuitable opportunity. The following are some of the fundamentals on which a prospective purchaser should take a firm up front view.

Location

Be absolutely clear which alternative locations for the business are acceptable. To be certain, you may need to research quite widely. For example, if you are looking for a tourist-based business in a coastal area, you may rule out Scotland, and the north-east and south-east of England before you start, but that still leaves large areas of Wales, East Anglia, the south coast and all of the south-west. As your research proceeds you will be able to zero-in on one or two more closely-defined locations, such as 'within twenty miles of Truro'. The scope of your research will encompass the environment, living conditions, a preliminary survey of the local market for the kinds of business that you have in mind and going market values.

Role of the investor

The primary differentiator in your approach as a purchaser will be whether you want to purchase a rural business solely as an investor, or whether you and your family intend to play an active part in running the business. In the first instance, your priorities will be the estimated return on investment (ROI) and likely appreciation in capital value. Since the business you buy will require management, you will also be taking a view on the availability of suitable tenants or managers. A poor tenant or, worse still, an incompetent manager, will damage your investment and may ruin your ROI.

The second instance demands total confidence that you and your family really want to run a business of the kind you have chosen, and whether you have the capability to do so. For example, before setting out to acquire a village shop on the north coast of Cornwall, are you sure that you can accept the long hours and monotonous work involved in high season, let alone all the year round? If you have that confidence, then the ROI which you demand from such a business may be tempered by the benefits 'in kind' which you can expect from the business and the ability to draw earned income for yourself and family members who work in the shop.

Price

Earnings-based valuations

There are a number of alternative formulae in common usage for pricing a private business, but invariably they are earnings-based or asset-based. Earnings-based formulae are usually a simple multiple of pre- or post-tax net profits based on recent years' financial results, current year performance or both. Remembering that profit multiples are the reciprocal of investment returns, it follows that a purchase price representing, say, four times pre-tax profits will deliver a return on the purchaser's total investment of 25 per cent before the tax payable on the business's profits and the investor's own income tax.

However, there are two issues that can be confusing and about which purchasers should be especially wary: the valuation of future earnings; and credit for owners' remuneration in kind.

Either issue or both may be put forward by the vendor of a business or his advisers as a means of raising the price. In the case of a village shop, for example, where planning consent has just been granted for the construction of 200 new holiday homes (a 10 per cent increase on the total number of homes within the shop's catchment area) the vendor might argue that sales are likely to increase accordingly and that an allowance should be made in the purchase price for the future increase in profits. The purchaser's response should be that the projection is not relevant to the present value of the business. He might also suggest that the additional population may justify a new regular bus service to the local town where residents will be able to shop at a nationally branded supermarket in place of the village shop. Realistically, it may be reasonable to give some credit in the purchase price for an improvement which the vendor has generated himself but which has not yet come into effect, such as an off-licence to sell beer, wines and spirits, where there the benefit to the business is assured. On the other hand, the purchaser should never factor into his valuation the benefits of any improvements that he will make post-acquisition.

The second issue of 'benefits in kind' that the owner has received from the business is more insidious. Salary paid to family members is readily identifiable and it is not too difficult to decide whether such payments were a substitute for profit distribution or whether they represent genuine remuneration for services rendered, which would have to be hired externally at an equivalent cost if not provided by members of the owner's family. However, other expenses against the business that were wholly of benefit to the owner and his family and not essential to the operation of the business, such as motoring expenses, building repairs and decoration or kitchen equipment may be harder to substantiate and may be ignored by the purchaser in pricing the business. It may be argued that the reward is sufficient if the vendor has received such benefits tax-free during his ownership of the business, and that he has no logical entitlement to their value being written back to arrive at an estimate of maintainable future profits.

Asset-based valuations

Asset-based valuations relate to the net assets of the business, evidenced preferably by its audited balance sheet. They are applied in preference to earnings-based valuations where losses have been incurred, the profit stream has been erratic, or where the business is highly personalised and its future is dependent on the owner-manager's personal relationships with providers of work. If the business is incorporated, the provision of a current balance sheet should present no problem, although small companies are not compelled to file balance sheets with their annual report and accounts. The company's accountants can be tasked to prepare a balance sheet which, if unaudited, can be warranted by the directors. In valuing the business on the basis of its asset value, the purchaser and his advisers will look at the net shareholders' funds equivalent to tangible assets net of any balance sheet goodwill, with the addition of any surplus in market value of the fixed assets over their balance sheet value.

If the business is not incorporated but is run as a sole trader business or partnership and there is no balance sheet, a statement of the business's net tangible assets should be constructed from the accounting records.

There used to be a convention among some advisers that valuation could be based on net tangible assets plus a provision for goodwill calculated as a multiple of several years' post tax profits. This approach is now generally regarded as too generous to the vendor, except where there are assets included in the sale which are separate from and unused by the business. For example, in the case of the sale of a farm and its business consisting of the farmhouse plus redundant agricultural businesses converted into a restaurant, it would be valid to value the whole as the sum of the farmhouse at residential market value plus the restaurant on the basis of a multiple of earnings.

Cash flow considerations

Remember that the cash that you have to provide as owner of the business for its operation may be significantly more than the balance sheet indicates. As a prospective purchaser, you should examine closely the cash flow of the business, particularly in cases where the level of business is highly seasonal. The balance sheet numbers may be deceptive depending on whether the accounting year-end is in or out of high season. The cash demands of the business should be factored into the total investment that you are prepared to make.

INVESTIGATION AND NEGOTIATION

Market research

The role of market research in developing the parameters for a post-acquisition business plan is already referred to in Chapter 3.2

and ways and means of how that may be carried out are discussed in Chapter 2.10. In valuing a business this task cannot be avoided and to rely on any projections submitted by the vendor or his advisers would be unwise.

Financial due diligence

As purchaser you may wish to use your own accountants to examine the accounts of the business and to ensure that the information with which you have been provided is accurate. If there are no audited accounts, a more detailed examination of actual accounting records will be necessary. Your accountant will pay particular attention to stock valuation methods, the adequacy of provisions for bad and doubtful debts, depreciation of assets and for periodic expenses such as rent and utilities in forward projections. The terms of bank borrowings will be examined and the tax affairs of the business will come under scrutiny. If you are intending to purchase a company you will need to be sure that there are no unprovided liabilities to corporation tax and that PAYE and national insurance payments in respect of past and present employees are up to date, as are all statutory filings. Finally, your accountant will form a view as to whether the business you are buying is adequately funded.

Legal due diligence

At some stage you will need to engage a solicitor to prepare the purchase contract but, before that, there is work to be done in examining all material contracts relating to the business which you are evaluating. If you are purchasing the shares of a company, the contracts to which it is a party will normally remain in force when the shares are transferred. However, as in the case of a sole trader or partnership business, there may be some contracts in the name of the owner(s) that will need to be assigned to the new owner. A lease of premises, for example, may be in the name of an individual rather than the company and assignment to the new owner is likely to require the consent of the landlord. In any case, you will want your lawyer to check the terms of all leases and to verify that there is a clean title to any freehold property offered. Equally, equipment leases and hire purchase or lease purchase agreements should be scrutinised.

External consents of one sort or another may also be required in relation to particular types of business such as licensed premises, as described in Chapter 2.2. Even contracts with some customers or suppliers where performance has been guaranteed by the owner of the business may require consent to ensure continuity.

Your solicitor should also check that all planning consents are in order and that the current business, with any additions or variations which you intend, does not infringe any by-laws, or any health and safety and environmental law requirements. You should also check that adequate insurance cover is in place to meet statutory requirements and third party liabilities as well as the protection and replacement of assets.

Warranties and indemnities

It is normal for the purchaser to seek protection from the vendors of a business in the form of warranties against the integrity of information supplied, including statements of account, asset and liability values, pensions and other employee matters, and environmental and planning issues. The time limit for making a warranty claim is generally two to three years. Protection against future unprovided tax liabilities may be covered by a separate tax deed which may run for up to six or seven years. Usually, a limit will be set to the amount of any one or the total of all warranty claims often expressed as a percentage of the purchase consideration. Indemnities are similar and refer to undertakings made by the vendors to reimburse the purchaser for the cost of specific contingencies that may arise after the transaction.

Vendors can provide relief for themselves against warranty and indemnity claims by declaring specific circumstances or events that may affect the business adversely, known as 'disclosures', against which they will not warrant or indemnify. From the purchaser's point of view the demand for protection serves the purpose of flushing any skeletons out of the cupboard in the form of disclosures which can be taken into account when agreeing the final purchase price.

Restrictive covenants

Assuming that the vendors are leaving the business upon completion, the purchaser needs to be protected against the vendor setting up in competition and enticing existing employees and customers or clients away. Therefore, it is normal practice to include a restrictive covenant in the purchase agreement. Be aware in drafting such covenants that they may not be legally enforceable if too restrictive in terms of geographical area or duration.

THE SELLER'S STANCE

Taking on board the likely requirements of a well-briefed purchaser, it is clear that the seller of a business should be equally prepared and there are a number of key issues to be addressed well in advance of offering the business for sale.

Accounts and accounting records

If your business is operated through a limited liability company, ensure that full audited accounts for the most recent financial year are available and monthly trading accounts since the year-end. The same applies if you operate as a partnership and, in this case, be sure that a balance sheet is included.

If you operate as a sole trader, it is important to distinguish clearly between the business and your personal finances. Although there may be disadvantages to you in terms of personal taxation, you should consider, for at least 12 months and preferably several years before the intended sale, maintaining separate bank accounts and completely separate accounting records. As already discussed, no prudent purchaser will allow you credit for those items of expenditure not strictly necessary for the progress of the business which have been debited against pre-tax income. Expenditure that is partly attributable to the business and partly for the benefit of the owners should be allocated reasonably. Again, regular balance sheets should be drawn up in which all the assets and liabilities of the business are correctly entered.

Taxation

Be sure that past year's taxation has been fully assessed and that current tax liabilities of the business are correctly declared.

Property

If the business owns freehold or long leasehold property to be included in the sale which is included in the balance sheet at less than current market value, consider having a formal professional valuation made which can be included in the documents made available to purchasers. If the business is to occupy premises of which you will be the freeholder or superior tenant after sale, instruct your solicitor to draft a lease on terms that are acceptable to you. The lease does not have to be signed until completion of the sale.

Contracts

Make sure that all material contracts to which the business is a party or from which the business benefits remain in force after transfer of the business or are assignable to a new owner.

Warranties and indemnities

Before entering into negotiations decide the limit of warranties and indemnities that you are prepared to provide and list the disclosures that you intend to make. There is merit in declaring disclosures early on in negotiations so that they do not become a bargaining chip in later discussions about price.

Pricing the business

Take advice on what is a fair valuation for the business and measure that against the 'drop dead' price at which you are prepared to sell and walk away. Then develop an asking price which can be supported by the evidence and which is stiff but not unrealistically exorbitant. Unless there is heavy competition to buy your business or you are an exceptionally talented negotiator, the probability is that you will not achieve the asking price. Therefore, you should set a price that is at least 15 per cent above the 'drop dead' price, after allowing for the professional fees you will have to pay to your advisers.

Memorandum of particulars

In preparation for the selling process you and your advisers should prepare a memorandum for prospective purchasers, rather like an estate agent's particulars of sale, which provides a short history of the business and its management, any relevant local information and circumstances of interest to buyers and identifies the supporting documentation, such as audited accounts and property valuation which will be made available to interested parties. Do not include an asking price in the memorandum. Your views on asking price may change and you should wait until prospective purchasers ask you.

Confidentiality letter

You will not want the details of your private business affairs circulated widely and discussed by all and sundry. Therefore, you are recommended to have your solicitor draft a standard form of confidentiality letter, to be signed by any interested party who wishes to be recognised as a prospective purchaser and who wants to examine the details of the business beyond the original memorandum. The letter will commit signatories to treating all information received in confidence and to returning documents at the termination of negotiations. Confidentiality letters help to sort the wheat from the chaff by identifying those with serious intent.

USING PROFESSIONAL ADVISERS

Both purchaser and vendor will need to use solicitors at the contract stage in the sale of a business. In this chapter we have also identified tasks which are best carried our by lawyers in the preparatory phases. The vendor will probably be taking advice from accountants in the preparation of accounting information about the business and very possibly in setting pricing expectations. A purchaser may decide to rely on the audited and warranted financial information provided by the vendor without employing his own accountants; alternatively, he may require more detailed investigation under the heading of financial due diligence.

In choosing these advisers, there are two main considerations: quality and cost. In some respects, buying or selling a smaller business involves a more exacting advisory role. There will be a strong subjective element in the whole negotiation process and in arriving at a final decision. It is of the utmost importance, whether you wear the purchaser's or vendor's hat, that you have a high level of confidence in your advisers' judgements. If you don't feel comfortable with the solicitor or accountant you first approach, look for an alternative adviser and go on looking until you are satisfied.

The cost of professional advice only becomes a contentious issue if you shirk addressing it up front. Lawyers and accountants should be asked to quote like any other service provider. This involves a discussion to specify the work that may be carried out on your behalf and to price each element. In this way you will know the fees to which you are committed throughout the progress of the preliminaries and the later stages of the transaction. This approach is greatly preferable to agreeing an hour or day rate without a definition of time to be spent, which will leave you vulnerable to a 'taxi fare' system of charging.

There is a third category of professional adviser to be considered: the business broker specialising in the sale and purchase of small- and medium-sized businesses. The advantages to the vendor of employing a business broker are threefold. First, the broker acts as a medium of exchange. Through his network of business contacts and associates he will have an awareness of prospective purchasers for your kind of business whom he can approach in confidence. Second, if he is a successful broker he will have knowledge of the current marketplace in terms of prices realised and will be able to advise you on asking price and pricing expectations. His knowledge of purchasers' requirements and attitudes will also be useful in drafting the memorandum of particulars. Third, the business broker will act as your intermediary, negotiating on your behalf, and acting as a buffer between purchaser and vendor. At the very least, this will help to take the pressure off you to react instantly to points and proposals that the purchaser may throw at you. The advantages to a purchaser of using a business broker are less obvious, other than the value of being on business broker mailing lists.

As with accountants and lawyers, the need for trust and confidence is paramount in selecting a business broker. Before choosing, you should check that the firm is properly registered as a financial intermediary and ask for references from previous clients. It is not essential that you like your business adviser, but affinity is helpful as you go through the sale process together.

The cost of the consultant's services will be related to the sale price achieved and is normally paid by the vendor on completion as a percentage of the consideration paid. Most business brokers will also ask for a retainer at the beginning of the assignment to cover their preparatory work and expenses, which may be deductible from the finder's fee when the business is sold. When negotiating fees you should not expect that the business broker's involvement will reduce the chargeable work by your accountant or solicitor. The consultant's value resides in his ability to generate *bona fide* purchasers and to help you to negotiate a satisfactory price.

3.4 Insolvency – management and mitigation

Matthew Howard, Larking Gowen

Insolvency can affect individuals with or without a business and also corporate entities.

Many people consider themselves or their interests to be immune from insolvency. However, circumstances change over time and sometimes insolvency problems do occur. This may be as a result of things out of the individual's control, and sometimes through no fault of that person.

The keys to avoiding these problems are:

□ to understand the basic principles of the insolvency legislation and terminology so that we understand what we are trying to avoid;
□ to recognise the warning signs of a potential insolvency problem, if and when they occur;
□ to act on the warning signs and seek professional help at an early stage.

UNDERSTANDING THE BASICS OF INSOLVENCY LEGISLATION

Broadly there are four tests of insolvency:

□ *The Balance Sheet test* – where liabilities exceed assets;
□ *The Commercial Insolvency test* – where debts cannot be paid when they fall due;
□ *Unsatisfied Statutory Demand* – where a written demand has been served for a sum of £750 or more and remains unsatisfied after 21 days;
□ *Unsatisfied Judgement* – where an execution or other process issued on judgement is returned unsatisfied in whole or in part.

The insolvency terminology used will depend on the entity that is insolvent. Administration, receivership and liquidation relate to companies. Bankruptcy is the procedure related to individuals. This is irrespective of whether or not the individual traded as a business. Contrary to popular belief, companies do not go bankrupt; nor do individuals. Sole trader businesses or partnerships go into liquidation.

In appropriate circumstances it may be possible for companies and individuals to enter into informal arrangements or formal voluntary arrangements with their creditors, as an alternative to, say, liquidation or bankruptcy, respectively. This may allow time for payments to creditors to be organised and may in some circumstances mean that creditors do not receive payment in full. Generally, however, the payment will provide a better likely outcome than would liquidation or bankruptcy. Creditors must agree to these proposals and, in the case of a formal voluntary arrangement, have the opportunity to vote on and potentially modify the proposals at a specially called creditors meeting.

Generally, the primary objective of an insolvency procedure is to maximise the return to creditors. However, some procedures work specifically for one particular class of creditor; for example, in an Administrative Receivership, where the Insolvency Practitioner is appointed by the holder of a floating charge for the purpose of realising funds for that chargeholder (subject to payment first of preferential creditors – see below).

Maximising the return to creditors may mean rescuing a company or business and allowing it to continue to trade either with the existing management or by achieving a going concern sale. In other circumstances it can mean the break up and sale of the company's or individual's assets.

In any insolvency, a strict order of payment is applied, as follows:

1. any individual or organisation holding a fixed charge security over an insolvent individual's or company's assets;
2. preferential creditors (such as some claims of the Inland Revenue, HM Customs & Excise, employees' wages arrears and holiday pay entitlements);
3. holders of floating charges over assets;
4. unsecured, non-preferential creditors;
5. shareholders or, in bankruptcy, the debtor themselves (after payment of statutory interest on the above debts).

RECOGNISING THE WARNING SIGNS

The warning signs, as with the terminology addressed above, vary depending on the entity involved.

Personal debt problems

If individuals can identify with any of the following problems they may need help with personal debt problems:

☐ Owing more money on credit cards or store cards than can comfortably be afforded each month.

☐ Changes in personal circumstances (such as divorce, long-term illness or unemployment) are having a negative effect on the financial position.

☐ The bank is threatening to dishonour cheques and/or withdraw overdraft facilities.

☐ The bank is stating that it is unable to offer further advice.

☐ Creditors are starting to exert pressure and possibly threatening to commence Court proceedings.

☐ Mortgage arrears are growing.

Business debt problems

If individuals trading an unincorporated business as a sole-trader or in partnership with others can identify with any of the following problems they may need help with business debt problems:

☐ Suppliers are insisting on cash terms or threatening legal action.

☐ Creditors are threatening to commence Court proceedings.

☐ The bailiff and/or sheriff is attempting to seize assets.

☐ VAT and PAYE arrears are growing.

☐ The bank is threatening to dishonour cheques and/or withdraw overdraft facilities.

☐ The bank is stating that it is unable to offer further advice.

☐ There is danger of personal credit ratings being negatively affected.

☐ Changes in personal circumstances (such as divorce, long-term illness or unemployment) are having a negative effect on the financial position.

☐ Mortgage arrears are growing.

☐   The balance between personal and business financial commitments is becoming a struggle.

Problems with company affairs

If directors trading a company can identify with any of the following problems they may need help with company affairs:

☐   Suppliers are insisting on cash terms or threatening legal action.
☐   Creditors are threatening to commence Court proceedings.
☐   The bailiff and/or sheriff is attempting to seize assets.
☐   VAT and PAYE arrears are growing.
☐   There is danger of the company's credit rating being negatively affected.
☐   The bank is threatening to dishonour cheques and/or reduce or withdraw the overdraft facility.
☐   The bank is requesting further security over company's assets.
☐   The bank is stating that it is unable to offer further advice.
☐   Directors are concerned over their potential personal liability for the company's debt.

ACTING ON THE WARNING SIGNS

In every situation, early action will greatly increase the chance of you or the company being able to avoid formal bankruptcy or liquidation proceedings, respectively. There are a number of options available to you or the company if action is taken early enough. Each scenario is unique and therefore it is necessary to identify the situation and adopt a solution to the specific circumstances of the case.

Personal debt

For individuals with personal debt problems, it may be possible to:

☐   Negotiate an informal arrangement with your creditors, whereby you pay all or part of your debts based upon what you can realistically afford to contribute.
☐   Restructure your debts or re-mortgage your property to help you avoid formal insolvency procedures.
☐   Prepare and implement an 'Individual Voluntary Arrangement' – a Court-backed procedure whereby you pay all or part of your

debts and receive protection to prevent your creditors from taking further action against you.

☐ If there is no viable alternative, seek advice on your rights and responsibilities in the event of bankruptcy and obtain guidance regarding your home and other assets.

Business debt

For individuals with business debt problems, it may be possible to:

☐ Ease your cash flow problems by obtaining help in chasing your problem debts.

☐ Change the way that your business manages its cash flow to help ease your financial problems.

☐ Obtain help to liase with your creditors to offer you breathing space, giving you time to consider your options.

☐ Negotiate an informal arrangement with your creditors, whereby you pay all or part of your debts based upon what you can realistically afford to contribute.

☐ Restructure your debts or re-mortgage your property to help you avoid formal insolvency procedures.

☐ Prepare and implement an 'Individual Voluntary Arrangement' – a Court-backed procedure whereby you pay all or part of your personal and business debts and receive protection to prevent your creditors from taking further action against you, while allowing you the option to continue trading.

☐ If there is no viable alternative, seek advice on your rights and responsibilities in the event of bankruptcy and obtain guidance regarding your home and other assets.

Individuals with or without businesses need to avoid getting themselves and the business, if applicable, further into debt. However, this is sometimes easier said than done and the prospect of losing your business and facing bankruptcy is a very daunting one. A common misconception for individuals trading an unincorporated business is that the business financial affairs are separate from their personal financial affairs. However, this is not true as business and personal assets are available to *all* creditors, and *all* business and non-business non-preferential, unsecured creditors rank equally.

Company's affairs

For directors with concerns over the company's affairs and viability, it may be possible to:

☐ Change the way that you manage the company cash flow and obtain help to chase problem debts, which will help to ease its financial problems.

☐ Obtain help to liase with creditors to offer breathing space, giving you time to consider the company's options.

☐ Obtain help to make better-informed decisions on the company's behalf by allowing an Insolvency Practitioner to attend creditors' meetings for you.

☐ Negotiate on the company's behalf an informal arrangement with its creditors, whereby the company pays all or part of its debts based upon what it can realistically afford to contribute.

☐ Prepare and implement a 'Company Voluntary Arrangement' – a Court-backed procedure whereby the company pays all or part of its debts and receives protection to prevent its creditors from taking further legal action, whilst allowing it to continue trading.

☐ If there is no viable alternative but to cease trading, obtain assistance to wind the company down in a controlled way and receive advice on the disposal of assets. This may include obtaining advice to help the company to enter into voluntary liquidation.

In many circumstances, directors will have some personal liability for the company's liabilities, which in turn may lead to financial concerns for their personal affairs. Furthermore, a director's conduct is reviewed on the insolvency of a company and a report is made by the office-holder (eg liquidator) on this conduct and may in due course result in director's disqualification proceedings being brought against the individual concerned.

In addition, some transactions may be overturned in an insolvency, or a civil recovery action may be brought personally against the director. This may result in the director being asked to contribute financially to the insolvent's assets from personal funds or may lead to bankruptcy proceedings being brought if the individual is unable to pay.

A further concern for a director should be the potential criminal charges that can be brought in relation to conduct. The nature of the charges may result in fines or imprisonment or both.

Obviously, the potential seriousness of the above demonstrates that directors should seek professional advice if there is any possibility that the company may enter into insolvency.

This advice should include:

☐ ascertaining your responsibilities and potential personal liabilities as a director;

☐ obtaining assistance to minimise the risk to your personal financial situation, for example, if you have given personal guarantees;

☐ obtaining assistance with the completion of director's conduct questionnaires;

☐ obtaining legal representation in the event of director's disqualification proceedings being commenced.

Transactions that may be overturned

A common mistake made by individuals and directors under financial pressure is to panic and to try to hide things from creditors and from the authorities. Trying to 'hide things' may include transactions such as selling assets at less than their true market value (often cars sold for negligible value to relatives or friends) or transferring the company's interest in property or a personal interest in a house to an associate or a connected party.

These transactions may be legal while the individual or company is solvent, but can be overturned at a later date in formal insolvency proceedings, when they are known as voidable transactions. It is also possible that paying one creditor in favour of another can also he unravelled. The Insolvency Practitioner may in this scenario seek to have the position restored to how it was before the payment was made. This could include asking the Courts to request the return of assets or cash transferred.

The Insolvency Practitioner or Official Receiver will look back at the transactions that have taken place in a given time frame. The length of this time frame will depend on the parties involved. If the parties are deemed to be connected or associated then the time frame is longer. For example, in bankruptcy the transfer of a matrimonial home to a spouse might be looked at if it took place in the five years prior to the date of the bankruptcy order.

Attempting to hide cash from creditors is often something else discovered by Insolvency Practitioners. The motivation for this is understandable, as people are naturally anxious to put money aside to re-establish their business or company, since it is their future livelihood. Again, these transactions may be unravelled and overturned.

Accordingly, to prevent any problems at a later date, the directors of a company, the partners or a sole trader should engage advisors to get debtors in order and attempt to improve cash flow or perhaps restructure loans. Seeking and acting on professional advice at an early stage serves by taking the stress off the person or people who are being burdened by financial pressure. It also provides time for the options to be discussed and considered and may prevent individuals or directors being forced into a corner where there will probably be only one option.

Seeking professional help

Taking the plunge to ask for assistance is a very difficult step for some people to take. Many people are frightened to seek advice or genuinely believe that circumstances will improve next week, next month or next year...

There is also a huge pride issue; people who have traded the business or company for many years do not want to face up to a potential failure.

Sadly, however, the national survey undertaken by R3, the Association of Business Recovery Professionals, shows that poor management is the biggest cause of business failure today. The research shows that throughout the 1990s, almost 70,000 businesses failed because of incompetent managers. R3 also comments that many insolvencies could have been avoided if professional advice had been sought earlier and state that: 'the longer a company waits before seeking help, the more likely it becomes that the company or its business will not be rescued. Likewise, the longer an individual waits before seeking advice, the greater that individual's debts are likely to be'.

Most Insolvency Practitioners offer a free initial consultation. That meeting provides an opportunity for the Insolvency Practitioner to gain an understanding of the present problem, together with the history that has led up to this point. Up to a point, the history is relevant, as is who is to blame and why it has all gone wrong; however, the most relevant point is where the business is today and what can be done to improve the situation. The potential clients of an Insolvency Practitioner need solutions to their problems and guidance as to the best way forward.

The role of an Insolvency Practitioner often has similarities to the role of a counsellor; the advisor will be leading people through one of the lowest times in their lives.

Taking the initial leap to discuss financial affairs is a big step, but at least when the step has been taken the first hurdle is down because the individual or director has begun to face up to the fact that they have a problem.

Part Four:

Country Business
Case Histories

Introduction

The seven case histories in this final part of the book have been chosen for their variety. In no way are they intended to be representative of the business developments and diversifications in which country dwellers can engage in order to add value to their farming, residential or business assets. However, readers who are seeking ideas of how to generate additional income or are exploring how to put their ideas into practice may find herein practical examples, which are applicable to their particular circumstances, of what can be achieved and how to set about the business development process.

The case histories are arranged in roughly ascending order in relation to the size of non-farming business generated. With the exception of the final case, each charts the progress of the business from either a farming or an agricultural building base. The seventh history focuses on a long-established agricultural business, the livestock centre at York, and how it has been restructured and adapted for survival to meet the winds of change.

OVERVIEW

The first three case histories tell very different stories of farmers who have branched out from their core activity and have developed redundant agricultural buildings successfully. In the case of Robert and Jean Henly at Looe in Cornwall, diversification has taken the form of converting farm buildings into quality holiday accommodation that has produced an entirely new income stream. In the case of John Maxted at East Ilsley, Berkshire, and David Fleming in Essex, the conversion and development of agricultural buildings into residential and commercial property has become a specialist development activity in its own right. The common ground for all three families is that they have retained their farming interests and remain rooted in the land.

The four remaining cases are each highly individual. The Barn Brasserie at Great Tey, is an outstanding conversion of a listed agricultural building by Michael Xenakis who gave up working in the City of London to pursue his highly profitable business concept in rural Essex. At Wetherby, Yorkshire, Gareth Gaunt is developing a leading edge renewable energy feedstock business, while at Aynho, Oxfordshire, Richard Stephenson has created his award-winning 'Day in the Country' corporate hospitality and conference mix with optional leisure activities. Finally, James Stephenson has diversified the new York Auction Centre into a wide range of markets and business services, while retaining its traditional business of selling livestock.

Four of the seven are winners of the coveted CLA Farm and Country Buildings Award in the 2002 national architectural award scheme, but what else do these projects and their protagonists have in common? In addition to an overriding focus on quality and a respect for old buildings, it is evident that they each have a strong entrepreneurial instinct. However, the main lesson for all those who wish to follow their examples and add value to their rural assets is that a professional approach is essential. Business development in the countryside is a demanding occupation and not a sideline to be undertaken lightly.

4.1 Holiday accommodation

Bucklawren Farm, St Martin by Looe, Cornwall

In 1987 Robert and Jean Henly moved from farming in Wiltshire to Bucklawren Farm, three miles from Looe on the south Cornwall coast. In purchasing their 500-acre mixed beef and arable farm, they recognised from the outset that an additional income stream was necessary. There was immediate scope to offer Bed & Breakfast accommodation in the six-bedroom farmhouse with the possibility of converting three stables and a large redundant barn into holiday cottages.

The story of their development and commercial experience at Bucklawren Farm must be typical of the rural holiday industry in Devon and Cornwall over the past fifteen years and includes a number of tips and lessons for those who are contemplating similar transfers to England's ever-popular coastal region.

PHASED DEVELOPMENT

In their first year of occupation, the Henlys offered three bedrooms for bed and breakfast and gained their first experience of this essentially seasonal activity. The following year they added two further bedrooms, with Jean Henly providing the breakfast catering. In 1991 they set about converting three stables into a holiday cottage, but their initial detailed planning application was rejected on the grounds that the buildings were too close to the working part of the farm. Consultation with Agricultural Development Agency Services (ADAS) and the local Planning Officer helped to resolve the problem and on second application approval was granted.

In 1997 a further bedroom downstairs in the farmhouse was turned over to B&B and the following year the Henlys started to discuss with the local planning authority the conversion of the slate-roofed stone barns into holiday letting accommodation and a restaurant. Initially, there was opposition from the District Planning Officer, who ruled that no apertures would be allowed in the south side of the larger two-storey barn that the Henlys wished to convert to self-catering units for eight persons. However, they enlisted the help of their local District Councillor, who supported their proposal and, employing a different architect from the 1991 application, submitted their detailed applications for this conversion and a separate application for the conversion of a smaller barn to the restaurant. Throughout the negotiation process the Henlys were careful to keep the Highways Authority fully informed, although there were no issues regarding access and egress and there was ample provision in the plans for parking.

The application for the conversion to holiday accommodation succeeded but a decision on the restaurant development was deferred with requests for more information on its commercial viability and on the tourism and residential aspects. Accordingly, conversion of the larger barn was carried out in 1999.

GOVERNMENT GRANTS

At this point in 1998, the Henlys investigated the grants that might be available for their planned developments. They had received a small grant in 1991 for the conversion of stabling, but more substantial funding was available now up to 25 per cent of total investment cost from the European Union Objective Fund 5B, for which South-West Tourism is the local UK facilitator. A further small grant was secured from the South-West Rural Development Agency.

Given the current drive to develop tourism and new employment opportunities in the south-west in the wake of the 2001 Foot and Mouth crisis, the availability of government grants and loans is at a high water mark. Robert Henly points out the dangers of being tempted by funds availability into diversification ventures that are not commercially viable. The conversion of redundant agricultural buildings into offices seems particularly risky in relation to local employment markets, which are far from buoyant.

It is also likely that capital investment in self-catering is at a level which may result in over-capacity.

THE RESTAURANT EXPERIENCE

In order to address the planners' concerns and to support funding, an ADAS feasibility study was commissioned for the proposed restaurant of 90 covers, of which 40 would be in the main dining room. In retrospect the conclusions of the study were slightly optimistic but the ADAS endorsement did clinch the argument and planning consent was granted.

Attempting to operate the restaurant themselves without previous experience was plainly not an acceptable management solution for the Henlys, although they were prepared to undertake the business management. With plenty of part-time labour available locally for table staff, the critical appointment was that of chef, and the recruitment and retention of a competent trained chef became the Achilles heel of the enterprise. Although sales turnover has reached a financially viable level, fixed overheads – particularly commercial rates and insurance premiums – are a heavy burden and, when the last chef left in February 2003, Robert and Jean Henly decided to rethink their strategy. They are now recruiting either a chef-proprietor or tenant to lease the restaurant from them.

AT THE END OF THE DAY

The high quality of the holiday accommodation development is emphasised by the CLA Farm and Country Buildings Award that Bucklawren Farm received in the 2002 national architectural award scheme.

Jean Henly continues to operate the Bucklawren B&B business and self-catering holidays, and Robert continues farming. As a dedicated farmer since graduating from Reading University, Robert Henly is able to continue in his chosen occupation and the additional income from holiday accommodation enables them both to maintain their chosen lifestyle. For many families today similar diversification and extensions of activity will provide the means to continue living and working on the land.

4.2 Development-funded farming

Manor Farm, East Ilsley, Berkshire

John Maxted has been a farmer all his working life. He graduated in farming studies from Leicester University and invested in his first tenanted farm in Oxfordshire in 1961, with the help of a family-guaranteed bank overdraft. For the first 29 years his efforts were focused on the development and expansion of his farming activities, but in the 1990s, after a profitable first experience in barn conversion, became increasingly more involved in the regeneration of rural buildings as a means of extracting additional value from the family's farming assets.

What makes the story unusual is John's fine sense of timing and an instinct which he has followed in exploiting development potential to support his farming business and generate family wealth, well before it became apparent that the bottom would fall out of profitable farming and that most farmers would need alternative income sources in order to maintain their life support systems.

EARLY EXPANSION AND DEVELOPMENT EXPERIENCE

By 1982 the Maxted farming enterprise had expanded into three separate farming ventures. In 1969 John Maxted bought into Oak House, a 1,200-acre tenanted farm at Hampstead Norrey's, Berkshire, moving from Oxfordshire, and in 1974 purchased 500 adjoining acres. The Milkhill Pig Co Ltd was formed in 1972 through which the pig-fattening unit at Oak House was operated. In 1979, further expansion was undertaken with the purchase of Woodlands Park Farm in Hampshire, a 250-acre all-grass holding eventually carrying 300 head of cattle and making 1,000 tons of silage with only 100 units per acre of nitrogen – no mean feat from a unit of this size.

In 1982 the Maxteds purchased Tuxwell Farm, Somerset, with 350 red land acres on the edge of the Quantocks, where the manager transferred from Woodlands Park Farm combined mixed arable farming with sheep, achieving outstanding yields. Unfortunately, the manager was headhunted locally and in 1990 John Maxted decided to sell, after first securing planning consent for residential development on a large barn. The price realised for the barn, farmhouse and 20 acres was double the investment cost, with the woodlands and arable land sold separately for an additional profit. This was his first experience of the enhanced value which planning consent could yield to farm buildings.

The final acquisitions of farmland were made in 1994/5 when the 1,000-acre Manor Farm at East Ilsley was bought, just three miles from Hampstead Norrey's, and to which the adjoining Beech Tree Farm was added in 1998, bringing in a further 500 acres. During this period, Woodlands Park Farm was sold in 1995 after completing a barn conversion, which recovered the original price of the holding, and in 1998 the Oakhurst tenancy was relinquished.

Today, the Maxted farming business comprises 2,000 acres, all owned, of which 1,700–1,750 acres are arable. There is a 600 sow unit with the progeny transferred to a fattening unit on the 500 acres remaining at Hampstead Norrey's, while the grassland at Manor Farm, which includes a site of special scientific interest (SSSI), supports an Aberdeen Angus suckler herd of 30 cows.

However, the focus of interest in the Maxted experience is the four successive planning and development projects that John has undertaken at East Ilsley and Woodend, the remaining holding at Hampstead Norrey's. In John Maxted's assessment, the net return from farming on tenants' capital is no more than 2–3 per cent and the only profit on arable farming is from government aid.

FARM BUILDING DEVELOPMENT

Manor Farm was purchased with a history of two planning applications, both failed by West Berkshire planning authority on the grounds that the farm was outside the village envelope. Undeterred by these precedents, John Maxted laid siege to the planning authorities with a low-key campaign of informal meetings with the Planning Officer, the Highways Officer and, as progress was made, with the Building Officer responsible for the approval of materials employed in building or conversion. Essentially, his intention was to regenerate in stages a series of dilapidated farm buildings within the area of the original farmyard, involving limited conversion but mainly redevelopment.

One factor that must be allowed for in protracted planning negotiations is that there is no continuity in Planning or Highway Officers, whose appointment is permanently subject to change. Each officer is likely to have his/her own priorities and to lay differing emphasis on the particular features of each development. For this reason alone, John Maxted advises would-be developers to go for full planning in one application rather than enter an outline application first. Outline approval does not ensure that detailed planning consent will be forthcoming.

After nearly three years' discussion, during which particular requirements such as restrictions on the level and height of buildings and exterior lights were established, John felt sufficiently comfortable to enter his first detailed planning application. Key issues that were agreed by the planners during prior negotiation were:

☐ the farmyard was admitted as a 'brownfield site';
☐ the 'footprint' of the existing buildings could not be exceeded – developed areas could not exceed the square meters occupied by buildings to be replaced;
☐ the planners would accept a 'village approach' to the front of the site so that terraced houses might be built;
☐ office accommodation might be acceptable under current government policy to create employment opportunities in rural communities.

The first application was to replace existing buildings with eight terraced houses and, behind them, five 'executive homes' and, at the same time, to convert stabling close to the farmhouse into office accommodation. The residential build was undertaken in partnership with a national developer, MJ Gleason, which took responsibility for development and sale of the executive homes, the provision of funding and the construction of the terraced housing through its building firm. The freehold interest in the retained terraced housing is vested in a Maxted family trust.

Every effort was made to involve the planners and planning committee in the detail of the application, with site visits and continuing consultation – another important element in maintaining continuity and developer-friendly relations. During this process the Highway Officer's requirements on access from the main road and the roadway that had to be built emerged as crucial and were accommodated in the plans. The planning application was approved in March 1999 and the residential development completed in November 2001.

Meanwhile, the conversion of stabling at Woodend into three units of residential accommodation formed a separate project. The same attention was paid to detailed consultation prior to planning application and paid dividends with a relatively smooth passage. The same architect was used for this development as for the previous barn conversion in Hampshire.

At East Ilsley the second phase of development took the form of an application to demolish an unsightly barn in poor condition at the rear of the former farmyard and to replace it with a 5,500 sq. ft. office block. As with the residential development the choice of traditional brick and tile materials and the configuration of the building were crucial in securing consent, as was acceptance of the planners' previous demand on the roadway and entrance to the site. The planning application was approved in January 2002 and the consent provides for flexible accommodation internally, depending on the number of tenants secured and their requirements.

This further development is speculative in that no space was pre-let prior to the initial construction. However, John Maxted is confident that the office accommodation, with its proximity to Newbury, Reading and the M4/A34 corridor will prove attractive to small businesses seeking to escape the urban environment and, no doubt, his commercial instinct will again prove reliable.

FURTHER CHALLENGES

There is still some scope for development at Manor Farm, East Ilsley: a smithy to be converted with an appropriate change of use; but this project seems unlikely to absorb John Maxted's attention for long. That entrepreneurial spirit will surely seek out some further challenge soon.

4.3 The Minerva Centre

Roundbush Farm, Essex

D Fleming & Son have been active in barn conversions for more than 15 years, starting with their own farm buildings, and have used the same firm of builders specialising in conservation work throughout. They have always used traditional materials and methods in their conversions, which have all fallen under the jurisdiction of Essex County Council. Of the two planning authorities which have been involved, Chelmsford has a more relaxed approach to redevelopment, whereas Maldon is more attuned to granting planning consents on existing buildings. Past developments have involved the conversion of a five-barn complex that was no longer suitable for agricultural use into commercial use including workshops for a Formula 1 and Indy motor racing team, and showrooms. Another two buildings were combined to form a house for Robert Fleming.

In the case of one barn, the Council listed the building after conversion. In addition to the conversion activities, David and Robert remain farmers. They are now engaged in contract farming in partnership, originally on 750 acres since 1996, but this was increased to 1,650 acres in 2003.

THE MINERVA CENTRE PROJECT

From the moment when David and Robert Fleming bought Roundbush Farm the development of its redundant buildings was on their agenda. Recognising that the costs would be substantial and that, in this case, speculative development would involve an unacceptable risk, the Flemings decided that they would apply for outline planning consent first, and then secure a tenant before proceeding to a detailed planning application. Previously, they had adopted the strategy of applying for detailed planning approval in the first instance and were accustomed to a 12-month cycle between first discussions with the local planning authority and the receipt of formal consent.

The Maldon planning department was the relevant authority for Roundbush Farm and the Flemings opened their campaign by submitting two applications: the first for residential development and the second for a change of use from agricultural to industrial and office accommodation, in the knowledge that the latter was likely to be the more acceptable to the planners. This strategy proved successful and outline planning consent was granted in 2000 for conversion of the original barns to commercial use.

The next step was more complex. The Flemings were resolved to apply for detailed planning consent only after identifying and securing a specific tenant. In the event, FPD Savills found a prospective blue chip tenant in the form of the Minerva Centre (NHS Trust), which was searching for office premises with conference facilities locally.

THE TENANCY

The basic terms of the tenancy negotiated were a fully repairing 10-year lease with a break clause in favour of the tenant only in the fourth year. The most critical element of the negotiation was to arrive at a rental which would support the total investment, including the cost of converting the barns to the tenant's specification and to the requirements of the planning authority in terms of materials and quality of construction.

Another difficulty was that it was necessary to be specific about the timing of construction, including the detailed planning application process, and the occupation date after providing some leeway for changes in the tenant's specification.

Another tenant demand that had to be accommodated was a requirement that all contractors engaged in the development had to carry collateral warranties and professional indemnities. The lease, and contractors' contracts, also contained provisions to fix and make good any defects in the first 18 months. For this purpose, a 10 per cent retention of contract value was retained by D Fleming & Son.

SATISFYING THE PLANNERS

Although the quality of internal materials was affected by cost parameters, there was no compromise in the quality of the conversion work. The specification provided that the main frame timbers would be pegged rather than bolted and that the brickwork in the small element of new building and any re-pointing of old brickwork would be carried out using lime mortars. Within the barn, new timber would be used to repair the building, leaving much of the original structure exposed so that there would always be a clear distinction between new and old. For example, replacement roof trusses were built over the originals but the old trusses were left exposed.

A local conservation architect, Hilary Brightman, was engaged, who had prior experience working for the Maldon planning authority and whose judgement on the conversion of old buildings was respected. The design included the installation of a new mezzanine floor in part of the barns using new materials in a quite different style, but this development feature has been very effective and is not in offensive contrast with the original.

Planning consent was granted and the work carried out successfully to schedule over a 12-month period. The Minerva Centre has been occupied and running since December 2001. In September 2002, D Fleming & Son's development was recognised in the Farm and Country Buildings Awards of the Country Land and Business Association (CLA) and also received an award from Maldon District Council.

WHAT NEXT?

No doubt D Fleming & Son will be engaging in more conversion and development projects in the future. As David says, they are fascinated by the way in which old agricultural buildings are constructed and like to research their history and that of the people who worked in them.

Nevertheless, conversion and development opportunities in Essex are changing. The local authorities are focused on 'encouraging the re-use of redundant agricultural buildings' for social and affordable housing in the countryside. Larger scale housing development demands a significant financial capability beyond the Flemings' capacity.

However, they have gained a reputation locally over the years for shrewd, high-quality developments and planning expertise. A third career in development consultancy beckons.

4.4 The Barn Brasserie

Great Tey, Colchester

Unlike other rural entrepreneurs whose exploits are featured in these case histories, Michael Xenakis does not have a farming background himself, although his wife Elizabeth's family have been farming for some generations. Having worked in the City of London for 25 years, Michael's experience of rural development prior to the development of the Barn Brasserie was confined to a previous barn conversion 14 years ago for his family's weekend occupation.

However, in 1998 Michael Xenakis opted out of the luxury cruise liner group of which he had been a main board director for 15 years, and decided to move permanently out of the corporate world to develop a business venture in Essex in the area where he and his family now resided. The choice of business would be determined by his own knowledge and experience in the design, operation and business economics of catering for large numbers on cruise liners.

THE BARN BRASSERIE CONCEPT

In considering suitable venues for establishing a restaurant of consequence, Michael Xenakis was guided by the necessary conditions he had established for success. First, a building of striking design and quality development were essential. Relying on his personal eating out experience rather than structured market research, Michael had concluded that people do not rate food and drink as the prime objective of going out for meals, although high quality food, wines and service are an essential accompaniment. Eating out, he maintains, is one of the very few opportunities to communicate with family and friends in a relaxed environment away from the pressures of work and modern living in smaller spaces, cluttered with entertainment systems and IT. In the United States, for example, 65 per cent of food is consumed outside the home. The same need to 'escape' drives adults into garden centres and DIY stores at the weekend.

Following this logic, Michael Xenakis's concept of a relaxed ambience embraced the need for an open, airy restaurant space, unencumbered by the ancillary service facilities of kitchen and cloakrooms with a construction design and décor using natural materials: glass, timber and steel, and natural colours.

The Grade II listed Brook barn, one of the largest thatched barns in England, was a clear but challenging choice, satisfying the main criteria for a restaurant of distinction and potentially providing a 'destination' and sense of experience which would draw eaters-out from a catchment area which Michael Xenakis characterises as 20 minutes driving distance. With four years' experience, the Barn Brasserie attracts diners from the Colchester, Witham, Chelmsford and Sudbury areas, as well as more local custom and 'ladies who lunch' from far and wide. But first, it was necessary to negotiate with the planners and to evaluate the development cost carefully in order to ensure that a restaurant could be created which satisfied fully the Xenakis concept.

A SUPPORTIVE PLANNING PROCESS

Up to 1999 Brook barn was a redundant agricultural building of historic interest that had fallen into disrepair. The building was largely in its original condition with the oak frame erected on bare soil ground. For this reason the approach for change of use and conversion by Michael Xenakis and his architect, Mark Perkins, was received positively by the local authority planning office. The main Xenakis requirements for ample windows and a vast open space, and a refusal to include kitchens in the existing building were accepted.

However, the planners were concerned that there should be sufficient car parking and insisted that disabled toilets should be accommodated within the building. The car parking requirement was satisfied by establishing a car park in an adjacent green field and a compromise was reached on the second requirement by constructing a mezzanine floor within the building which provided sufficient space for all the washrooms. As with many planning applications the requirements of the county Highways Authority on access, exit and car parking were in many ways the most demanding.

The construction work involved jacking up the original oak frame with brick foundations and the use of reclaimed and original materials, in particular black weather-boarding, timber floors and interior oak beams. The completed development was recognised in the CLA national architectural award scheme, Farm and Country Buildings Awards. The judges praised the stylish, light modern feel of the magnificent restaurant within this historic building.

OPERATIONAL ASPECTS OF THE BRASSERIE

The Barn Brasserie has a seating capacity for 150 people and employs 50. All table staff are given a compulsory two days off each week to ensure that they remain bright and attentive. Typically, the restaurant serves 2,000 meals each week, all of which are cooked to order from fresh food ingredients. The menu includes fish, meat and vegetarian specialities with modern European and spiced Asian dishes. Prices range from full á la carte menu to £5.95 two-course lunchtime specials. There is a wine list of more than 100 wines.

Michael Xenakis acknowledges that there is a drink and drive factor, which has affected dining out habits. There is a greater use of taxis and a noticeable trend to drinking less but more discriminately. However, he doubts that there has been much impact on dining out frequency.

During the start-up phase, the Brasserie was marketed heavily in the local press and radio. Local radio was initially effective but it has become difficult to find fresh 'punch' messages that attract attention. The restaurant's overall performance has surpassed the original business plan reaching break-even point in the eighteenth month of operation. Michael Xenakis's own involvement in day-to-day management is now reduced from full-time to about one hour a day.

A BROADER HORIZON

Michael Xenakis has proved that his restaurant concept is valid and is ready to apply the formula elsewhere. However, suitable buildings and locations are difficult to find. The formula relies on selecting a striking older building which can be restored and converted into a 'destination' of interest with a dining capacity of 150 which will attract eaters out from a distance.

The location can be urban or rural, provided that it is 'within 20 minutes of the chimney pots'. Therefore, readers who have a disused warehouse or decommissioned chapel on their hands and are looking for an alternative use are welcome to contact Michael on michaelxenakis@aol.com.

4.5 Diversification into renewable energy

Carlshead Farms, Wetherby, Yorkshire

Gareth Gaunt's story is quite different from the other experiences related in this collection of case histories. Qualified as a veterinary surgeon and specialising as a horse vet in Yorkshire and further afield, Gareth was drawn back home to the 500-acre Carlshead Farms six years ago after his father underwent a kidney transplant operation. In order to generate a steady source of income, Gareth decided to put down 150 acres to short-term coppice willow which produced a three-year crop of tall timber which could be harvested and converted into biomass fuel for the ARBRE renewable energy project at nearby Eggborough, Selby.

This R&D project, promoted by a private water company, was subsidised with £10 million of EU funding and encouraged by the UK government. Its objective is to develop fuel sources that can be used to replace fossil fuels such as coal for gasification and to drive steam turbines for large power producers. The British Government has committed itself to satisfy 3 per cent of national fuel requirements from the output of renewables with a further target of 10 per cent by 2010.

At the same time, Gareth Gaunt embarked on a more conventional project to convert two 300-year-old barns at Carlshead Farms into offices linked by a modern new build. The two projects were compatible but not interdependent.

RENEWABLE ENERGY FEEDSTOCK PRODUCTION

Willow Coppice is harvested in the winter months when the sap is down using a converted sugar cane harvester. The harvester cuts the crop into a 50 mm billet in one pass; the billets are then allowed to air dry for two to three months, reducing their moisture content from 55 per cent to below 30 per cent. The crop is now ready to use as a fuel feedstock.

The revenue parameters for this activity are a yield of 20 to 30 oven-dried tons per hectare and a selling price of about £45 per oven-dry ton. Given the growing cycle and process time from harvest to delivery, there is a cash flow issue but this is addressed by DEFRA grants for planting, down payments from long-term contracts and set-aside claims.

The ARBRE project was *the* pilot project for Biomass in the United Kingdom. Other local farmers have taken the opportunity to follow Gareth Gaunt's example and have formed a syndicate, the Renewable Energy Growers, to satisfy the feedstock requirement of the local Selby plant. The syndicate plans to expand its collective growing area beyond 1,300 hectares, to raise commercial funding for the producer group and to engage in agronomy, farmer promotion, the provision of advice, government lobbying and group marketing.

THE OFFICE DEVELOPMENT

As other owner-developers in this group of case studies have indicated, the conversion of redundant farm buildings, particularly those that are centuries old, requires painstaking pre-work with the local planners, in Gareth Gaunt's case the Harrogate Planning Authority. Early discussion made it clear that this planning authority's prime objectives were to approve a development involving the new section connecting the two old barns, which would be both sustainable and environmentally friendly.

The tactic Gareth chose was to put in, as a stalking horse, an initial application based on a thoroughly boring design which he knew the planners would not like and then to change to an architect whom they recommended to enter a more sympathetic design for 7,500 sq. ft. of accommodation with reception, boardroom and leisure area. The only point of contention related to the access, where the Highways Authority demanded an altered junction. However, the planners proved helpful in negotiations, the junction was left as it was, and the planning consent was granted. The single tenant for the completed office development is The Program Management Group, which was secured by marketing through Rural Business Centres.

The choice of architect was rewarding in an unexpected sense. Like other barn conversions featured in these case studies, the development received a CLA Farm and Country Buildings Award in the 2002 national architectural award scheme.

The rest of the farm has just been entered for an extensive Countryside Stewardship Scheme, which will dovetail nicely with a new Educational Trust set up this year.

THE OUTLOOK FOR RENEWABLE ENERGY

With fossil fuel prices climbing steadily and a Government committed to reducing greenhouse gasses, the future for renewables looks bright. Wood heating technology is commonplace in countries such as Austria and Denmark; the boilers are highly efficient (typically 90 per cent), automated, and able to run on woodchips or wood pellets. Pellets have the advantage of fuel standardization and density, and will be suited to the domestic market. Larger woodchip systems such as the Talbott C3 range will be more suited to on-farm projects heating offices and houses. In the near future, small on-farm Biomass Generators, such as the Bioflame unit, will be able to produce heat and power, enhancing the value added for farmers. Small wonder, therefore, that Michael Meacher, the DEFRA minister, spent a day at Carlshead Farm recently and is planning to chair a seminar there for Rural District Authorities and County Councils later in 2003.

For Gareth Gaunt, what started as an opportunistic diversification from farming is fast becoming a new career with his appointment as Vice Chairman of the Renewable Energy Group, with the mandate to develop the undertaking into a major commercial enterprise. And, as a footnote, it comes as no surprise that the offices and houses at Carlshead Farm are heated by a 150 kilowatt biomass-fuelled boiler.

4.6 A Day in the Country and the Great Barn

Upper Aynho Grounds, Aynho, Banbury, Oxfordshire

In 1985, when Richard and Di Stephenson bought Upper Aynho Grounds, a 270-acre farm with a fine 17th century stone farmhouse, magnificent barns, cottages, a number of outbuildings, fish ponds and pheasant covers, they recognised that the amenity value of the estate probably exceeded its potential as a farming enterprise. Neither Richard nor Di had farmed previously, although there were farming interests in the family and their son Jeremy had trained at agricultural college. Richard's main occupation as senior partner in a busy North Oxfordshire medical practice was a major constraint on available time for development at Upper Aynho Grounds so that the successful ventures of the last 18 years reflect boundless energy, as well as business acumen in abundance.

EARLY ACTIVITY

The immediate priority on taking occupation was to make arrangements for the farming. From the outset all the arable land was contract farmed. A pair of farm buildings were set up for pig-breeding, which Jeremy Stephenson managed. However, the industry's general move towards outdoor pig-farming and the effect on prices helped to make the Aynho unit unviable and the activity was discontinued after five years.

A row of cottages – built originally for agricultural workers – linked by an arch to the house and forming one side of the original farmyard, was in poor condition but an obvious candidate for holiday lettings. They were duly repaired and improved but the Stephensons decided that due to their proximity to the main house and in view of their plans for the use of the adjoining barn, an imposing unused stone structure of 40 m by 8 m with a leaky roof but having potential as an entertainment location on a grand scale, it would be better to rent the cottages on short leases to more permanent or carefully selected tenants.

Before arriving at a strategy for the profitable use of the barn, the Stephensons focused on reorganising the existing fishing arrangements. Richard decided to continue with game fishing, which was run on a seasonal subscription basis between April and October with re-stocking of the three trout lakes every three weeks. The game fishing runs as a club with 40 members and is a profitable sideline. Coarse fishing was considered as an alternative as this is more profitable, but taking into consideration the position of the lakes and the possibility of using them for corporate entertainment it was decided to continue with game fishing for trout. It should be emphasised that licenses from the Environment Agency are required for stocking and fishermen require a Rod Licence to fish on private water.

By now the idea was forming of developing a corporate entertainment package, which would offer a combination of country activities with catering facilities as an attractive alternative to more conventional corporate events for clients and customers or staff meetings and celebrations. A key factor in Upper Aynho Grounds' market potential was its location and parking space for up to 200 cars. Situated 5 minutes from junction 10 of the M40 and 25 minutes from junction 15A of the M1, one hour from Heathrow and 45 minutes from Birmingham International airport and the NEC, the catchment area included then the major conurbations of Oxford, Northampton and Milton Keynes. Important population centres within reach now include Newbury, Aylesbury, Leamington Spa and Warwick, as well as nearby Banbury and Bicester.

In the late 1980s clay-pigeon shooting grew rapidly in popularity as a competitive hobby and as a leisure pastime for 'townies'. Country people had always shot clays in the late summer as a practice warm-up for the shooting season. Now in North Oxfordshire, licensed and unlicensed clay shoots in farmer's fields open to the public became commonplace in the winter months. Therefore, it was a natural extension from game fishing to introduce clay-pigeon shooting at Upper Aynho Grounds as a second country pursuit. It is important to remember that permission is required from the Firearms Licensing Department to approve the site, in order that a person may use a shotgun on the designated area of land without holding a shotgun certificate, in accordance with Section 11(6) of the Firearms Act 1968–1997.

A DAY IN THE COUNTRY CONCEPT

Most of 1986 was spent in planning and preparation. By the year's end the concept of 'A Day in the Country' as a new form of quality corporate entertainment had emerged. Richard and Di Stephenson were clear from the outset that the quality of the catering would be crucial to penetrating the corporate hospitality market. Three-course sit-down lunches in the ambience of a comfortable traditional building with fine wines served in cut glass goblets rather than instant coffee in plastic beakers were the necessary accompaniment to fly fishing for trout and clay shooting, however good the sport or competent the expert instruction provided. To attract City bankers and multinational corporate managers and their clients and customers, oak smoked Scottish salmon at lunch would be as important as the size of the morning's catch and marksmanship at the clays would count for less than the quality of the claret.

And so the Day in the Country Programme evolved. Over the years additional optional activities were added to the game fishing and clay shooting, including Land Rover 4-wheel driving on a 'jungle track', archery, pistol shooting and Pacer Pirates 'sand buggies'. Horse carriage or tractor driving, sheep dog trialing and cow milking – even falconry, skydiving and hot air ballooning – are among the additional rural pursuits that can be provided on request. Clients can order in advance the combination of activities that appeals most to them and their guests, together with the menus for snacks on arrival, lunch, tea and dinner – for those wishing to continue the entertainment into the evening.

During 1986, the Stephensons realised they needed some professional help with marketing and management expertise. Richard invited an old friend Nicholas Price to become a partner in the business. Nicholas had recently sold his hotel company and was an ex-chairman of the Best Western Hotel Group. He had considerable marketing experience with many contacts in the hospitality industry. Richard's own experience in the improvement and refurbishment of old buildings was more than sufficient for the initial task of making the first half of the barn inhabitable; primarily roof repair, draught proofing and the installation of fireplaces and chimneys. Management of the medical practice had given him the necessary business administration experience.

There were no kitchens attached to the barn and, to begin with, Di Stephenson and a small staff of part-time helpers recruited locally had their work cut out in serving freshly cooked meals for parties of 30 or more from the farmhouse kitchen across the yard in all seasons and weather conditions. As the business grew, kitchen facilities were installed in an outbuilding adjacent to the barn and the same part-time staff employed.

EVOLUTION OF THE CORPORATE HOSPITALITY MARKET

The business traded as a partnership until 1990, when on professional advice the business was incorporated into A Day in the Country Ltd. The heady days of lavish corporate entertainment peaked in the late 1980s towards the end of the Thatcher era but, as the megabuck market for high profile hospitality events such as Ascot and Wimbledon faded, demand for comparatively modest and competitively priced, but still upmarket, A Day in the Country packages remained buoyant.

The market was changing in other respects too. The early 1990s saw a weeding out of many corporate hospitality organisers, as public interest dwindled and other outdoor activities in the countryside aimed at the fashionable 'corporate bonding' market, such as paint ball war games, flourished for a year or two before the fad faded.

A Day in the Country was able to survive this tough trading period, as it was still able to offer its quality product at a competitive rate, owing to its low and controllable overheads. In the corporate field, two converging trends opened up new market opportunities for the company. On the one hand, cost-conscious corporates were moving towards 'away days' in which staff seminars could be combined with an element of relaxation among colleagues. On the other hand, the combination of corporate entertainment with conferences, presentations and product launches to major clients and customers was recognised as a cost-effective way of strengthening business relationships purposefully with a degree of informality. And so the concept of mixed days evolved from the original Day in the Country. Corporate customers could bring their staff or clients to Upper Aynho Grounds for a half-day of meetings, first class food and drink and a few hours of country sports.

Although this hybrid form of hospitality increased the company's ability to provide more days on which the activities could be offered as a half-day event combined with catering, the barn now had to be used both as a restaurant and a meeting room. There was also an emerging demand for a more formal meeting area with auditorium seating and audio-visual facilities. Fortunately, there was the opportunity to satisfy this demand by opening up the second half of the barn, an identical floor area to the original area which had served A Day in the Country so well.

THE GREAT BARN

By 1997 the annual turnover of A Day in the Country was such that Richard Stephenson was sufficiently confident of the market opportunities to apply for planning consent in two stages for the whole barn and extended, permanent change of use to conference centre and civil wedding venue – another developing market. The planning application included new draught-proof entrances to the whole barn, heating and insulation throughout and the addition of a luxury toilet and restroom facilities suite. After receiving planning consent, the work was carried out by local building contractors under Richard's close supervision. Car parking was also extended.

The new conference suite, named the Croughton Room after another local village, has a seating capacity of 120 (60 in classroom format) while the original Aynho Room maintains its seating capacity of 100. Receptions using both rooms can accommodate up to 300. With the expansion of activity to include large party events not involving country pursuits, such as conferences and wedding receptions, the original trading name was not always appropriate and the title 'The Great Barn' was adopted for those events, with hospitality occasions still focused on country pursuits offered under the original 'A Day in the Country' trading name.

CONTINUING OPERATIONS AND OUTLOOK FOR THE FUTURE

As the business heads towards it eighteenth year of profitable operation, it is possible to begin assessing strengths and weaknesses. The flexibility of the hospitality events, meeting and catering facilities that are on offer at Upper Aynho Grounds is clearly a major factor in its continuing appeal to a wide range of profitable corporate and private function markets. At one extreme, The Great Barn can accommodate conferences plus catering of 120, at the other, small exclusive corporate days of 10 or more people.

This flexibility addresses business conditions where market prices have scarcely changed over the past ten years and the Great Barn and A Day in the Country can continue to compete against mainline prestige events at about only one-third of their prices. Local large-party catering competition has increased, but few are able to offer the range and flexibility of the Upper Aynho Grounds product mix.

Wisely, Richard Stephenson has maintained a policy of maintaining overhead costs at a minimum. Richard and Di were joined by their son, Jeremy Stephenson, on a full-time basis after the Great Barn expansion in 1997 and Jeremy's primary function is now marketing and operations director for the business as Nick Price nears retirement. However, he also farms the 200 acres of arable land which have been taken back in hand. Aside from the three family members, the business employs a marketing assistant. The catering is now wholly subcontracted to a local firm set up by catering professionals that maintains Richard and Di's exacting standards.

A marketing budget of around 3 per cent of sales is allocated mainly to mail shots, yellow page and business magazine advertising with an Internet website which Richard and Jeremy regard as an essential promotional tool. Despite the focus on economy, rising establishment costs such as business rates and insurance premiums, which more than trebled in 2002 after 9/11, take their toll. Fortunately, whatever the economic climate the demand for wedding receptions is constantly increasing at such an attractive venue. Because of rising fixed costs the company has to operate for 12 months in the year as opposed to barely 6 months in the year prior to 1997. Many private functions also now take place throughout the year.

Nevertheless, the business at Upper Aynho Grounds continues to prosper and, barring an economic downturn, turnover looks set to increase yet again. In 2002 Richard Stephenson retired from medical practice and whilst keeping a watchful eye on the business does not wish to be involved in the long and unsociable hours associated with the catering industry. He can now devote his attentions to improving the amenities on this small estate.

The attention to detail and maintenance of the highest standards has resulted in the company winning five major awards in the last five years. For the third time the company won the coveted 'Venue of the Year Award' in 2002.

In conclusion, one must look at the advantages and disadvantages of opening up one's own home to the general public. All forms of diversification carry an element of intrusion and the proximity of the hospitality area to the main house has been a disadvantage, minimised by putting the entrance and car parks away from the private area. Weddings and evening parties can mean long hours and some noise but conference and corporate functions are more dependent on the economy and have a short lead time whereas weddings can be booked up to two years in advance. The main advantage is that this is now a viable unit with a turnover that equates to a farm with many more acres than the 250 it has at present. This has enabled them to maintain and improve the property and provide a livelihood for the family. They may not spend large amounts on farm machinery but re-roofing the Great Barn, furnishing a conference centre or buying a generator are expensive alternatives. Above all they have derived great satisfaction from seeing clients return on many occasions to enjoy the hospitality. To do it, you have to enjoy it yourself.

4.7 Livestock markets – dead or alive? A study of York Auction Centre

James Stephenson, Stephenson & Co., York

A GRAND OLD TRADITION

There was a time when every market town in England would have an actual trading market where farm products including animals were sold. With increasing pressure on town centres most of the markets have gradually vanished over the years, although a few steadfastly remain such as the ones at Malton and Darlington in North Yorkshire.

Selling by auction is a tradition that is almost unique to this country and one that has been put under near terminal pressure in recent years. This case study looks at the problems faced by the partners of York Livestock Centre and the ways in which they seek to resolve them.

HISTORY OF YORK MARKET

Ever since Roman times there has been a market in the City of York, which established itself just outside the walls where local farmers could gather their stock to sell them profitably to the Roman Garrison.

More or less in the same location, the market continued until 1971 selling cattle, sheep and pigs on two days each week, with the premises owned by the City Corporation. At one stage in the 1930s there would be eight auctioneers licensed to sell and all were vying for the farmers' trade.

In addition to the live auction, York was also a major centre for the sale of imported Irish cattle, which were shipped to Holyhead and transported by train to the Corporation farm on the outskirts of the city. Up to 2000 cattle could turn up and they were walked along the road from the Corporation farm to the pens which ran round the outside of the Bar walls. The Irish cattle were actually shown to the farmers by turning them into the street for inspection and it wasn't long before the citizens and motorists raised more than eyebrows at the inconvenience.

In 1971 two of the old established auctioneering firms, English & Son of Pocklington and Stephenson & Son of York, got the opportunity to purchase a site on the new ring road and the old premises were quickly developed to boost the Civic coffers. The original site purchased by the auctioneers extended to 15 acres, to which a further 50 acres of adjoining lairage ground was added over the years. York was the first modern market to be built and set the tone for many that followed.

Reg Stephenson, the doyen of the firm, placed great emphasis on the flow of people, livestock and traffic. There are five acres of car park at the front for the public, two acres of lorry park at the back for the hauliers and two acres of covered accommodation in between for the animals.

The centre became hugely popular and expanded rapidly to a peak between 1980 and 1985. At this time there was a period in the spring of 1983 when they sold over 1,000 fat cattle for each of five consecutive weeks; and at the same time the fat pig market was accommodating up to 4,000 pigs a day, which were put through a sale ring with a revolutionary moving floor on the weighbridge.

The yearly turnover reached £40 million, but Isaac Newton's prophetic law would inevitably take its toll. This is Stephenson & Son's story.

THE CHANGING YEARS

An unwelcome wind of change was about to blow through the auction pens and there was little the market operators could do to halt it. There were three major factors that brought about the decline of the traditional auction market as we knew it.

Plagues & disease

The auctioneer's 'El Nino' carried with it a series of disease outbreaks that were all notifiable and highly contagious. We went from TB to Swine Fever, Scrapie, SVD, Blue-Ear, and then through the spectre of BSE to the disastrous calamity of Foot and Mouth Disease. Each outbreak was automatically punctuated by an immediate cessation of business for the auction market, which was perceived as a potential carrier of disease.

There was no compensation for losing business and we could be closed for as long as 12 months at a time. Inevitably each time controls were lifted, lost business had to be regained but some had found other marketing channels on a permanent basis.

There was and still is little excuse for all the epidemics that break out amongst our domestic animal kingdom. We are an island and like New Zealand we could quite easily keep out the trouble. Being British and having politicians with diminishing affinity to agriculture, we operate an almost open door policy, although I do note that the current Minister of Agriculture is raising the number of sniffer dogs at ports from two to six!

Suffocating 'red tape'

Every industry complains about its paperwork but I think that agriculture has been hit harder than most and what makes matter worse is that farmers are not equipped to deal with it.

As markets, not only do we have to have a licence for the premises but we are also obliged to comply with all the regulation surrounding the identification and movement of animals.

Currently every beast that comes through our gates has to carry an individual passport, which in turn has to correspond with its ear tag number and for which we have to send back notification of movement to DEFRA.

The same controls are about to be introduced for sheep, heaven help us, and so it goes on. The continuous imposition of red tape has for certain reduced any margin of profit and in many cases persuaded market operators to cease altogether.

Changing trade patterns

There has been a move for the bigger producers to sell their own stock. This has been stimulated and encouraged by the larger abattoirs, which in turn supply the major supermarkets. The supermarket domination has been a key factor in diverting stock away from the open Auction Market into a channel where the buyer has more control over price. Most believe this is not to the benefit of the industry but it is a fact of life and has brought about the demise of a lot of markets.

When the new York market was built in 1971 there would be round about 300 auctions still going in the country. Today there are 180 members of the Livestock Auctioneers Association. At its lowest point following the FMD crisis, York was reduced to trading around 200 fat cattle a week and its pig numbers had dropped from a peak of 4,000 down to 250.

It was time to change or die.

DIVERSIFICATION IN ALL DIRECTIONS

We have had a continuous development programme at York, which has been drip-fed into our operation as and when the core livestock business receded.

Listed below is a range of activities that we have or hope to have established at the newly titled York Auction Centre.

Machinery sales

This was one of the first enterprises we introduced onto the site about 15 years ago and we now have one of the largest collective sales of agricultural machinery in the country, with our last catalogue comprising over 5,000 lots in eight simultaneous auctions. We draw in customers from both home and abroad and have even sold items over the Web.

Our Machinery Sale website attracts an average 20,000 visits for catalogues each sale.

Horse sales

We have constructed a purpose built Equestrian Sales Complex with a heated ring, cage box stabling and a show paddock. We operate around 15 sales each year, selling up to 100 horses at each sale.

Motor auctions

We have struck out into the grey world of car auctions operating a weekly sale on a Wednesday evening and utilising the same facilities as for the horse sales. We now have specialist sales for 4x4 vehicles, light commercials and motor bikes.

Sunday car-boot and table-top sale

To take advantage of the national sport of retail therapy, we opened the gates on a Sunday for car-booters and this operates all year round with over 100 stalls and the cafeteria serving 500 lunches of roast beef & Yorkshire pud.

Farmers' market

York was one of the first and leading markets in the North of England, expanding last year to a twice-monthly operation with up to 70 stalls. This provides the opportunity for local producers to market their goods – predominantly food but including some crafts.

The market has recently undergone a full Soil Association inspection and achieved certified status under the National Association of Farmers' Markets rules.

City Lorry Park

The Lorry Park for the city had been in the centre where it was becoming increasingly inaccessible and unacceptable for local residents. With the financial support of the Council we have recently opened a new floodlit Lorry Park for 30 vehicles to stop overnight, with catering facilities and security available. This dovetails with our daytime operations, providing extra income from the site during the dead hours of night.

Computer training

One project that appeals to current Government thinking is computer education and with grant assistance we have set up a Computer Suite. We offer to farmers and others a tutored course at any level of computer literacy and at a Yorkshire price!

Currently all seven computer stations are occupied on two evenings a week with our secretaries earning well-deserved extra money.

The Food Hall

We have carried out an analysis of covered space that is used and there is a serious under-utilisation, which we are addressing. One project will be to create a purpose-built Food Hall that will incorporate the Farmers' Market, taking it onto its next stage of development.

The Food Hall would initially be open for the whole weekend from Friday night to Sunday lunchtime and provide a regular shopping venue for the discerning clientele who want to taste what they eat and know where it's come from.

The Food Hall would include a permanent cold room where food could be stored overnight rather than taking it backwards and forwards. The promotion of Yorkshire produce with strict rules of qualification could well attract a regional grant.

Auction store and chattel sales

We have built up a good programme of Chattel Auctions, which range from mundane household goods through to respectable antiques; and more recently we have introduced sales of electrical white goods and even carpets.

We try to hold these sales on the same days as a Farmers' Market in order to have as large a footfall as possible, and they have been remarkably successful. It is our intention to develop a permanent store and sales area for these auctions.

Country Store

With the ever-increasing number of visitors to the York Auction Centre we are looking at the opportunity of establishing a Country Store to sell clothing and equipment. There is the possibility of a joint venture and we would hope that this could also market products manufactured in our Yorkshire region.

Business starter units

There is a strong demand for small offices, workshops and studio units for new businesses and we are planning a fully serviced and managed workspace that would be available on an easy in/easy out basis without formal long lease commitments. The service provisions would include reception and central switchboard, computer network links, photocopying, boardroom and cafeteria facilities.

The way ahead

The sixth generation of the Stephenson family is now a partner in the business and we are hoping that all the changes will provide a platform for our family in the future. The core business of selling livestock remains but it will occupy only 20 per cent of our facilities in the future.

Appendix I: Recommended reading list

CLA ADVISORY HANDBOOKS

CLA advisory handbooks provide unparalleled technical treatment of significant tax, legal, land management and business issues for CLA members. The handbooks are prepared by CLA advisers and draw on their technical expertise and experience of handling members' queries.

Serial No.	Date published	Title
CLA1	1992	Share Farming (3rd Edition)
CLA2	1993	Access to Neighbouring Land Act 1992
CLA3	1993	CGT Roll Owner Relief
CLA4	1994	CGT Retirement Relief
CLA5	1994	Provision of Living Accommodation to Employees
CLA6	1999	Agricultural Tenancies Act Farm Business Tenancies
CLA7	1995	Environmental Protection Act
CLA8	1995	Inheritance Tax Agricultural Property Relief
CLA9	1995	Reclassification of Roads Used as Public Paths
CLA10	1995	Rights of Way – Rebutting Deemed Dedication
CLA11	1997	A Campaigners Guide to Compulsory Purchase
CLA12	1997	Metal Detecting and the Treasure Act 1996
CLA13	1999	Grazing Agreements
CLA14	1999	Housing
CLA15	1999	Minerals and Waste Guidelines
CLA16	2000	Diversification Survey on Tenanted Land
CLA17	2000	Employment Law
CLA18	2000	Farm Business Tenancies for a Fixed Term of Two Years or Less
CLA19	2000	Horses and the Law
CLA20	2000	Taxation of Furnished Holiday Accommodation

Serial No.	Date published	Title
CLA21	2001	Business Tenancies on Farms
CLA22	2001	Model Storage Licence Agreement
CLA23	2001	Telecommunication Towers
CLA24	2001	The Lands Tribunal – Resolving Disputes on Statutory Compensation
CLA25	2001	Wind Farms
CLA26	2001	Cables and Wires
CLA27	2001	Law Relating to Livestock and Domestic Animals
CLA28	2001	Pipes and Sewers
CLA29	2001	Shooting Lease
CLA30	2002	Biomass
CLA31	2002	Rating and Council Tax
CLA32	2003	New Transport Schemes

CLA GUIDANCE NOTES

These Guidance Notes are free to CLA members and can be down-loaded from the CLA website: www.cla.org.uk

GN Ref	Date published	Title
GN01/01	2001	Damage to Water Pipes: liability and how to avoid it
GN01/02	2002	Rules on interest on compensation payable under compulsory purchase
GN02/02	2002	Recommended BT wayleave payments from 1/4/01 to 31/3/06
GN03/02	2002	Crichel Down Rules: Disposal of surplus government land – obligation to offer land back to former owners or their successors
GN04/02	2002	The implementation of national planning policy guidance PPG7 in relation to the diversification of farm business
GN05/02	2002	Choosing an agent in respect of a proposed telecommunications tower
GN06/02	2002	Landfill and waste disposal advice
GN07/02	2002	Payment for cables in the highway
GN08/02	2002	Indirect Betterment: the treatment of income gained from borrow pits, site offices, etc

GN Ref	Date published	Title
GN09/02	2002	Necessary wayleaves and the owner's rights to require removal or relocation of electricity industry equipment
GN10/02	2002	Principles adopted by electricity companies for payment for equipment on private land
GN11/02	2002	Climate change levy as it affects rural businesses
GN12/02	2002	Recommended payments for optic fibre cables installed on overhead electricity apparatus
GN13/02	2002	_WindWorks_ licence: guidance on the offer made by windworks to rent land for turbines
GN14/02	2002	CROW Act 2000: the right of access – initial action for owners
GN15/02	2002	Private easements for water and drainage pipes: guidance for when a new private right is required
GN16/02	2002	Electricity wayleaves : recommended rates of payment
GN17/02	2002	186k or FPL Telecom Ltd – proposed fibre optic telecommunications line (a subsidiary of BG Transco) recommended payments for telecom cables
GN18/02	2002	Development control and agriculture: guidance on what farm developments are exempt from formal planning permission
GN19/02	2002	The lifting of agricultural ties (limiting occupation to farm workers) from farm dwellings: guidance on removing them
GN20/02	2002	Late payment of commercial debts (Interest) Act 1998: guidance on when applicable and rates chargeable
GN21/02	2002	2002 Suckler Cow Premium Scheme Quota National Reserve Application Period
GN22/02	2002	Agricultural tenancies and the definition of agriculture (Jewell v McGowan and another)
GN23/02	2002	Certificates of lawfulness of existing use or development (CLEUD): guidance on the rules for existing uses that do not have formal planning consent
GN24/02	2002	Guidance on conversion of rural buildings to business use

GN Ref	Date published	Title
GN25/02	2002	Energy crops: drafting a supply contract – checklist for growers when making supply agreements
GN26/02	2002	Share Farming and Contract Farming
GN27/02	2002	Telecommunication mast sites – rental & capital values
GN28/02	2002	Compulsory purchase compensation code
GN29/02	2002	Diversification – reuse of farm and rural buildings
GN30/02	2002	The CLA/RICS Mediation Scheme
GN31/02	2002	Sewer pipes – Ransom values and Kettering BC v Anglian Water plc
GN32/02	2002	The Telecommunications Code
GN33/02	2002	Nitrate Vulnerable Zones
GN34/02	2002	Lead Shot Ban
GN35/02	2002	Electricity substations
GN36/02	2002	NVZ News
GN37/02	2002	Capital payments for electricity equipment
GN38/02	2002	Consideration of heads of terms for telecommunications leases
GN39/02	2002	Installation of new public water pipes
GN40/02	2002	The Rural Land Register
GN41/02	2002	Farm diversification and rates
GN42/02	2002	NVZ appeals, slurry stores & farm waste grants
GN43/02	2002	Minimum wage increase, protection of fixed-term contract employees
GN44/02	2000	CROW Act 2000, CLS lobbying achievements
GN45/02	2000	CROW Act 2000 – a summary
GN46/02	2001	CROW Act – the right of access
GN47/02	2001	CROW Act, commencement of provisions
GN48/02	2001	CROW Act – the right of access, initial action for owners
GN49/02	2002	CROW Act – mapping of access land (summary)
GN50/02	2002	CA/CCW consultations on draft access land maps – grounds for making representations
GN51/02	2002	CA draft access land map consultation – mapping region 3, central souther England
GN52/02	2002	Beaters and the operation of PAYE by shoots
GN53/02	2002	CroW Act 2000, mapping of access land, making an appeal
GN54/02	2002	RSPCA – Enforcement of Animal Welfare Legislation

GN Ref	Date published	Title
GN55/02	2002	New Policy Governing Movements of Cattle (TB)
GN56/02	2002	National Grid Plc and Telecommunications Companies
GN57/02	2002	2003 Sheep Annual Premium Scheme: Application period opens
GN58/02	2002	Joint guidance note: BT wayleaves and backpayments
GN59/02	2002	Rural Payments Agency Review of 2001 Bovine Subsidies
GN01/03	2003	Roads Used as Public Paths – Redesignation as restricted Byways under the Countryside and Rights of Way Act
GN02/03	2003	Notification under the Data Protection Act 1998
GN03/03	2003	Images of England
GN04/03	2003	Employment Law Update
GN05/03	2003	Livestock Worrying
GN06/03	2003	The prohibition of keeping or release of live fish
GN07/03	2003	The Commission's Proposals for the Mid Term Review of the Common Agricultural Policy (CAP)
GN08(a)/03	2003	Spring Interim Animal Movement Regime
GN08(b)/03	2003	Transitional Arrangements for Agri-Environment Schemes
GN09/03	2003	Right to Request Flexible Working
GN10/03	2003	Professional fees in compensation cases (Ryde's scale)
GN11/03	2003	Electricity Wayleaves – Rates of Payment from 01/04/03 to 31/03/04
GN12/03	2003	Employment Law Update (This supersedes GN04/03 and GN43/02)
GN13/03	2003	RPA Announces 2003 IACS Arrangements
GN14/03	2003	The Water Resale Order 2001
GN15/03	2003	Control of Asbestos at Work Regulations 2002
GN16–03	2003	Rebated Fuel – Red Diesel
GN17–03	2003	Rating of Stables
GN18/03	2003	Planning For The Introduction of an Entry-Level Agri-environment Scheme
GN 19/03	2003	Animal By Products Regulation and the Ban on Burial of Fallen Stock
GN20/03	2003	Water or Sewerage Service Complaints
GN21/03	2003	CROW Act Appeals – Costs Issues
GN22/03	2003	Shotgun Cartridges – Homeloading

GN Ref	Date published	Title
GN23/03	2003	The Rating (Former Agricultural Premises and Rural Shops) Act 2001
GN24/03	2003	EH – Images of England Exemption Scheme
GN25/03	2003	Environmental Impact Assessment (EIA) Regulations for the Use of Uncultivated Land or Semi-Natural Areas for Intensive Agricultural Purposes

Country Land and Business Association publications may be ordered from:

Publications Department, CLA, 16 Belgrave Square. London SW1X 8PQ. Tel: 020 7235 0511.

KOGAN PAGE AND OTHER PUBLICATIONS

Accounting for Non-Accountants, 5th edition, Graham Mott (Kogan Page)
All About Selling, A Williams (McGraw Hill)
The Allied Dunbar Tax Guide, W I Sinclair (Longman, published annuallly)
Be Your Own Boss! David McMullan (Kogan Page)
Be Your Own PR Man, Michael Bland (Kogan Page)
British Rate & Data (monthly)
The Business Property Handbook (Royal Institution of Chartered Surveyors)
Compensation and Case B Notices to Quit, October 1999, Joint Guidance Note (CLA, Tenant Farmers' Association and National Farmers Union)
Croner's Reference Book for the Self-employed and Smaller Business, (Croner Publications)
Directory of Enterprise Agencies (Business in the Community)
Doing Business on the Internet, 3rd edition, Simon Collin (Kogan Page)
E-business for the Small Business, John G Fisher (Kogan Page)
An Economic Evaluation of the Agricultural Tenancies Act 1995, April 2002, (University of Plymouth Department of Land Use and Rural Management)
Effective PR Management, 2nd edition, Paul Winner (Kogan Page)
Fair Deal: A Shopper's Guide (Office of Fair Trading)
Financial Management for the Small Business, 4th edition, Colin Barrow (Kogan Page)
Forming a Limited Company, 7th edition, Patricia Clayton (Kogan Page)
Good Non-retirement Guide, 17th edition, Rosemary Brown (Kogan Page)
Going Freelance, Godfrey Golzen (Kogan Page)
A Guide to Franchising, Martin Mendelsssohn (Cassell)

A Guide to Sources of Finance for SMEs, Michael Brand (Kogan Page)

A Guide to Working for Yourself, 22nd edition, Godfrey Golzen and Jonathan Reuvid (Kogan Page)

How to Prepare a Business Plan, 3rd edition, Edward Blackwell (Kogan Page)

How to Run Your Own Restaurant, B Sim and William Gleeson (Kogan Page)

How to Set Up and Run Your Own Business, 16th edition, Helen Kogan (Kogan Page)

Looking Ahead: A Guide to Retirement, Fred Kemp and Bernard Buttle (Springfield)

Managing for Results, Peter F Drucker (Pan Books)

Practical Marketing and PR for the Small Business, 1998, 2nd edition, Moi Ali (Kogan Page)

The Pubs, Bars and Clubs Handbook 6th edition, Danny Blyth (Kogan Page)

Report of the Policy Commission on the Future of Food and Farming, January 2002 (Cabinet Office website www.cabinet-office.gov.uk/farming)

Running a Home Based Business, Diane Baker (Kogan Page)

Self-Employment in the United Kingdom, Nigel Meager (Institute of Employment Studies)

Setting up a Workshop (Crafts Council)

The Small Business Casebook, Sue Birley (Macmillan Press)

The Small Business Guide, S Williams (Penguin)

Start Your Own Business in 30 Days, Gary Grappo (Kogan Page)

Start Up and Run Your Own Business, Jonathan Reuvid and Roderick Millar (Kogan Page)

Successful Marketing for Small Businesses, 5th edition, Dave Patten (Kogan Page)

Survey of Farm Landlords & CLA Data Analysis, April 2002, National Farm Research Unit

Taking up a Franchise, 2003, Iain Murray (Kogan Page)

Writers' and Artists' Yearbook (A & C Black)

Kogan Page books may be ordered direct from the website: kogan-page.co.uk or from:

Littlehampton Book Services
PO Box 53
Littlehampton BN17 7BU
Tel: 01903 828 800
Fax: 01903 828 802
E-mail: orders@lbsltd.co.uk

Appendix II: Selected information sources

**Agricultural Wages Board
(England and Wales)**
Ergon House
17 Smith Square
London SW1P 3JR
Tel: 020 7238 6540

**British Institute of
Agricultural Consultants**
The Estate Office
Torry Hill
Milstead
Sittingbourne
Kent ME9 0SP
Tel: 01795 830100

Countryside Agency
Head Office: John Dower
House
Crescent Place
Cheltenham
Gloucestershire GL50 3RA
Tel: 01242 521381

**DEFRA (Department for
Environment, Food and Rural
Affairs)**
Nobel House
17 Smith Square
London SW1P 3HX
Tel: 020 7238 3000

English Nature
Northminster House
Peterborough PE1 1UA
Tel: 01733 455000

Environment Agenccy
Rio House
Waterside Drive
Aztec West
Almondsbury
Bristol BS32 4UD
Tel: 01454 624400

**Health and Safety Executive
Information Services**
Caerphilly Business Park
Caerphilly
Wales CF83 3GG
Tel: 08701 545500

Historic Houses Association
2 Chester Street
London SW1X 7BB
Tel: 020 7259 5688

Lantra
Lantra House, NAC
Kenilworth
Warwickshire CV8 2LG
Tel. 024 7669 6996

The National Assembly for Wales Agriculture Department
Crown Building
Cathays Park
Cardiff CF10 3NQ
Tel: 02920 825111

The Planning Inspectorate
Temple Quay House
2 The Square
Temple Quay
Bristol BS1 6PN
Tel: 0117 3728000

The Planning Inspectorate (Wales)
Room 1–004, Cathays Park,
Cardiff CF10 3NQ
Tel: 029 2082 33866

Planning Officers Society
Wycombe District Council
Queen Victoria Road
High Wycombe HP11 1BB
Tel: 01494 461000

Planning Officers Society (Wales)
Ceredigion County Council
Penmorta
Aberaevon
Ceredigion SA46 DPA
Tel: 01545 570881

Royal Institution of Chartered Surveyors
12 Great George Street
London SW1
Tel: 020 72222 7000

Royal Town Planning Institute
41 Botolph Lane
London WC3R 8DL
Tel: 020 7929 9494

Scottish Landowners' Federation
Stuart House
Eskmills Business Park
Musselburgh
East Lothian EH21 7PB
Tel: 01311 653 5400

Town and Country Planning Association
17 Carlton House Terrace
London SW1Y 5AS
Tel: 020 7930 8903

Appendix III: Contributors' contact details

CLA contributors

Brian Castle — Senior Taxation Adviser
Jeffrey Hansen — Formerly Legal Advisor
Oliver Harwood — Head of Rural Economy
Sean Johnson — Senior IT Analyst
Dr. Karen Jones — Chief Legal Adviser
Mark Jones — Formerly Senior Planning Advisor
Helen Shipsey — Senior Legal Adviser
Duncan Sigournay — Senior Legal Adviser
Charles Trotman — Rural Economics Adviser

Country Land and Business Association (CLA)
16 Belgrave Square
London SW1X 8PQ
Tel: 020 7235 0511
Fax: 020 7235 4696
Website: www.cla.org.uk

CLA regional offices

CLA North West Regional Office
Dalton Hall Stable Yard
Burton
Carnforth
Lancashire LA6 1NJ

CLA Yorkshire Regional Office
Malt Shovel House
Spring Street
Easingwold
York YO61 3BJ

CLA West Midlands Regional
  Office
The Business Centre
Bleak House Farm
Knightley
Woodseaves
Staffordshire ST20 0JW

CLA East Midlands Regional
  Office
The Lodge
Sutton Bassett
Market Harborough
Leics LE16 8HL

CLA regional offices (*continued*)

CLA Eastern Regional Office
Aspen House
Assington Green
Stansfield
Sudbury
Suffolk CO10 8LY

CLA South East Regional Office
Brookfields House
Westridge
Highclere
Newbury
Berkshire RG20 9RX

CLA South West Regional Office
Hartham Park
Corsham
Wiltshire SN13 0RP

CLA Wales Office
Hoddell Farm
Kinnerton
Presteigne
Powys LD8 2PD

External contributors

Philip Coysh
National Business Manager
Farming & Agricultural
   Finance Ltd.
PO Box 4115
Hornchurch
Essex RM12 4DS
Tel/Fax: 01453 767644
Email: philip.coysh@rbs.co.uk

Matthew Howard
Licensed Insolvency Practitioner
Larking Gowen, Chartered
   Accountants
King Street House,
15 Upper King Street,
Norwich NR3 1RB
Tel: 01603 624181
Fax: 01603 667800
Email: matt.howard@
   larking-gowen.co.uk

Stuart Rootham
Commercial Director
R K Harrison Brokers Ltd.
The Maktings, Lurke Street,
Bedford MK40 3HH
Tel: 01234 305555
Fax:01234 408676
Email: Stuart.Roothaam@
   rkharrison.co.uk

James Stephenson
Senior Partner
Stephenson & Son
York Auction Centre
Murton
York YO19 5GS
Tel: 01904 489731
Fax:01904 489782
Email: jfs@stephenson.co.uk

Kogan Page contributors

Roderick Millar, Author
Jonathan Reuvid, Consultant Editor and Author
Kogan Page Limited
120 Pentonville Road
London N1 9JN
Tel: 020 7278 0433
Fax: 020 7837 6348
Website: www.kogan-paage.co.uk